101 ESSAYS
that will
CHANGE
the way
YOU THINK

Brianna Wiest

INTRODUCTION

In his book *Sapiens*, Dr. Yuval Noah Harari explains that at one point, there were more than just *Homo sapiens* roaming the Earth[1]. In fact, there were likely as many as six different types of humans in existence: *Homo sapiens, Homo neanderthalensis, Homo soloensis, Homo erectus*, etc.

There's a reason Homo sapiens still exist today and the others didn't continue to evolve: a prefrontal cortex, which we can infer from skeletal structures. Essentially, we had the ability to think more complexly, thus were able to organize, cultivate, teach, practice, habituate and pass down a world suited for our survival. Because of our capacity to imagine, we were able to build Earth as it is today out of virtually nothing.

In a sense, the notion that thoughts create reality is more than just a nice idea; it's also a fact of evolution. It was because of language and thought that we could create a world within our minds, and ultimately, it is because of language and thought that we have evolved into the society we have today—for better and for worse.

Almost every great master, artist, teacher, innovator, inventor, and generally happy person could attribute some similar understanding to their success. Many of the world's 'best' people understood that to change their lives, they had to change their minds.

These are the same people who have communicated to us some of the longest-standing conventional wisdom: that to believe is to become, that the mind is to be mastered, that the obstacle is the way[2]. Often, our most intense discomfort is what precedes and necessitates thinking in a way we have never conceived of before. That new awareness creates possibilities that would never exist had we not been forced to learn something new. Why did our ancestors develop agriculture, society, medicine, and the like? To survive. The elements of our world were once just solutions to fears.

In a more cerebral context, if you consciously learn to regard the "problems" in your life as openings for you to adopt a greater understanding and then develop a better way of living, you will step out of the labyrinth of suffering and learn what it means to thrive.

1

I believe that the root of the work of being human is learning how to think. From this, we learn how to love, share, coexist, tolerate, give, create, and so on. I believe the first and most important duty we have is to actualize the potential we were born with—both for ourselves and for the world.

The unspoken line of everything I write is: "This idea changed my life." Because ideas are what change lives—and that was the first idea that changed mine.

Brianna Wiest — July 2016

---

1 Harari, Yuval Noah. *Sapiens: A Brief History of Humankind. 1st Edition.* 2015. Harper.
2 Holiday, Ryan. *The Obstacle Is The Way.* 2014. Portfolio.

SUBCONSCIOUS
BEHAVIORS
that are
KEEPING YOU
from HAVING
THE LIFE
YOU WANT

Every generation has a "monoculture" of sorts, a governing pattern or system of beliefs that people unconsciously accept as "truth."

It's easy to identify the monoculture of Germany in the 1930s or America in 1776. It's clear what people at those times, in those places, accepted to be "good" and "true" even when in reality, that was certainly not always the case.

The objectivity required to see the effects of present monoculture is very difficult to develop. Once you have so deeply accepted an idea as "truth" it doesn't register as "cultural" or "subjective" anymore.

So much of our inner turmoil is the result of conducting a life we don't inherently desire, only because we have accepted an inner narrative of "normal" and "ideal" without ever realizing.

The fundamentals of any given monoculture tend to surround what we should be living for (nation, religion, self, etc.) and there are a number of ways in which our current system has us shooting ourselves in the feet as we try to step forward. Here, 8 of the most pervasive.

01. You believe that creating your best life is a matter of deciding what you want and then going after it, but in reality, you are psychologically incapable[1] of being able to predict what will make you happy.

    Your brain can only perceive what it's known, so when you choose what you want for the future, you're actually just recreating a solution or an ideal of the past. When things don't work out the way you want them to, you think you've failed only because you didn't re-create something you perceived as desirable. In reality, you likely created something better, but foreign, and your brain misinterpreted it as "bad" because of that. (Moral of the story: Living in the moment isn't a lofty ideal reserved for the Zen and enlightened; it's the only way to live a life that isn't infiltrated with illusions. It's the only thing your brain can actually comprehend.)

02. You extrapolate the present moment because you believe that success is somewhere you "arrive," so you are constantly trying to take a snapshot of your life and see if you can be happy yet.

You convince yourself that any given moment is representative of your life as a whole. Because we're wired to believe that success is somewhere we get to—when goals are accomplished and things are completed—we're constantly measuring our present moments by how "finished" they are, how good the story sounds, how someone else would judge the elevator speech. We find ourselves thinking: "Is this all there is?" because we forget that everything is transitory, and no one single instance can summarize the whole. There is nowhere to "arrive" to. The only thing you're rushing toward is death. Accomplishing goals is not success. How much you expand in the process is.

03. You assume that when it comes to following your "gut instincts," happiness is "good" and fear and pain are "bad."

When you consider doing something that you truly love and are invested in, you are going to feel an influx of fear and pain, mostly because it will involve being vulnerable. Bad feelings should not always be interpreted as deterrents. They are also indicators that you are doing something frightening and worthwhile. Not wanting to do something would make you feel indifferent about it. Fear = interest.

4

04. You needlessly create problems and crises in your life because you're afraid of actually living it.

The pattern of unnecessarily creating crises in your life is actually an avoidance technique. It distracts you from actually having to be vulnerable or held accountable for whatever it is you're afraid of. You're never upset for the reason you think you are: At the core of your desire to create a problem is simply the fear of being who you are and living the life you want.

05. You think that to change your beliefs, you have to adopt a new line of thinking, rather than seek experiences that make that thinking self-evident.

A belief is what you know to be true because experience has made it evident to you. If you want to change your life, change your beliefs. If you want to change your beliefs, go out and have experiences that make them real to you. Not the opposite way around.

06. You think "problems" are roadblocks to achieving what you want, when in reality they are pathways.

Marcus Aurelius sums this up well: "The impediment to action advances action. What stands in the way becomes the way." Simply, running into a "problem" forces you to take action to resolve it. That action will inevitably lead you to think differently, behave differently, and choose differently. The "problem" becomes a catalyst for you to actualize the life you always wanted. It pushes you from your comfort zone, that's all.

07. You think your past defines you, and worse, you think that it is an unchangeable reality, when really, your perception of it changes as you do.

Because experience is always multi-dimensional, there are a variety of memories, experiences, feelings, "gists" you can choose to recall...and what you choose is indicative of your present state of mind. So many people get caught up in allowing the past to define them or haunt them simply because they have not evolved to the place of seeing how the past did not prevent them from achieving the life they want, it facilitated it. This doesn't mean to disregard or gloss over painful or traumatic events, but simply to be able to recall them with acceptance and to be able to place them in the storyline of your personal evolution.

08. You try to change other people, situations, and things (or you just complain/get upset about them) when anger = self-recognition. Most negative emotional reactions are you identifying a disassociated aspect of yourself.

Your "shadow selves" are the parts of you that at some point you were conditioned to believe were "not okay," so you suppressed them and have done everything in your power not to acknowledge them. You don't actually dislike these parts of yourself, though. So when you see somebody else displaying one of these traits, it's infuriating, not because you inherently dislike it, but because you have to fight your desire to fully integrate it into your whole consciousness. The things you love about others are the things you love about yourself. The things you hate about others are the things you cannot see in yourself.

---

1 Gilbert, Daniel. *Stumbling on Happiness*. 2007. Random House.

The PSYCHOLOGY
of DAILY ROUTINE

The most successful people in history—the ones many refer to as "geniuses" in their fields, masters of their crafts—had one thing in common, other than talent: Most adhered to rigid (and specific) routines.

Routines seem boring, and the antithesis to what you're told a "good life" is made of. Happiness, we infer, comes from the perpetual seeking of "more," regardless what it's "more" of. Yet what we don't realize is that having a routine doesn't mean you sit in the same office every day for the same number of hours. Your routine could be traveling to a different country every month. It could be being routinely un-routine. The point is not what the routine consists of, but how steady and safe your subconscious mind is made through repetitive motions and expected outcomes.

Whatever you want your day-to-day life to consist of doesn't matter, the point is that you decide and then stick to it. In short, routine is important because habitualness creates mood, and mood creates the "nurture" aspect of your personality, not to mention that letting yourself be jerked around by impulsiveness is a breeding ground for everything you essentially do not want.

Most things that bring genuine happiness are not just temporary, immediate gratifications, and those things also come with resistance and require sacrifice. Yet there is a way to nullify the feeling of "sacrifice" when you integrate a task into the "norm" or push through resistance with regulation. These, and all the other reasons why routine is so important (and happy people tend to follow them more).

01. Your habits create your mood, and your mood is a filter through which you experience your life.
It would make sense to assume that moods are created from thoughts or stressors, things that crop up during the day and knock us off-kilter. This isn't so. Psychologist Robert Thayer

argues that moods are created by our habitualness: how much we sleep, how frequently we move, what we think, how often we think it, and so on. The point is that it's not one thought that throws us into a tizzy: It's the pattern of continually experiencing that thought that compounds its effect and makes it seem valid.

02. You must learn to let your conscious decisions dictate your day—not your fears or impulses.

An untamed mind is a minefield. With no regulation, focus, base or self-control, anything can persuade you into thinking you want something that you don't actually. "I want to go out for drinks tonight, not prepare for that presentation tomorrow" seems valid in the short-term, but in the long-term is disastrous. Going out for drinks one night probably isn't worth bombing a super important meeting. Learning to craft routine is the equivalent of learning to let your conscious choices about what your day will be about guide you, letting all the other, temporary crap fall to the wayside.

03. Happiness is not how many things you do, but how well you do them.

More is not better. Happiness is not experiencing something else; it's continually experiencing what you already have in new and different ways. Unfortunately as we're taught that passion should drive our every thought move and decision, we're basically impaled with the fear that we're unhappy because we're not doing "enough."

04. When you regulate your daily actions, you deactivate your "fight or flight" instincts because you're no longer confronting the unknown.

This is why people have such a difficult time with change, and why people who are constant in their habits experience so much joy: simply, their fear instincts are turned off long enough for them to actually enjoy something.

05. As children, routine gives us a feeling of safety. As adults, it gives us a feeling of purpose.

9

Interestingly enough, those two feelings are more similar than you'd think (at least, their origin is the same). It's the same thing as the fear of the unknown: As children, we don't know which way is left, let alone why we're alive or whether or not a particular activity we've never done before is going to be scary or harmful. When we're adults engaging with routine-ness, we can comfort ourselves with the simple idea of "I know how to do this, I've done it before."

06. You feel content because routine consistently reaffirms a decision you already made.

If said decision is that you want to write a book—and you commit to doing three pages each night for however long it takes to complete it—you affirm not only your choice to begin, but your ability to do it. It's honestly the healthiest way to feel validated.

07. As your body self-regulates, routine becomes the pathway to "flow[2]."

"Flow" (in case you don't know—you probably do) is essentially what happens when we become so completely engaged with what we're doing, all ideas or worries dissolve, and we're just completely present in the task. The more you train your body to respond to different cues: 7 a.m. is when you wake up, 2 p.m. is when you start writing, and so on, you naturally fall into flow with a lot more ease, just out of habit.

08. When we don't settle into routine, we teach ourselves that "fear" is an indicator that we're doing the wrong thing, rather than just being very invested in the outcome.

A lack of routine is just a breeding ground for perpetual procrastination. It gives us gaps and spaces in which our subconscious minds can say: "well, you can take a break now," when in fact, you have a deadline. But if you're used to taking a break at that point in time, you'll allow it simply because "you always do."

---

2 Csikszentmihalyi, Mihaly. *Flow: The Psychology of Optimal Experience*. 2008. Harper Perennial Modern Classics.

10 THINGS
EMOTIONALLY
INTELLIGENT
PEOPLE
do not DO

Emotional intelligence is probably the most powerful yet undervalued trait in our society.

We believe in rooting our everyday functions in logic and reason, yet we come to the same conclusions after long periods of contemplation as we do in the blink of an eye[3]. Our leaders sorely overlook the human element of our sociopolitical issues and I need not cite the divorce rate for you to believe that we're not choosing the right partners (nor do we have the capacity to sustain intimate relationships for long periods of time).

It seems people believe the most intelligent thing to do is not have emotions at all. To be effective is to be a machine, a product of the age. A well-oiled, consumerist-serving, digitally attuned, highly unaware but overtly operational robot. And so we suffer.

Here are the habits of the people who have the capacity to be aware of what they feel. Who know how to express, process, dismantle, and adjust their experience as they are their own locus of control. They are the true leaders, they are living the most whole and genuine lives, and it is from them we should be taking a cue. These are the things that emotionally intelligent people do not do.

01. They don't assume that the way they think and feel about a situation is the way it is in reality, nor how it will turn out in the end.

    They recognize their emotions as responses, not accurate gauges, of what's going on. They accept that those responses may have to do with their own issues, rather than the objective situation at hand.

02. Their emotional base points are not external.

Their emotions aren't "somebody else's doing," and therefore "somebody else's problem to resolve." Understanding that they are the ultimate cause of what they experience keeps them out of falling into the trap of indignant passivity: Where one believes that as the universe has done wrong, the universe will ultimately have to correct it.

03. They don't assume to know what it is that will make them truly happy.

Being that our only frame of reference at any given time is what's happened in the past, we actually have no means to determine what would make us truly happy, as opposed to just feeling "saved" from whatever we disliked about our past experiences. In understanding this, they open themselves up to any experience that their life evolves toward, knowing there are equal parts good and bad in anything.

04. They don't think that being fearful is a sign they are on the wrong path.

The presence of indifference is a sign you're on the wrong path. Fear means you're trying to move toward something you love, but your old beliefs, or unhealed experiences, are getting in the way. (Or, rather, are being called up to be healed.)

05. They know that happiness is a choice, but they don't feel the need to make it all the time.

They are not stuck in the illusion that "happiness" is a sustained state of joy. They allow themselves time to process everything they are experiencing. They allow themselves to exist in their natural state. In that non-resistance, they find contentment.

06. They don't allow their thoughts to be chosen for them.

They recognize that through social conditioning and the eternal human monkey-mind, they can often be swayed by thoughts, beliefs, and mindsets that were never theirs in the first place. To combat this, they take inventory of their beliefs, reflect on their origins, and decide whether or not that frame of reference truly serves them.

07. They recognize that infallible composure is not emotional intelligence.

They don't withhold their feelings or try to temper them so much as to render them almost gone. They do, however, have the capacity to withhold their emotional response until they are in an environment wherein it would be appropriate to express how they are feeling. They don't suppress it; they manage it effectively.

08. They know that a feeling will not kill them.

They've developed enough stamina and awareness to know that all things, even the worst, are transitory.

09. They don't just become close friends with anyone.

They recognize true trust and intimacy as something you build, and something you want to be discerning with whom you share. But they're not guarded or closed as they are simply mindful and aware of who they allow into their lives and hearts. They are kind to all, but truly open to few.

10. They don't confuse a bad feeling for a bad life.

They are aware of, and avoid, extrapolation, which is essentially projecting the present moment into the foreseeable future—believing that the moment at hand constitutes what your entire life amounted to, rather than just being another passing, transitory experience in the whole. Emotionally intelligent people allow themselves their "bad" days. They let themselves be fully human. It's in this non-resistance that they find the most peace of all.

---

3 Gladwell, Malcolm. *Blink: The Power of Thinking Without Thinking.* 2007. Back Bay Books.

HOW *the* PEOPLE WE ONCE LOVED *become* STRANGERS AGAIN

It's interesting to think about how we make people who used to be everything into nothing again. How we learn to forget. How we force forgetting. What we put in place of them in the interim. The dynamics afterward always tell you more than what the relationship did—grief is a faster teacher than joy—but what does it mean when you cycle out to being strangers again? You never really stop knowing each other in that way. Maybe there's no choice but to make them someone different in your mind, not the person who knew your daily anxieties and what you looked like naked and what made you cry and how much you loved them.

When our lives revolve around someone, they don't just stop doing so even if all that's left is some semblance of their memory. There are always those bits that linger. The memories that are impressed on the places you went and the things you said and the songs you listened to remain.

We all eventually find ourselves standing in the checkout line, hearing one of those songs come on and realizing that we're revolving around them again. And maybe we never stopped.

Do you ever really forget your lovers' birthdays, or all your first times, intimate and not? Do your anniversaries ever become normal days of the year again? Are the things you did and promises you made ever really neutralized? Do they become void now that you're broken up or do you decidedly ignore them because there's simply no other choice? The mind tells you to go on and forces your heart to follow suit, I guess.

I want to believe that you either love someone, in some way, forever, or you never really loved them at all. That once two reactive chemicals cross, both are changed. That the wounds we leave in people are sometimes too raw to risk falling back into them. I don't want to believe that we write each other off because we simply don't matter anymore. I know love isn't expendable. I wonder, and maybe hope, if we ever just force it to be out of necessity.

Maybe it's just that we're all at the centers of our own little universes, and sometimes they overlap with other people's, and that small bit of intersection leaves some part of it changed. The collision can wreck us, change us, shift us. Sometimes we merge into one, and other times we rescind because the comfort of losing what we thought we knew wins out.

Either way, it's inevitable that you expand. That you're left knowing that much more about love and what it can do, and the pain that only a hole in your heart and space in your bed and emptiness in the next chair over can bring. Whether or not that hole will ever again include the person who made it that way...I don't know. Whether or not anybody else can match the outline of someone who was so deeply impressed in you...I don't know that, either.

We all start as strangers. The choices we make in terms of love are usually ones that seem inevitable anyway. We find people irrationally compelling. We find souls made of the same stuff ours are. We find classmates and partners and neighbors and family friends and cousins and sisters and our lives intersect in a way that makes them feel like they couldn't have ever been separate. And this is lovely. But the ease and access isn't what we crave. It isn't what I'm writing about right now. It isn't what we revolve around after it's gone. We are all just waiting for another universe to collide with ours, to change what we can't ourselves. It's interesting how we realize the storm returns to calm, but we see the stars differently now, and we don't know, and we can't choose, whose wreckage can do that for us.

We all start as strangers, but we forget that we rarely choose who ends up a stranger, too.

15

16 SIGNS
of a SOCIALLY
INTELLIGENT
PERSON

While you may not know what makes someone socially intelligent, you have likely experienced the kind of social tone-deafness that leaves you feeling frustrated at best, and physically uncomfortable at worst.

Manners are cultural social intelligence. Yet it seems traditional "politeness" is beginning to lose its appeal—it can conjure images of washing out your personality in favor of more uniform behavior. While we want to be able to engage with people in a mutually comfortable way, we shouldn't have to sacrifice genuine expression in favor of a polite nod or gracious smile. The two are not mutually exclusive.

People who are socially intelligent think and behave in a way that spans beyond what's culturally acceptable at any given moment in time. They function in such a way that they are able to communicate with others and leave them feeling at ease without sacrificing who they are and what they want to say. This, of course, is the basis of connection, the thing on which our brains are wired to desire, and on which we personally thrive.

Here, the core traits of someone who is socially intelligent:

01. They do not try to elicit a strong emotional response from anyone they are holding a conversation with.

    They don't communicate in such a way that aggrandizes their accomplishments to incite a response of awe or exaggerates their hardships to incite a response of sympathy. This usually occurs when the topic in question is not actually deserving of such a strong response, and therefore makes others uncomfortable because they feel pressured to fake an emotional reaction.

02. They do not speak in definitives about people, politics, or ideas.

The fastest way to sound unintelligent is to say, "This idea is wrong." (That idea may be wrong for you, but it exists because it is right to someone else.) Intelligent people say, "I don't personally understand this idea or agree with it." To speak definitively about any one person or idea is to be blind to the multitude of perspectives that exist on it. It is the definition of closed-minded and short-sightedness.

03. They don't immediately deny criticism, or have such a strong emotional reaction to it that they become unapproachable or unchangeable.

Some of the most difficult people to be in relationships with are those who are so threatened by even the slightest suggestion that their behavior is hurtful that they actually end up getting angry at the person suggesting it, reinforcing the problem altogether. Socially intelligent people listen to criticism before they respond to it—an immediate emotional response without thoughtful consideration is just defensiveness.

04. They do not confuse their opinion of someone for being a fact about them.

Socially intelligent people do not say, "He's a prick" as though it is fact. Instead, they say: "I had a negative experience with him where I felt very uncomfortable."

05. They never overgeneralize other people through their behaviors.

They don't use "you always" or "you never" to illustrate a point. Likewise, they root their arguments in statements that begin with "I feel" as opposed to "you are." They do this because choosing language that feels unthreatening to someone is the best way to get them to open up to your perspective and actually create the dialogue that will lead to the change you desire.

17

06. They speak with precision.

They say what they intend to say without skirting around the issue. They speak calmly, simply, concisely, and mindfully. They focus on communicating something, not just receiving a response from others.

07. They know how to practice healthy disassociation.

In other words, they know that the world does not revolve around them. They are able to listen to someone without worrying that any given statement they make is actually a slight against them. They are able to disassociate from their own projections and at least try to understand another person's perspective without assuming it has everything to do with their own.

08. They do not try to inform people of their ignorance.

When you accuse someone of being wrong, you close them off to considering another perspective by heightening their defenses. If you first validate their stance ("That's interesting, I never thought of it that way...") and then present your own opinion ("Something I recently learned is this...") and then let them know that they still hold their own power in the conversation by asking their opinion ("What do you think about that?"), you open them up to engaging in a conversation where both of you can learn rather than just defend.

09. They validate other people's feelings.

To validate someone else's feelings is to accept that they feel the way they do without trying to use logic to dismiss or deny or change their minds. (For example: "I am sad today." "Well, you shouldn't be, your life is great!") The main misunderstanding here is that validating feelings is not the same thing as validating ideas. There are many ideas that do not need or deserve to be validated, but everyone's feelings deserve to be seen and acknowledged and respected. Validating someone's emotions is validating who they really are, even if you would respond differently. So in other words, it is validating who someone is, even if they are different than you.

10. They recognize that their "shadow selves" are the traits, behaviors, and patterns that aggravate them about others.
One's hatred of a misinformed politician could be a projection of their fear of being unintelligent or underqualified. One's intense dislike for a particularly passive friend could be an identification of one's own inclination to give others power in their life. It is not always an obvious connection, but when there is a strong emotional response involved, it is always there. If you genuinely disliked something, you would simply disengage with it.

11. They do not argue with people who only want to win, not learn.
You can identify that this is the case when people start "pulling" for arguments or resorting to shoddy logic only to seem as though they have an upper hand. Socially intelligent people know that not everybody wants to communicate, learn, grow or connect—and so they do not try to force them.

12. They listen to hear, not respond.
While listening to other people speak, they focus on what is being said, not how they are going to respond. This is also known as the meta practice of "holding space."

13. They do not post anything online they would be embarrassed to show to a parent, explain to a child, or have an employer find.
Aside from the fact that at some point or another, one if not all of those things will come to pass, posting anything that you are not confident to support means you are not being genuine to yourself (you are behaving on behalf of the part of you that wants other people to validate it).

14. They do not consider themselves a judge of what's true.
They don't say, "you're wrong"; they say, "I think you are wrong."

15. They don't "poison the well" or fall for ad hominem fallacy to disprove a point.

    "Poisoning the well" is when someone attacks the character of a person so as to shift the attention away from the (possibly very valid) point being made. For example, if a person who eats three candy bars a day says: "I don't think kids it's healthy for children to eat too much candy each day," a socially intelligent person wouldn't respond, "Who are you to say?"; they would be able to see the statement objective from the person who is saying it. Usually, it is people who are most inflicted with an issue that are able to speak out on the importance of it (even if it seems hypocritical on the surface).

16. Their primary relationship is to themselves, and they work on it tirelessly.

The main thing socially intelligent people understand is that your relationship to everyone else is an extension of your relationship to yourself.

6

UNCOMFORTABLE FEELINGS
that actually
INDICATE
you're on the
RIGHT PATH

Discomfort is what happens when we are on the precipice of change. Unfortunately, we often confuse it for unhappiness and cope with the latter while running from the former. It usually takes a bit of discomfort to break through to a new understanding, to release a limiting belief, to motivate ourselves to create real change. Discomfort is a signal, one that is often very helpful. Here are a few (less than desirable) feelings that may indicate you're on the right path after all:

01. Feeling as though you are reliving your childhood struggles.
    You find that you're seeing issues you struggled with as a kid reappear in your adult life, and while on the surface this may seem like a matter of not having overcome them, it really means you are becoming conscious of why you think and feel so you can change it.

02. Feeling "lost" or directionless.
    Feeling lost is actually a sign you're becoming more present in your life—you're living less within the narratives and ideas that you premeditated and more in the moment at hand. Until you're used to this, it will feel as though you're off-track (you aren't).

03. "Left brain" fogginess.
    When you're utilizing the right hemisphere more often (you're becoming more intuitive, you're dealing with emotions, you're

1

creating) sometimes it can seem as though "left brain" functions leave you feeling fuzzy. Things such as focusing, organizing, and remembering small details suddenly become difficult.

04. Having random influxes of irrational anger or sadness that intensify until you can't ignore them anymore.
When emotions erupt it's usually because they're "coming up" to be recognized, and our job is to learn to stop grappling with them or resisting them and to simply become fully conscious of them (after that, we control them, not the opposite way around).

05. Experiencing unpredictable and scattered sleeping patterns.
You'll need to sleep a lot more or a lot less, you'll wake up in the middle of the night because you can't stop thinking about something, you find yourself full of energy or completely exhausted, and with little in between.

06. A life-changing event is taking place or just has.
You suddenly having to move, getting divorced, losing a job, having a car break down, etc.

07. Having an intense need to be alone.
You're suddenly disenchanted with the idea of spending every weekend out socializing, and other people's problems are draining you more than they are intriguing you. This means you're recalibrating.

08. Intense, vivid dreaming that you almost always remember in detail.
If dreams are how your subconscious mind communicates with you (or projects an image of your experience), then your mind is definitely trying to say something. You're having dreams at an intensity that you've never experienced before.

09. Downsizing your friend group; feeling more and more uncomfortable around negative people.
The thing about negative people is that they rarely realize they are negative, and because you feel uncomfortable

22

saying anything (and you're even more uncomfortable keeping that in your life), you're ghosting a bit on old friends.

10. Feeling like the dreams you had for your life are collapsing.
What you do not realize at this moment is that it is making way for a reality better than you could have thought of, one that's more aligned with who you are, not who you thought you would be.

11. Feeling as though your worst enemies are your thoughts.
You're beginning to realize that your thoughts create your experience, and it's often not until we're pushed to our wits' end that we even try to take control of them—and that's when we realize that we were in control all along.

12. Feeling unsure of who you really are.
Your past illusions about who you "should" be are dissolving. You feel unsure because it is uncertain! You're in the process of evolving, and we don't become uncertain when we change for the worse; we become angry and closed off. In other words: If what you're experiencing is insecurity or uncertainty, it's usually going to lead to something better.

13. Recognizing how far you still have to go.
When you realize this, it's because you can also see where you're headed; it means you finally know where and who you want to be.

14. "Knowing" things you don't want to know, such as what someone is really feeling, or that a relationship isn't going to last, or that you won't be at your job much longer.
A lot of "irrational" anxiety comes from subconsciously sensing something, yet not taking it seriously because it isn't logical.

15. Having an intense desire to speak up for yourself.
Becoming angry with how much you've let yourself be walked on or how much you've let other people's voices get into your head is a sign that you're finally ready to stop listening and love yourself by respecting yourself first.

23

16. Realizing you are the only person responsible for your life and your happiness.

This kind of emotional autonomy is terrifying, because it means that if you mess up, it's all on you. At the same time, realizing it is the only way to be truly free. The risk is worth the reward on this one, always.

7

WHAT *the*
FEELINGS
you most
SUPPRESS
are trying to
TELL YOU

Emotional intelligence is not how infrequently you feel anything "bad" because you've developed the discipline and wisdom "not to." It's not how easily you choose what you think, how you let it affect you, or how placidly you react to any given situation.

Real emotional maturity is how thoroughly you let yourself feel anything. Everything. Whatever comes. It is simply the knowing that the worst thing that could ever happen...is just a feeling at the end of the day.

That's it! A feeling. Imagine the very worst, the only thing bad about it is...how you would feel about it. What you would make it out to be, what you'd assume the repercussions mean, and how those would ultimately affect...how you feel.

A sense of fear, a pinch or throb or sting. A hunger pang or ego kick. The sense of worthlessness, the idea of not belonging. (Interesting how physical feelings are always quick and transient, but the ideas we hold of pain always seem to stick around...)

But we avoid feeling anything because we have more or less been taught that our feelings have lives of their own. That they'll carry on forever if we give them even a moment of our awareness.

Have you ever felt joy for more than a few minutes? What about anger? No? How about tension, depression, and sadness? Those have lasted longer, haven't they? Weeks and months and years at a time, right?

That's because those aren't feelings. They are symptoms. But we'll get to their causes in a minute.

What you have to know is that suffering is just the refusal to accept what is. That's it. Etymologically, it comes from the Latin word to "from below to bear." Or, to "resist, endure, put under."

So healing is really just letting yourself feel.

It is unearthing your traumas and embarrassments and losses and allowing yourself the emotions that you could not have in the moment that you were having those experiences. It's letting yourself filter and process what you had to suppress at the time to keep going, maybe even to survive.

We all fear that our feelings are too big, especially in the moment we're actually having them. We were taught not be too loving, we'd get hurt; too smart, we'd get bullied; too fearful, we'd be vulnerable. To be compliant with what other people wanted us to feel. As kids we were punished for crying out if our emotional experience wasn't in accordance with our parents' convenience. (No wonder we still respond the way we do.)

The point is that you aren't the one who is afraid of feeling too much. It's the people who called you crazy and dramatic and wrong. The people who don't know how to handle it, who want you to stay where you are. Those are the people who want you to keep not feeling. Not you. You know how I know?

Because your numbness isn't feeling nothing, it's feeling everything, and never having learned to process anything at all. Numbness is not nothing, neutral is nothing. Numbness is everything at once.

Because your sadness is saying, "I am still attached to something being different." Your guilt is saying, "I fear I have done bad in someone's eyes," and your shame, "I fear I am bad in someone's eyes."

Your anxiety is your resistance to the process, your last grasps at a control you are becoming more and more aware that you do not have. Your tiredness is your resistance to who you really are, the person you actually want to be. Your annoyance is your repressed anger. Your depression, biological factors aside of course, is everything coming to the surface, and you bellowing down to stow it away.

26

And your arrival at the conclusion that you cannot go on like this, that you're missing out, that you're off-track and feeling stuck and lost, is you realizing that you need not change your feelings. You just have to learn to lean into them and see what they are trying to tell you.

Trying to change how you feel is like finding a road sign that points in the opposite direction of where you had intended to go and getting out to try to turn the sign, rather than your course of action.

And what happens when we stow away the emotions that accompany our experiences, never give ourselves time to process, try to force ourselves into feeling any given way at any given time, is we disregard what will give us the ultimate peace: just allowing, without judgment.

So it's not about changing how you feel. It's about listening. Not accepting what they appear to mean—that's important—but really following your instincts down to what they are trying to signal. They are how you communicate with yourself.

Every feeling is worthwhile. You miss so much by trying to change every one of them away, or thinking there are some that are right or wrong or good or bad or that you should have or shouldn't, all because you're afraid that you'll tell yourself something you don't want to hear.

The feelings you most suppress are the most important ways you guide yourself. Your apprehension to listen is not your own desire. It's fear of being something more or less or greater or worse or simply different than those around you have implied they will accept.

When you choose to value having other people's acceptance over your own, you accept a fate of battling your instincts to assimilate to the needs of other people's egos. In the meantime, a world and lifetime of listening, leaning, allowing, following, perceiving, feeling, and experiencing... constantly eludes you.

Sadness will not kill you. Depression won't, either. But fighting it will. Ignoring it will. Trying to escape it rather than confront it will. Denying it will. Suffocating it will. Allowing it no place to go other than your deep subconscious to embed and control you will. Not that you'll take your life or destroy everything "good" you do receive (though you might).

But it will kill you in that it will rob you of every bit of life you do have: You either let yourself feel everything or numb yourself into feeling nothing. You cannot select emotions. You are either in accord with their flow or in resistance to their nature. In the end, the choice is yours.

8

THE PARTS
of you that
AREN'T "I"

Let's pretend for a moment that we pulled apart all of your organs and laid them on a table.

Feel your heartbeat; imagine it outside of you. You would not look at your heart and think: "That is me." You think: "That is my heart."

Now feel your breath. Feel it in tandem with your heartbeat, neither of which you are often conscious of, both of which are in constant motion. You do not say, "I am my breath." You say: "I am breathing."

Think about your liver. And your kidneys. Think about your bones and your blood. Think about your legs and your fingers and your hair and your brain. You see them objectively. They're just parts. They're ultimately (mostly) removable and replaceable and they're all entirely temporary. You don't think of them and see "I." You think of them and you see things. If you pulled them apart, they'd just be compilations of cells. You don't see them and think: "That's me!" You think: "Those are mine."

Why is it any different when we compile and attach them?

There is a concentration of energy, of heavy presentness, in your chest and throat and maybe a little in your head. It is centered. You don't feel yourself in your legs. You don't have emotions in your arms. It's at the core.

In that same space coexist the organs we don't identify with and the energy we do. If we removed the latter, what would be left? What would be there? What exists when you don't?

Have you ever sat in that? Have you ever sat with that? Have you ever felt each part of your body and realized the parts are not "I?" Have you ever felt the presentness that is somehow livened when attached? Have you ever identified the difference between what you call yours and what you call yourself?

29

Knowing who you are is grounding; it gives you a sense of trajectory. But when we assign words and meanings to what we know we like and value and want, we create attachments. We then strive to keep things within the parameters of which we've already accepted. Out of that, we create failure. We create suffering over self. We begin to believe that a static idea can represent a dynamic, evolving being. The ways we don't live up to the ideas in our minds become our greatest grievances.

I think sometimes we get attached to the structures because we don't like the contents. We're more invested in how we're perceived than who we are, in the idea of what the title means than the day-to-day work of the job, in the "do you promise to love me forever?" than the actual day-to-day loving. This is to say: We're more comforted by ideas of what things are as opposed to what they really are. We like to think of ourselves as bodies because that doesn't leave us with the open-ended "what else."

But what if the "what else" isn't the end-thought, but the beginning? What if awareness of it frees us of so many things, quells so many thoughts, balms so many aches? What if healing yourself is not fixing an attitude, not changing an opinion, not altering an aesthetic, but shifting a presence, an awareness, an energy?

In this case, fixing the parts does not heal the whole.

The only thing that changes you and your life is the awareness of the parts that are not "I." It is the whole, it is where you end up, it is where you began, it is the one thing, the only thing, that shifts, and raises, and facilitates the spark of awareness that made you question the elements of its vessel.

I'm not really asking you to consider the theories. I'm just asking whether or not you feel it.

30

9

20 SIGNS
you're doing
BETTER
than you think
YOU ARE

01. You paid the bills this month and maybe even had extra to spend on nonessentials. It doesn't matter how much you belabored the checks as they went out; the point is that they did, and you figured it out regardless.

02. You question yourself. You doubt your life. You feel miserable some days. This means you're still open to growth. This means you can be objective and self-aware. The best people go home at the end of the day and think: "or...maybe there's another way."

03. You have a job. For however many hours, at whatever rate, you are earning money that helps you eat something, sleep on something, wear something every day. It's not failure if it doesn't look the way you thought it would—you're valuing your independence and taking responsibility for yourself.

04. You have time to do something you enjoy, even if "what you enjoy" is sitting on the couch and ordering dinner and watching Netflix.

05. You are not worried about where your next meal is coming from. There's food in the fridge or pantry, and you have enough to actually pick and choose what you want to eat.

06. You can eat because you enjoy it. It's not a matter of sheer survival.

07. You have one or two truly close friends. People worry about the quantity but eventually tend to realize the number of

people you can claim to be in your tribe has no bearing on how much you feel intimacy, acceptance, community, or joy. At the end of the day, all we really want are a few close people who know us (and love us) no matter what.

08. You could afford a subway ride, cup of coffee, or the gas in your car this morning. The smallest conveniences (and oftentimes, necessities) are not variables for you.

09. You're not the same person you were a year ago. You're learning, and evolving, and can identify the ways in which you've changed for better and worse.

10. You have the time and means to do things beyond the bare minimum. You've maybe been to a concert in the last few years, you buy books for yourself, you could take a day trip to a neighboring city if you wanted—you don't have to work all hours of the day to survive.

11. You have a selection of clothing at your disposal. You aren't worried about having a hat or gloves in a blizzard, you have cool clothes for the summer and something to wear to a wedding. You not only can shield and decorate your body but can do so appropriately for a variety of circumstances.

12. You can sense what isn't right in your life. The first and most crucial step is simply being aware. Being able to communicate to yourself: "Something is not right, even though I am not yet sure what would feel better."

13. If you could talk to your younger self, you would be able to say: "We did it, we made it out, we survived that terrible thing." So often people carry their past traumas into their present lives, and if you want any proof that we carry who we were in who we are, all you need to do is see how you respond to your inner child hearing, "You're going to be okay" from the person they became.

14. You have a space of your own. It doesn't even have to be a home or apartment (but that's great if it is). All you need is a room, a corner, a desk, where you can create or rest at your

discretion; where you govern who gets to be part of your weird little world, and to what capacity. It's one of the few controls we can actually exert.

15. You've lost relationships. More important than the fact that you've simply had them in the first place is that you or your former partner chose not to settle. You opened yourself to the possibility of something else being out there.

16. You're interested in something. Whether it's how to live a happier life, maintain better relationships, reading or movies or sex or society or the axis on which the world spins, something intrigues you to explore it.

17. You know how to take care of yourself. You know how many hours of sleep you need to feel okay the next day, who to turn to when you're heartbroken, what you have fun doing, what to do when you don't feel well, etc.

18. You're working toward a goal. Even if you're exhausted and it feels miles away, you have a dream for yourself, however vague and malleable.

19. But you're not uncompromisingly set on anything for your future. Some of the happiest and best-adjusted people are the ones who can make any situation an ideal, who are too immersed in the moment to intricately plan and decidedly commit to any one specific outcome.

20. You've been through some crap. You can look at challenges you currently face and compare them to ones you thought you'd never get over. You can reassure yourself through your own experience. Life did not get easier; you got smarter.

BREAKING *your* "UPPER LIMIT,"
and how
PEOPLE HOLD THEMSELVES
back from real
HAPPINESS

Most people don't want to be happy, which is why they aren't. They just don't realize this is the case.

People are programmed to chase their foremost desire at almost any cost. (Imagine the adrenaline-fueled superhuman powers people develop in life-or-death emergencies.) It's just a matter of what that foremost desire is. Often enough, it's comfort. Or familiarity.

There are many reasons people thwart the feeling of happiness, but a lot of them have to do with assuming it means giving up on achieving more. Nobody wants to believe happiness is a choice, because that puts responsibility in their hands. It's the same reason people self-pity: to delay action, to make an outcry to the universe, as though the more they state how bad things are, the more likely it is that someone else will change them.

Happiness is not a rush of positive emotion elicited by random events that affirm the way you think something should go. Not sustainable happiness, anyway. The real stuff is the product of an intentional, mindful, daily practice, and it begins with choosing to commit to it.

Everybody has a happiness tolerance—an upper limit—as Gay Hendricks coins it[4]. It is the capacity for which we allow ourselves to feel good. Other psychologists call it the "baseline," the amount of happiness we "naturally" feel, and eventually revert back to, even if certain events or circumstances shift us temporarily.

The reason we don't allow those shifts to become baselines is because of the upper limit—as soon as our circumstances extend beyond the amount of happiness we're accustomed to and comfortable feeling, we unconsciously begin to self-sabotage.

We are programmed to seek what we've known. So even though we think we're after happiness, we're actually trying to find whatever we're most accustomed to, and we project that on whatever actually exists, over and over again. These are just a few of many psychological impediments that hold us back from the emotional lives we claim to want. Here are a few others:

01. Everybody has a limited tolerance for feeling good.
    When things go beyond that limit, we sabotage ourselves so we can return to our comfort zones. The tired cliché of stepping outside them serves a crucial purpose: It makes people comfortable with discomfort, which is the gateway to expanding their tolerance for happiness.

02. There is a "likability limit" that people like to remain under: Everybody has a level of "success" that they perceive to be admirable—and unthreatening to others.
    Most things people do are in an effort to "earn" love. Many desires, dreams, and ambitions are built out of a space of severe lack. It's for this reason that some of the most emotionally dense people are also the most successful: They use their desire for acceptance, love, wholeness, as fuel—for better and for worse.
    The point is: Once people surpass the point at which they think people will judge and ridicule them for their success (as opposed to praise them for it), they promptly cut themselves off, or at minimum severely downplay/minimize it so as to keep themselves in good standing with those from whom they desire approval. (It's ultimately not that people value ego and material over love, but that they think those things will earn them love.)

03. Most prefer the comfort of what they've known to the vulnerability of what they don't.
    Even when "what they don't" is, objectively, much better. If we redefine "happiness" in terms of what human beings innately

36

desire (comfort, inclusiveness, a sense of purpose, etc.), we can then make the choice to seek comfort from things that are ultimately aligned with what we want to achieve.

04. Many people are afraid that "being happy" = giving up on achieving more.

Happiness is, in an essential form, acceptance. It's arriving at the end goal, passing the finish line, letting the wave of accomplishment wash over you. Deciding to be that way every day can make it seem as though the race is already over, so we subconsciously associate "happiness" and "acceptance" with "giving up." But the opposite is true: The path to a greater life is not "suffering until you achieve something," but letting bits and pieces of joy and gratitude and meaning and purpose gradually build, bit by bit.

05. People delay action once they know truth—and the interim between knowing and doing is the space where suffering thrives.

Most of the time, it's not about not knowing what to do (or not knowing who you are). It's about the resistance between what's right and what's easy, what's best in the long v. short term. We hear our instincts; we just don't listen. This is the single most common root of discomfort: the space between knowing and doing. We're culturally addicted to procrastination, but we're also just as enamored by deflection. By not acting immediately, we think we're creating space for the truth to shift, when we're really only creating discomfort so that we can sense it more completely (though we're suffering needlessly in the process).

06. People believe that apathy is safety.

We're all afraid of losing the pieces and people that make up our lives. Some people try to cut ahead of the pain-curve and don't let themselves feel as though they wanted or liked those things in the first place. The undercurrent here is the sense that everything ends and all is impermanent and while those things are more or less true, there is something just slightly truer, and it is that death gives life meaning. It's the fact that we can lose what we have that makes it sacred and precious and wonderful. It's not about what pain you suffer; it's about what you suffer for. You can choose to cut yourself off from feeling good so as to buffer the sense of loss and suffer from numbness, or you can have an incredible life and mourn wildly when it's over, but at least there was a means to that end.

07. Few know how to practice feeling good (or why it's necessary).

It is almost essential to raising your upper limit, augmenting your baseline, and ultimately assimilating to the new chapter(s) of your life without destroying them out of unfamiliarity. Practicing feeling good is simply taking a moment to literally let yourself feel. Extend that rush just a few seconds longer, meditate on some things you're grateful for, and let it wash over you as much as possible. Seek what's positive, and you'll find that your threshold for feeling it expands as you decide it can.

08. People think happiness is an emotional response facilitated by a set of circumstances, as opposed to a choice and shift of perception/awareness.

It seems that the people who are steadfast in their belief that circumstances create happiness are not to be swayed—and that makes sense. It's for the same reason that we buy into it so much: It's easier. It's the way to cut corners on your emotional life. It's seemingly logical and fairly easy to attain, so why not stand by it fiercely? Because it's ultimately false. It maintains that you must wait to feel happy, and as we know, unless you are cultivating your baseline to be all-around higher, you'll spend the rest of your life bopping from one perceived high to another. Some of the statistically happiest countries in the world are nearly impoverished. Some of the most notable and peaceful individuals to grace the Earth died with only a few cents to their name. The commonality is a sense of purpose, belonging, and love: things you can choose to feel and cultivate, regardless of physical/material circumstance.

09. Most people don't know that it's possible to shift their baseline, since it's always framed in a way of being "how one naturally is."

If I've heard it once I've heard it a thousand times: the woman with anxiety who says, "It's just the way I am." The man with a dozen irrational fears who attributes them to "his personality." The thing is that nothing has to be an essential part of you unless you decide it is—least of all anxiety and fear. In fact, those things are never essentially part of who someone is; they are learned behaviors. They are ego-reactions that go unchecked. They are flashing lights and waving flags from our innermost selves that something is not right, but we're avoiding making the shift (mostly by deflecting on the circumstance being out of our control).

10. People believe that suffering makes them worthy.

To have wonderful things in our lives without having suffered for them somehow translates to us feeling as though we haven't truly "earned" them and therefore, they are not completely ours. On the flip side: The idea that beautiful, joyous things could simply be ours without any conscious creation of them on our part is terrifying, because the opposite could just as well be true.

11. Many people believe they can beat fear to the finish line.

Worry is the Western cultural pastime, and it's ultimately a deflection from the fact that we buoy between extremes: not caring about anything or caring so much about one thing it could break us altogether.

Worrying conditions us to the worst possible outcomes so they don't cause as much pain if they come to pass. We're thinking through every irrational possibility so we can account for it, prepare for it, before it surprises us. We try to imagine every "bad" thing a person could say about us so they're not the first to do it.

But this does not change anything. You still won't expect difficult things to arise. You will never know what people are really thinking, or how often. You will not be able to prepare to cope with your irrational fears, because there's no basis in a reality you could possibly get ready to deal with. You cannot beat fear to the finish line. You are not cheating your way around pain. You're actively pursuing more and more of it.

12. Happy people are often perceived as being naive and vulnerable.

If nothing else, happy people are stigmatized as being clueless and ill-informed and delusionally positive and disconnected from reality, but the only people who perceive them that way are people who do everything in their power to justify the negativity in their lives they feel they cannot control. It is people who don't choose a better life that are naive and truly vulnerable, as "happy people" may lose everything they have, but people who never choose to fully step into their lives never have anything at all.

---

4 Hendricks, Gay. *The Big Leap: Conquer Your Hidden Fear and Take Life to the Next Level*. 2010. HarperOne.

the HAPPINESS
of EXCELLENCE

Eric Greitens says that there are three primary forms of happiness: the happiness of pleasure, the happiness of grace, and the happiness of excellence[5]. He compares them to the primary colors, the basis on which the entire spectrum is created.

The happiness of pleasure is largely sensory. It's a good meal when you're hungry, the smell of air after it rains, waking up warm and cozy in your bed. The happiness of grace is gratitude. It's looking over to see the love of your life sleeping next to you and whispering, "thank you." It's taking inventory of what you do have. It's when you speak to something greater than yourself, expressing humility and awe.

And then there is the happiness of excellence. The kind of happiness that comes from the pursuit of something great. Not the moment you arrive at the top of the mountain and raise your fists in victory, but the process of falling in love with the hike. It is meaningful work. It is flow. It is the purpose that sears identity and builds character and channels our energy toward something greater than the insatiable, daily pursuit of our fleeting desires.

Just as removing one of the primary colors would make many others impossible (without yellow, you could not have any shade of green) without any one of these happinesses, it is almost impossible to thrive.

One cannot replace another. They are all necessary. But we try anyway.

To drink in excess, for example—the happiness of pleasure—is common when the happiness of excellence isn't being pursued. But it is not, and will never be, the solution.

"Lots and lots of red will never make blue. Pleasures will never make you whole."

The happiness of excellence is the work of emotional resilience. It's the highest ranking on Maslow's hierarchy. It is measured, deliberate, and consistent. It is often avoided because the discomfort is palpable, and the reward isn't instantaneous. There's no contact high during the first days of marathon training when your lungs are stinting and you want to vomit. But over time, you develop your skill. You begin to imagine what you could accomplish. You fall in love with the process.

Though all three of the happinesses are different, they are all shaped by context. Someone who has gone without food for three days is more attuned to the happiness of pleasure than people who consider meals and shelter givens.

Likewise, those who have never acquainted themselves with the power and pleasure of working toward something fueled not by the sparks of passion but with the embers of sober, consistent resolve, do not know that on the other side of exerted effort, there is profound reward.

Many of us are colorblind to the joys and complexities of our lives, and it is because we are missing a part of the foundation. We want to be authors but have no desire to develop the discipline it takes to sit down and write for four hours a day for years on end. We want to be legends and geniuses and masters, but care little to develop the discipline it would require to log our 10,000 hours—so to say.

Happiness is not only how we can astound our senses, but also the peace of mind that comes from knowing we are becoming who we want and need to be. That's what we receive from pursuing the happiness of excellence: not accomplishment, but identity. A sense of self that we carry into everything else in our lives. A technicolor pigment that makes the entire spectrum come alive.

---

5 Greitens, Eric. *Resilience: Hard-Won Wisdom For Living a Better Life.* 2016. Mariner Books.

the KNOWING-DOING GAP:
why we AVOID DOING
WHAT'S BEST FOR US,
and how to
CONQUER
RESISTANCE
FOR GOOD

The ancient Greeks called it Akrasia, the Zen Buddhists call it resistance, you and I call it procrastination, every productivity guru on the Internet calls it being "stuck." Jeffrey Pfeffer and Robert Sutton call it the "knowing-doing gap," or the experience of knowing the best thing to do, but doing something else anyway[6].

Common sense tells us that if we put another hour into novel writing each night, ate better, woke earlier, chose affirmative thoughts, spoke honestly and connected more genuinely, we'd live better lives. But the real question, and the real work, is not understanding what's good for us, but why we choose otherwise. Understanding the fabric of resistance is the only way we can unstitch it.

There are many reasons we self-sabotage, and most of them have something to do with comfort. Modern society (innovation, culture, wealth, success) is designed to convince us that a "good life" is one that is most comfortable, or able to provide us with a sense of being pain-free and secure. This is pretty directly related to the fact that human beings are hardwired to seek comfort, which translates to us as survival—we're physiologically designed that way. It only makes sense that in our more fully actualized intellectual and emotional lives, we'd want the same.

Moving yourself past resistance is a matter of shifting your perception of comfort. It's about considering the alternative. It's altering your mindset to focus on the discomfort you will face if you

43

don't do the thing in front of you, as opposed to the discomfort you will face if you do.

If left unchecked, the knowing-doing gap will leave you a shell of the person you intended to be. It will wreck your most intimate, passionate relationships, keep you from the kind of daily productivity required to achieve any goal worth working toward. It will keep you in a manic state of indecision (do I, or don't I? Which feeling do I let guide me?). You have to take control for yourself, and you can do so by considering the big picture. The alternative. The way your life will be if you don't do this thing.

How will you quantifiably measure this year? What will you have done? How many hours will you have wasted? If you had to live today—or any average day—on repeat for the rest of your life, where would you end up? What would you accomplish? How happy would you be? What relationships will you have fostered? Will you be looking back knowing you likely damn well missed out on what could have been the love of your life because you weren't "ready?" What about the hours you could have been playing music or writing or painting or whatever-ing? Where will those have gone?

You will never be ready for the things that matter, and waiting to feel ready before you start acting is how the knowing-doing gap widens. It's uncomfortable to work, to stretch the capacity of your tolerance, to be vulnerable with someone you care deeply about, but it is never more comfortable than going your whole life without the things you really want.

Anxiety builds in our idle hours. Fear and resistance thrive when we're avoiding the work. Most things aren't as hard or as trying as we chalk them up to be. They're ultimately fun and rewarding and expressions of who we really are. That's why we want them. Taking small steps will remind you that this is true. It will soothe you in a way that just thinking about taking action never will. It's easier to act your way into a new way of thinking rather than think your way into a new way of acting, so do one little thing today and let the momentum build.

And thank whatever force within you that knows there's something bigger for you—the one that's pushing you to be comfortable with less.

---

6 Pfeffer, Jeffrey. *The Knowing-Doing Gap: How Smart Companies Turn Knowledge Into Action*. 2000. Harvard Business School Press.

13

101 THINGS
more worth
THINKING
about than
WHATEVER'S
CONSUMING YOU

01. The way it will feel to have the life you want. The place you'll live, the clothes you will wear, what you will buy at the supermarket, how much money you'll save, what work you'll be most proud to have done. What you'll do with your weekends, what color your sheets will be, what you'll take photos of.

02. The parts of yourself you need to work on, not because someone else doesn't love them, but because you don't.

03. The fact that sometimes, the ultimate expression of self-love is admitting you don't like yourself and coming up with steps to change the things that you know you can and will do better.

04. A list of things that turned out to be very right for you, and what similar feeling accompanied each of them.

05. The way you will quantify this year. How many books you want to say you've read, how many projects you've completed, how many connections with friends and family you fostered or rekindled, how you spent your days.

06. The things in the past that you thought you'd never get over, and how insignificant they seem today.

07. What you will create today, what food you will eat, and who you will connect with. (These are the only things you carry with you.)

08. How you learn best, and how you could possibly integrate that form of comprehension into your life more often (do things that are more visual, or listen better, try to experiment more often, and so on).

09. The fact that you do not need to be exceptionally beautiful or talented or successful to experience the things that make life profound: love, knowledge, connection, community, and so on.

10. The cosmos, and how despite being insignificant specks, we are all essential to the core patchwork that makes up humanity, and that without any single one of us, nothing would exist as it is right now.

11. The proper conjugations for a language you could stand to speak conversationally.

12. The people you smiled at on the street this morning, the people whom you text regularly, the family you could stand to visit more—all the little bits of genuine human connection that you overlook because they've become givens.

13. How you will remember this time in your life 20 years from now. What you will wish you had done or stopped doing, what you overlooked, what little things you didn't realize you should have appreciated.

14. How few of your days you really remember.

15. How you likely won't remember this particular day 20 years from now.

16. Everything you honestly didn't like about the person you're no longer with, now that you're not emotionally obligated to lie to yourself about them.

17. A list of all the things you've done for yourself recently.

18. Little ways you can improve your quality of day-to-day life, such as consolidating debt, or learning to cook an easy signature meal, or cleaning out your closet.

19. The patterns in your failed relationships, and what degree of fault you can rightfully hand yourself.

20. What you subconsciously love about the "problems" you struggle to get over. Nobody holds onto something unless they think it does something for them (usually keeps them "safe").

21. The idea that perhaps the current problem in your life is not the problem, but that your perception is skewed, or you aren't thinking of solutions as much as you are focusing on your discomfort.

22. The ways you have sincerely failed, and how you can commit yourself to doing better, not only for yourself but for the people who love and rely on you.

23. The ways in which your current situation—though perhaps unplanned or unwanted—could be the path to the place you've actually always wanted to be, if only you'd begin to think of it that way.

24. Your mortality.

25. How you can more actively take advantage and appreciate the things that are in front of you while you still have them.

26. What your life looks like to other people. Not because you should value this more than you value your own feelings, but because perspective is important.

27. What you have already accomplished in your life.

28. What you want to be defined by when all is said and done. What kind of person you want to be known as. (Kind? Intelligent? Giving? Grounded? Helpful?)

29. What you could honestly be defined by at this point, based on your consistent actions and interactions, and whether or not that's what you really want.

30. How your unconscious assumptions about what's true and real are shaping the way you think of reality.

31. What other options exist outside of your default way of thinking; what would be true if the things you assumed were not.

32. The details of whatever it is you're working on right now.

33. How you can possibly put more effort into said work that deserves your time and attention and energy more than whatever you become distracted by does.

34. How you can help other people, even just by sitting down to speak with an old friend, buying someone dinner, sharing an article or a quote that resonated with you.

35. Other people's motivations and desires.

36. The fact that you do not think the exact way other people think, and that perhaps the issues you have with them are not issues, but lapses in your understanding of them (and theirs of you).

37. The patterns of the people you know, and what they tell you about whom they really are.

38. The fact that we assume people are as we imagine them—a compilation of the emotional experiences we've had with them—as opposed to the patterns they reveal to us in their behavior. It's more accurate to sum people up by what they repeatedly do.

39. What you would say if you could tell every single person in the world just one thing.

40. What you would say if you could tell your younger self just one thing.

41. The years of practice it takes to learn to play each instrument in your favorite song. The power and creativity it takes to simply come up with a melody, forget a piece of music that moves you to your core.

42. Where your food comes from.

43. What your big objective is. If you don't know what you generally want to do with your precious, limited time here, you're not going to do much of anything at all.

44. What you'd put in one box if you had to move to the other side of the country and could only bring that.

45. Getting to inbox 0.

46. How much your pet loves you.

47. How you can adequately and healthfully allow yourself to feel and express pain when it comes up (as opposed to just freaking out and trying to get rid of it as fast as possible).

48. Plot twists. The complexities and contradictions of your favorite characters in your favorite books.

49. Who you would be happy to also live for, if your own desires and interests were no longer your sole priority.

50. What your future self would think and say about whatever situation you're in right now.

51. An upcoming trip, whether it's booked or not. What you're going to do, what you're going to take pictures of, what you can explore, who you'll be with, who you'll meet.

52. The hardest nights of your life. What you would have done differently. What you would do if you could re-enter those hours and advise your past self.

53. The best nights of your life. Not only what you were doing and who you were with, but what you were thinking and what you were focusing on.

54. The fact that it is hard to do everything: It's hard to be in a relationship, it's hard not to be in one. It's hard to have to perform at a job you love and are emotionally invested in, it's hard not to be living your dreams by a certain age. Everything is hard; it's just a matter of what you think is worth the effort.

55. What you think is worth that effort. What you are willing to suffer for.

56. Aesthetics that you love. The kind of spaces you not only want to live and work in, but which make you feel most like yourself.

57. What actions, choices, and behaviors you think could have saved your parents.

58. Your singular, deepest fear.

59. What your singular, deepest fear tells you about your singular, deepest desire.

60. The little wonders. The smell of rain when the windows are open in the summer, your favorite T-shirt, songs you loved as a kid, your favorite food when you're hungry.

61. Your stories. The strange and simple and beautiful things you've experienced and how you can better share them with other people.

62. What you will be motivated by when fear is no longer an option.

63. What you are motivated to do when fear is no longer an option.

64. What "enough" means to you. What's enough money, enough love, enough productivity. Fulfillment is a product of knowing what "enough" is—otherwise you will be constantly seeking more.

65. Your dream moments. Having a birthday party in which all the people you love attend, or getting on a plane to Thailand, or losing the weight you've always wanted to, or being debt-free, or renovating a house.

66. What you'd do if you had $1,000 of extra disposable income each month.

67. What actions you could take to move yourself in the direction of the life you want—where you could search for networking opportunities, what friends in neighboring cities you could visit and explore, how you could get out more.

68. The feeling of sun on your skin.

69. The smell of spring.

70. What you can do with your minutes, as opposed to your hours, or days.

71. How much of your self-perception is built by culture, or expectations, or other people's opinions.

72. How much of your self-perception is sustained by culture, or expectations, or other people's opinions.

73. Who you are when nobody's around.

74. What you thought you'd be when you were younger. How the elements of that play into your life now.

75. How you'd behave differently if this entire time-space reality were in fact a holographic illusion over which you ultimately have control.

76. How you'd behave differently if your fate were dependent on the thoughts you think and the actions you take in any given moment.

77. The basic premise of various ancient philosophies, and which resonates with you the most soundly.

78. Melodies of songs that haven't been written yet.

79. The fact that the way to change your life is to change the way you think, and the way to change the way you think is to change what you read.

80. What you'd read if you chose books and articles based on what interested you, not what other people say is "good" literature.

81. What you'd listen to if you chose music based on what interested you, not what other people say is "good" music.

82. What genuinely turns you on.

83. What qualities you admire most in other people. (This is what you most like about yourself.)

84. What qualities you most dislike in other people. (This is what you cannot see, or are resisting, in yourself.)

85. How love would save your life, if it were capable of doing such things. (It is.)

86. How infinite the universe is; how infinitesimal we are; how perhaps each is a reflection, and extension, of the other.

87. How complicated the questions are; how simple the answers turn out to be.

88. What "yes" feels like to you. People very often focus on the warning signs that something is wrong, but not the subtle signals that something is right.

89. How many random, chance occurrences were involved in nearly every important advancement in your life.

90. A mantra, or many mantras, all of which work to support your unwavering conviction that the future will be different, and you will figure out how to make it so.

91. The fact that the kind of love worth choosing and keeping is the kind that ever so slightly tilts the axis on which your world spins, leaving nothing to ever be the same again.

92. How to fight better. How to eloquently communicate your thoughts and feelings without putting people on the defensive, and starting an argument where there should just be a deepening of connection.

93. What you'd live for, if your primary interest was no longer your own wants and needs.

94. The people who depend on you, and how absolutely devastated they would be if you were no longer in their lives.

95. Who and where you will be in five years if you carry on as you are right now.

96. The most important things you've learned about life so far.

97. How you came to learn the most important things you've learned so far.

98. How many people go to bed at night crying, wishing they had what you have—the job, the love, the apartment, the education, the friends, and so on.

99. How many times in your life you went to bed crying, wishing you could have what you have now—the job, the love, the apartment, the education, the friends, and so on.

100. What you can do to more consistently remind yourself of this.

101. What your most fully realized self is like. How your best self thinks. What they are grateful for, who they love. The first, and most important step, to being the person you were intended to be is to conceive of them. Once you've accomplished that, everything else falls in line.

EXPECTATIONS
YOU MUST
let go of
IN YOUR 20s

01. You're meant to be extraordinary.

    Extraordinary people are just that—rare. Recognizing this doesn't mean you're giving up on your potential, it means you're dissolving the illusions you have about what it means to be your whole self and live your best life. We tout the "one in a billion" success story as though it's the natural end goal of working hard and actualizing yourself. It's not. The real question is what work are you willing to do even if nobody claps? What will be worthwhile if it goes unacknowledged? How will you feel loved by a few people if you aren't recognized by many? Finding the exceptional in the ordinary is the real extraordinary.

02. You're at the beginning of your life.

    Some of you reading this will not make it through your 20s. Others won't make it past midlife, or even past this year. Keep a skull on your desk if you must—nobody assumes they'll die young, but that doesn't mean they don't.

03. Your faults are more forgivable, and your attributes are more exceptional.

    Believing that you're less responsible for your misgivings and that you're more exceptionally skilled at your strengths is the mindset to which many people default, but it ultimately just keeps you small. If you don't acknowledge the magnitude of the poor choices you've made, you're bound to justify doing them again; if you live and act as though you can slide by because you're ever so slightly better than everyone else, you'll never actually try.

04. You can literally be whatever you want.

If you don't have the IQ of a rocket scientist, you cannot be a rocket scientist. If you don't have the coordination to be a professional dancer, you won't be a professional dancer. Wanting something badly enough doesn't qualify you to have it.

You cannot be whatever you want, but if you work hard and don't give up and happen to be born to circumstances that facilitate it, you can maybe do something that crosses your abilities with your interests. And if you're really smart, you'll figure out how to be grateful for it, even on the difficult days.

05. You can outsmart pain.

You cannot think your way out of pain. You cannot predict it, or avoid it, or pretend you don't feel it. Doing so is living a fraction of the life you were meant to, and it will make you a fraction of the person you're supposed to be.

06. Love is something other people give you.

People cannot transmute emotions, which is interesting to consider when you realize how utterly consumed the human race is with the concept of getting other people to love us. This is because when we think other people love us, we give ourselves permission to feel love. It's a mind game, one in which we rely on everyone but ourselves to allow us to feel what's already inside us. (If you think love is something that exists anywhere but within your own mind and heart, you will never have it.)

07. Feeling something deeply means it's "meant to be."

The intensity with which you experience something (or someone) does not equate to how "destined" it is. Many people deeply feel they're called to be famous in their field, but they do not have the skills or the grit to make it; most people who get married feel deeply they're in the right relationship, but that doesn't mean it won't end in divorce someday.

Breakups are meant to be. Job losses and hurt feelings and disappointments are, too. How do we know this? Because they happen often, they are the most pivotal redirects. Forget the final picture you want your life to amount to. It will never exist the way you think it should, and in the meantime, it will only ensure that you waste what you do have in the moment. There's only one final destination here—the only thing you're rushing toward is the end of your life.

08. If you work on yourself enough, you won't struggle anymore.
If you work on yourself enough, you'll understand what the struggle is for.

09. You can control what other people think of you.
You can control how you treat people, but you cannot actually control what they think. The idea that behaving a certain way will elicit a certain response is a delusion that will keep you puppeteering through your life. It will distance you from the person you want to be and the life you want to live. And for what? People are going to judge, criticize, condemn, love, admire, envy, and lust based on their own subjective perceptions regardless.

10. Hard work guarantees success.
If you're looking for any one particular outcome as the end goal of your hard work, you're most likely going to end up disappointed. The point of hard work is to recognize the person it makes you, not what it "gets" you (the former you can control; the latter, you can't).

11. Your thoughts will change themselves when your circumstances change.
Most people assume that when their lives change, their thoughts will change. When they have someone who loves them, they'll think they're worthy of love. When they have money, they'll have a different attitude about it. Unfortunately, the opposite is true—when you adopt a new mindset about money, you'll start behaving differently, and then you'll be in a different fiscal position, for example. Your mind creates; it is not created.

12. Other people are responsible for your feelings.

The only place you have complete control over what's said to and around you is in your home. Otherwise, you exist in a diverse world of many people and opinions of which are likely to "offend" you at some point or another. If you want to assume you are the focal point of everyone's life and ascribe meaning to every passing comment and idea that doesn't soundly resonate with your own belief system, you're going to live a very difficult life. Changing how other people think and treat you is not a matter of how outraged you get, but how willing you are to explain, teach, and share. Defensiveness never precedes growth, it stunts it.

13. Emotional intelligence is infallible composure; self-esteem is believing you are supremely, completely "good"; happiness is a product of not having problems.

Emotional intelligence is the ability to feel, express, and interpret your feelings productively; self-esteem is believing you're worthy of loving and being loved despite not being supremely, completely "good" all of the time; happiness is a product of how you cope with your problems and whether or not you see them as the opportunities they are.

14. The right person will come at the right time.

You will not be ready when the love of your life comes along. You also probably won't be ready when you see the listing for your dream job, or to buy a house or maybe have a kid or maybe quit that job and try to write the book you keep thinking about or get sick or lose a relative or die yourself. If you wait on the feeling of "readiness," you'll be waiting forever, and worse, you'll miss the best of what's in front of you.

15. You can postpone your happiness or save it up like money in a bank.

People postpone their happiness to keep themselves safe. They dig for another problem to have to solve, another obstacle to overcome, another passageway until they can feel the happiness they know is in their lives. You cannot save up your happiness; you can either feel it in the moment, or you miss it. It's that simple. It's temporary regardless. The only variable is whether or not you ever felt it in the first place.

16. Anxiety and negative thinking are pesky irritants you just have to learn to thwart.
Anxiety is one of the main driving forces that has kept you—as well as our entire species—alive. Struggling with a crippling overabundance of it usually means you're not listening to it, or there's some major issue in your life you refuse to address or take action on. The power of negative thinking is that it shows us what matters and how we need to respond to our lives.

17. Focusing solely on your own needs will make you happiest.

Despite what many corners of the Internet would have you believe, self-sufficiency is just a precursor to happiness. It is the foundation. It is crucial, but it is not the connectedness on which human beings thrive. Committing, sacrificing, trying and trying again for the people you love and the things you believe in are what make a life feel worthwhile. Meeting your own needs is the first step, not the ultimate goal.

15

READ THIS
if you
"DON'T KNOW
WHAT YOU'RE
DOING"
with your
LIFE

If you ask any young adult what their primary stressor in life is, it's likely something that relates to uncertainty. If you were to boil it down to a sentence, it would be something along the lines of: "I don't know what I'm doing with my life."

How many times have you heard someone say that? (How many times have you said that?) Probably a lot. The idea that we should know is a heaping pile of socially crafted bullshit that's been superimposed on our psyches since kindergarten, and it's holding us back.

Nobody—not one of us—knows "what we're doing with our lives." We can't summarize the big picture, not yet. We don't know what we'll be doing in 5 years, and pretending that we can predict that isn't being responsible or ambitious, it's cutting ourselves off from living according to our inner navigation systems as opposed to the narrative we once thought would be right.

You owe nothing to your younger self.

You are not responsible for being the person you once thought you'd be.

But you do owe something to the adult you are today.

Do you know why you don't have the things you once thought you wanted? Do you know why you're not the person you once thought you'd be? Because you don't want those things anymore. Not badly enough. If you did, you'd have and be them.

If you're wondering "what you should do with your life," it's likely that you're in the limbo between realizing you don't want what you once did, and giving yourself permission to want what you want now.

Thinking you know what you're "doing with your life" quells your hunger. It soothes your mind with the illusion that your path is laid out before you, and that you no longer have to choose, which is another way to say, you're no longer responsible for becoming the person you want and need to be.

Hunger is important. Complete fulfillment is the fast track to complacency. People don't thrive when they're fulfilled. They stagnate.

So fuck knowing what you're "going to do with your life."

What are you doing today? Who do you love? What intrigues you? What would you do today if you could be anyone you wanted? If social media didn't exist? What do you want to do this weekend?

"What do I want?" is a question you need to ask yourself every day. The things that run true will weave through your life, the ones that pop back up again and again are the ones you'll follow. They'll become the places you remain, the people you're drawn to, the choices you make. The core truths will win out, even if other truths are lodged beside them.

Listening to it is saying: What do I want now?

16

8 COGNITIVE
BIASES
that are
CREATING
the way
YOU EXPERIENCE
YOUR LIFE

The good news is that your life is probably different than how you think it is. Unfortunately, that's the bad news, too. As Nobel Prize-winning psychologist Daniel Kahneman says: "The confidence people have in their beliefs is not a measure of the quality of evidence, but of the coherence of the story that the mind has managed to construct."

Yet the tools for that construction are not only our experiences, hopes, desires, and fears. There are psychological biases that prevent us from seeing an objective reality. In a sense, our collective reality is nothing but subjective experience v. subjective experience. The people who do not understand this believe their subjective experience is, in fact, objective. Our inability to coexist is not out of lack or inherent social dysfunction, but simply a lack of understanding of the most fundamental aspects of the bodies we inhabit.

This phenomenon has been studied since ancient Greek philosophy, and it's typically referred to as "naïve realism," the assumption that we see the world as it actually is, and that our impression is an objective, accurate representation of reality. Psychologist David McRaney summarizes it as follows:

"The last one hundred years of research suggest that you, and everyone else, still believe in a form of naïve realism. You still believe that although your inputs may not be perfect, once you get to thinking and feeling, those thoughts and feelings are reliable and predictable. We now know that there is no way you can ever know an "objective" reality, and we know that you can never know how much of subjective reality is a fabrication, because you never experience anything other than the output of your mind. Everything that's ever happened to you has happened inside your skull."

So what are these biases that affect us so deeply? Well, for starters, while there are many that are identifiable, there's nothing that says you can't create your own, unique biases—and in fact, it's likely that most people do. Yet those are likely derived from some combination of the following.

01. Projection

Because our sole experience of the world is only through the apertures of our senses and ultimately, our psyches, we inevitably project our own preferences and consciousness onto what we see, and interpret it accordingly. In other words: The world is not as it is, it is as we are. We overestimate how typical and normal other people are, based on how "odd" or "different" we feel. We assume that people think the way we do—because our internal narrative and process of the world is all we know.

02. Extrapolation

Extrapolation is what happens when we take the current moment we are in and then project those circumstances onto our lives as a whole. We make assumptions based on what our current circumstances "mean" about us, and then also begin to believe that things will always be the way they are—hence why tragedies feel so insurmountable, yet happiness feels so fleeting (in fearing that happiness won't last forever, we lose it—in fearing that grief will last forever, we create it).

03. Anchoring

We become too influenced by the first piece of information we hear. For example, our world views tend to be the culmination of our parents', not our most inherent beliefs. During a negotiation, the person who first puts an offer out creates a "range of possibility." If you've heard of three people getting their books published for about the same amount of

63

compensation, you begin to assume what will be possible for you, simply from your first frame of reference.

04. Negativity

We can't stop watching car crashes and pay more attention to bad news and find ourselves absolutely enthralled by the destruction and drama in people's lives—and it's not because we're morbid or completely masochistic. It's actually because we only have the capacity to be selectively attentive, and we perceive negative news to be more important and profound, therefore, what our attention should go to first. Part of the reason for this is an essence of mysteriousness (when we don't know the purpose of negativity in an existential sense, we become fascinated by it).

05. Conservatism

The sister of "anchoring," conservatism is believing something more only because we believed it first. In other words, it's an apprehension toward accepting new information, even if that information is more accurate or useful.

06. Clustering illusion

"Clustering" is when you begin to see patterns in random events because you have subconsciously decided to. This is what happens when you start seeing the car you want everywhere, or notice everyone wearing red when you're wearing it. You subconsciously create patterns that, to other people, would be seen as random, simply because you're seeking a confirmation bias.

07. Confirmation

One of the most commonly known biases, confirmation is what happens when we selectively listen to information that supports or proves our preconceptions of an idea or issue at hand. It's how we mentally insulate ourselves and our worldview. It's also how we self-validate.

08. Choice-supportive

When you consciously "choose" something, you tend to see that thing more positively, and actively disregard its flaws, more often than you would of a thing you did not choose for yourself. This is why the idea that we are autonomous in deciding what's right for us is so crucial—it dictates how we'll relate to that thing forever.

17

WHAT
EMOTIONALLY
STRONG
PEOPLE
do not
DO

01. They do not believe every feeling they have means something.
    They don't assign value to everything they feel. They know that conviction doesn't make something true.

02. They aren't threatened by not being right.
    They understand that having a misinformed belief or incorrect idea does not invalidate them as a person.

03. They do not use logic to deny their emotions.
    They validate their feelings by acknowledging them; they do not say someone "shouldn't" feel a particular way if they do.

04. They do not project meaning onto everything they see.
    Particularly, they do not assume that everything they see or hear has something to do with them. They do not compare themselves to other people, simply because the idea that other people exist in comparison to oneself is mindless at best and selfish at worst.

05. They do not need to prove their power.
    Rather than embody an inflated image of their invincibility, their disposition is predominantly peaceful and at ease, which is the mark of a truly secure person.

06. They do not avoid pain, even if they are afraid of it.
    They cope with discomfort in favor of breaking an old habit. They trace the root of a relationship issue rather than deflect

from the symptoms. They recognize that the discomfort is in avoiding the pain, not the pain itself.

07. They do not seek out other people's flaws in an effort to diminish their strengths.
They do not respond to someone's successes with observations about their failures.

08. They don't complain (too much).
When people complain, it's because they want others to recognize and validate their pain; even if it's not the real problem, it's still a form of affirmation.

09. They do not filter out certain aspects of an experience to catastrophize it.
People who jump A-Z and only think up worst-case scenarios usually do not have the confidence that they can take care of themselves if something unexpected were to arise—so they prepare for the worst and rob themselves of the best in the process.

10. They do not keep a list of things people "should" or "shouldn't" do.
They recognize that "right" and "wrong" are two highly subjective things and that believing there is a universal code of conduct to which all people need to adhere only makes the person who believes that consistently disappointed.

11. They do not consider themselves a judge of what's right or wrong.
Especially when it comes to offering friends advice, they don't assume their ideal response to a situation is the solution everyone needs.

12. They do not draw general conclusions from their personal experiences.
They do not draw their own generalized conclusions about the human race based on the small percentage of the world that they experience each day.

13. They do not change their personality based on who they're around.

    Everyone fears rejection, but not everyone gets to truly experience the kind of acceptance that comes from being yourself unconditionally.

14. They can stand up for themselves without being aggressive or defensive.

    Though it sounds like a contradiction, aggressiveness or defensiveness is indicative of insecurity. Calmly standing up for oneself is indicative of inner resolve and self-esteem.

15. They do not assume that this is always the way their life will be.

They are always conscious of the fact that their feelings are temporary, be they good or bad. This makes them focus on the positive and let the negative go with more ease.

18

10 KEY THINGS
WE MISUNDERSTAND
about EMOTION

01. The long-term effects of emotional abuse can be as bad, if not worse, than physical abuse[7].

    Emotional abuse is often not taken as seriously because it cannot always be "seen." But the severity of the long-term effects of any type of abuse aren't all that different. Emotional abuse is similar to physical abuse in that it systematically wears away at a person's self-confidence, worth, and concept. Emotional abuse can manifest in a variety of ways, including but not limited to controlling, threatening, degrading, belittling, criticizing, shouting, etc.

02. Emotions outlast the memories that created them.

    We take past emotions and project them onto situations that are in our current lives. This is to say, unless we heal what happened in the past, we're always going to be controlled by it. Furthermore, our irrational fears and most severe day-to-day anxieties can be traced back to a cause, which needs to be addressed to effectively stop the effect.

03. Creative people are depressed for a reason[8].

    The expression and experience of negative emotions are correlated with activation in the right frontal cortex (as well as in other structures such as the amygdala) or in other words, the same areas that are activated when consistently being creative and putting abstract meaning to the concrete reality of whatever your current experience is.

04. Fear doesn't mean a desire to escape. It means you're interested.

    The emotion most associated with fear is interest, believe it or not. It's even been said that fear has two invisible faces: one that wants to flee and the other that wants to investigate. This is to say, nothing is generally "scary" to us unless some part of us also wants to understand it, knows we are a part of it, and feels as though it will become part of our experience.

05. Feelings other than happiness are not marks of failure. Health is having a spectrum of emotion.

Negative emotions are good for you. In fact, maintaining a consistent experience of only "happiness"—or any emotion, really—would be a sign of mental illness. It's simply not how our minds and bodies are structured. In other words, you're not supposed to be happy all the time. Listen to what your body is telling you. Negative emotions are a signal that something isn't right. The emotion doesn't have to be fixed; the thing that it's signaling your attention to does.

06. Emotions can "predict the future," or in other words, gut feelings are real.

A study at Columbia University[9] which is being called the "Emotional Oracle Effect" essentially proved that people who trust their emotions can predict future outcomes. Because they tap into it regularly, they have a window into their subconscious mind, which is more or less just an unconscious well of information.

07. We can relive social pain more than we can physical pain, which is another reason some researchers believe it is, in a sense, more damaging.

When there aren't any psychological factors that play into physical pain, or rather, there's no innate instinct that we need to process or readjust ourselves to survive, we let the memory go. However, our brains will prioritize rejection or other social emotion or humiliation, because we need to remain in the "tribe" to survive.

08. Stress may just be the most dangerous emotion (especially when it's consistent) and yet it goes unaddressed more often than other feelings.

Relaxing isn't something you should do to pamper yourself; it's absolutely essential. Stress debilitates every part of you, and it's in one way or another interconnected with the top causes of death around the world: accidents, cancer, heart disease, suicide, etc.

09. Social media is actually making us more emotionally disconnected.

Consistently consuming soundbites of people's lives leads us to piece together a particular idea of reality—one that is far from the truth. We develop such anxiety surrounding social media (and whether or not we're really living up to the standards expected of us) that we begin to prioritize screen time over real-life face time. As beings who require human intimacy (romantic and not) to survive, it's becoming a more and more detrimental force in our culture.

10. "You cannot selectively numb emotion. When we numb [hard feelings], we numb joy, we numb gratitude, we numb happiness."

Brené Brown argues that you cannot numb yourself to one experience without numbing yourself to everything else[10]. You cannot disregard sadness without also making yourself immune to happiness. This is to say, it's healthier to experience everything, the good and the bad.

7 Spinazzola, Joseph. "Childhood Psychological Abuse as Harmful as Sexual or Physical Abuse." *Psychological Trauma: Theory, Research, Practice, and Policy.* 2014. American Psychological Association. http://www.apa.org/pubs/journals/tra/index.aspx

8 Adams, William Lee. "The dark side of creativity: Depression + anxiety x madness = genius?" CNN. 2014.

9 Lee, Leonard; Stephen, Andrew; Pham, Michel. "The Emotional Oracle Effect." *Journal of Consumer Research.* 2012. https://www8.gsb.columbia.edu/newsroom/newsn/1957/the-emotional-oracle-effect

10 Brown, Brené. *Daring Greatly: How the Courage to be Vulnerable Transforms the Way We Live, Love, Parent and Lead.* 2015. Avery.

19

THE LITTLE THINGS
you don't realize
ARE AFFECTING
how you feel
ABOUT YOUR BODY

01. How your parents felt about their bodies, and what they said about them—and others—even when you were little or they didn't think you were listening. So goes my favorite saying: "The way we talk to our children becomes their inner voice."

02. Photoshop so good you don't even realize there's Photoshop (and so your perception of "normal" is totally skewed).

03. The attitudes of the first people you dated/were intimate with, and whether or not they appreciated your body for the completely awesome thing it was (and is). For whatever reason, people's body hang-ups can often be traced back to those initial experiences, especially if they were negative.

04. How you judge other people. What you first reach to insult someone with—especially when it's physical—says infinitely more of you than them.

05. The way your friends treat their bodies and behave. In this case, it's less about what they say to you or about themselves, and much more what you pick up on through their actions. We begin to subconsciously adopt the collective mindset of the group of people we hang out with most.

06. What media you consume. The books and magazines you read, websites you visit, TV shows you binge-watch all combine to create your concept of what's "normal" and what's "ideal," and you usually derive these ideas from the characters you identify with most.

07. Your heritage and your hometown. Food is such an integral part of culture—it's largely the thing we socialize around—it is tied to the culture in which you were raised. Emotional eating can start young and passing judgments about your figure from not-ill-intentioned relatives can really settle into your psyche after a while.

08. Whether or not you've been in a relationship in which you felt that your connection was more than just skin-deep. It's hard to believe that love can exist without hinging on physical expectations, until you experience it, and you start to realize that appearance really doesn't matter most.

09. If you are associating fitness with being a means to an end—that end being a different body—as opposed to being something holistic to keep yourself running (PUN INTENDED).

10. How genuine your friendships are. If you only maintain relationships with people out of convenience—if you don't have anybody in your life to whom you know you are important for who you are and not what you do for them, your attentions will generally be focused on maintaining a physical, exterior kind of acceptability.

11. The comments people yell on the street—even if catcalls are "meant" to be complimentary (this is arbitrary, but bear with me), they still reduce your body to a commodity.

12. How much you understand about health v. genetic build, the fact that we don't ever lose fat cells, they just shrink, and the concept of big v. small/heavy v. light is completely subjective to each person. If you only gauge your body's acceptability by comparison, you'll never be enough.

13. An assignment of "good" and "bad" to foods in terms of how they'll make you look, how they'll make you feel or how good they'll be for you. It skews your idea of what's important for your body in general.

14. Not spending any time outside. The sun regenerates your body—we are as solar-powered as the foods we eat—and to deny your body that source of warmth and light is to deplete your feel-good hormones and everything else you were built to live in.

15. Not having anything more important to base your self-worth on. When you don't feel like you have anything more important to offer the world, it's inevitable that you get stuck on what's most easy to see and judge.

16. Unrequited love. It's easy to pin something physical to being the reason someone isn't interested, but someone who only loves you when you're 20 pounds thinner is not someone you want to be with anyway.

17. The constant attention given to celebrities' bodies, how frequently you consume it and how seriously you take it. Whether they're "bouncing back" after having a baby or simply going through the ebb and flow of life, they're under the kind of scrutiny that would almost make it seem that obsessing about 10 pounds after you've had a baby is normal. Part of their job is to endure this, and it's terrible, but you don't need to be another person entertaining yourself with it. It's not helping anybody. Hold yourself to your own standard.

18. Forgetting what our bodies were meant to do—laugh and play and jump and hug and love—and there is literally zero evolutionary advantage in having chiseled hipbones to help you do any of that.

20

GOALS TO SET
that are more
ABOUT ENJOYING
what you have
THAN CHASING
what you don't

Milestones are markers that you're evolving—they do not create emotional fulfillment in the way we think they will. This confusion is why with the dawn of each new year, our resolutions are to change our lives rather than to change ourselves. But what if we made goals that were more about loving what we have rather than chasing what we don't? What if we realized that it's what we were seeking in the first place? It's something to consider—if not even try just a little. Here are a few ideas to get you started:

01. Pick up where you left off. Finish the half-read books on your shelf. Eat what's in the cupboard. Wear what you own in ways you never thought of before. Apologize and mean it. Call old friends. Revisit old projects. Try other routes.

02. Seek out ways to appreciate the way people are, not the way you want them to be. It is not your job to judge who is deserving of your love and kindness. It is not your job to fix anybody. It is only your job to love them in whatever way is appropriate. You are not anybody else's god.

03. Make time for the friends you have more than you seek out the ones you don't. Stop counting how many people are in your life as though hitting a certain tally will make you feel loved. Start appreciating how rare and beautiful it is to even just have one close friend in life. Not everybody is so lucky.

04. Each day, write down one thing your body allowed you to do. Whether it was watching your favorite show or listening to the

sounds on the street on the way to work or being able to see a computer screen or hug someone you love, focus on what your body does more than what it looks like doing it.

05. Learn to love things that don't cost much. Learn to love simple food and cooking it, being outside, the company of a friend, going for walks, watching the sunrise, a full night's sleep, a good day's work.

06. Start a "journal of days" where you write down a sentence or two to sum up each day of your year. The reason keeping up with a journal is only sustainable for a week or so is that nobody has the time (or energy) to thoughtfully or extensively detail their everyday lives. Yet we miss out on the incredible opportunity to see how far we've come and what our lives are ultimately comprised of when we fail to—so make it easy for yourself. Just write down one sentence that sums up the day before bed. In a year, you'll be grateful you did.

07. Find meaning and joy in the work you do, not the work you wish you did. Finding fulfillment in work is never about pursuing your idea of what your "purpose" is. It is always about infusing purpose into whatever it is you already do.

08. Start your own holiday traditions. Make the most special days of the year reflect who you are and what you love and how you want to celebrate your life.

09. Do a "spend cleanse" where you only use what you have for a period of time. At once, teach yourself the art of denying immediate gratification for the sake of something more important, and show yourself that you already have everything you need, or at least, more than you think you do (even when it doesn't feel like it).

10. Give everything you own a "home"; it is essentially the key to feeling at peace in your space. Go through your belongings and only keep what's purposeful or beautiful to you—and then assign each of those things a "home," or a space to return to each night. It makes maintaining flow in your space effortless and calming.

11. Learn to live within your means—no matter how much money you make, your "percentage habits" will remain the same. If you're in the habit of seeing all of the income you make as "spending money" (as opposed to investing money, saving money, etc.) you will always revert to that habit, no matter how much you make. It is only by learning to live comfortably within your means that you're able to actually achieve your goals when you earn more.

12. Call your mom. Not everybody has the privilege.

13. Aspire to be someone who gives things meaning, not who seeks things to give them meaning. Rather than chasing "success," chase kindness. Rather than believe wealth is the mark of a life well lived, believe that intelligence is, or kindness is, or open-mindedness is.

14. Do the most important things immediately in the morning. Give your energy to what matters most, when you have the most of it. It also helps you define what really matters to you.

15. Shed what no longer serves you. Teach yourself to let go of the big things by learning to let go of the little ones. It is easier to bypass thoughts and emotions that are negative in nature when you're able to release belongings and objects with negative associations.

16. Pace yourself—if at any point you're doing anything in which you cannot feel your breath, you're moving too fast. Make physical relaxation a priority—no matter what you're doing. Keep track of your breath at all times. Be mindful, present and intentional with everything you do. It is not the quantity of what we accomplish, but the quality of it.

21

102 WAYS
to not let
IRRATIONAL
THOUGHTS
RUIN YOUR LIFE

01. Learn to differentiate what's actually happening from what you're currently thinking about.

02. Learn the difference between honesty and truth. The way you honestly feel can be different from how you truthfully feel—the former is usually temporary, the latter is deeper, and consistent.

03. Stop trying to navigate the path while the forest is dark. You'll most want to try to make changes to your life when you're consumed by emotion, but that's the worst time to do so. Do not make decisions when you're upset. Let yourself come back down to neutral first.

04. Fire can burn your house down, or it can cook you dinner each night and keep you warm in the winter. Your mind is the same way.

05. Recognize that anxiety stems from shame. It is the idea that who you are or what you are doing is "not right," therefore eliciting a rush of energy designed to help you "fix" or change it. You're suffering because there's nothing you can fix to make that urgent, panicked feeling go away. It's a mismanaged perception of who and how you are.

06. Remedy your tunnel vision by writing your narrative on a piece of paper. Start with: "My name is..." and then go on to list where you live, what work you do, what you've accomplished, who you spend time with, what you're working on, what you're proud of.

07. Realize that thoughts are illusions, but powerful ones. Take inventory of all the things you've thought and worried about that have turned out not to be real. Think of all the time you wasted preparing for outcomes that would never manifest and problems that were only in your head.

08. Practice negative visualization. Create tangible solutions for your intangible fears. Show yourself that you won't actually die if you lose a job or a boyfriend. Make a list of the things you worry about most, imagine the worst outcome, then make a plan for exactly how you would deal with it if that came to pass.

09. Stop being so cerebral. Do things with your hands. Cook, clean, go outside.

10. Evolve past one-dimensional thinking. People who worry a lot are usually very firm in their convictions of what is and isn't. They fail to see complexity, opportunity, the majority of the iceberg that is the reality they don't know and can't see.

11. Practice healthy discomfort. Learn to lean into your stress, not resist it.

12. Change your objective. The goal is not to feel "good" all the time, it's to be able to express a healthy range of emotion without suppressing or suffering.

13. Ask yourself the following questions when a thought upsets you: "Is this true? Can I absolutely know this is true?" Most of the time, the answer will be "no" to one or both.

14. Do more. If you have time to be regularly consumed by irrational, spiraling thoughts, you need more to focus on, more to work toward, more to suffer for. Make sure you're living more than you're thinking about living.

15. Accept the fact that everyone, everywhere, has weird, incorrect, disturbing thoughts that have no bearing on reality. You are not a freak. You are (probably) not sick. You just have to learn to not be intimidated by your own mind.

16. Freaking out is not usually what happens when something in your life actually needs to change. Depression, anger, resistance, sadness...that's what happens when something isn't right. Stop gauging how bad things are by how much you panic, and start by gauging what your emotional homeostasis is. That's how you know what's really wrong or right—what you consistently do and how you regularly feel.

17. When you are spiraling, be able to say out loud: "I am having a panic attack. I am having irrational thoughts." Doing so is the first step toward bringing yourself back to reality.

18. Identify your comfort zones, and step back into them now and again. Moving past the place that you're used to is a gradual process—going too quickly is a recipe for a breakdown.

19. Prove yourself wrong. Show yourself that your thoughts have no basis in truth. Go to the doctor and confirm that you aren't dying of some incurable disease. Ask someone how they feel about you if you don't know. Do not live in the grey area when answers are available.

20. Do not always trust yourself. Give yourself space to be wrong. Open yourself up to the idea that you don't know what you don't know. If your feelings are informed by irrational thoughts, they can very well be incorrect.

21. Trust what gives you peace. Even if the idea of an intimate relationship or a career in the field of your dreams scares you initially, if it's what you really want, it will also give you a feeling of "yes." Trust your "yes" feelings.

22. Take the instances in which you're most uncomfortable to mean that it's time you expand yourself. You need to learn to think differently, see differently, do differently. You need to open yourself. If you don't, you'll be stuck in the cocoon phase forever.

23. Fall in love with the unknown, for the fact that it will almost always bring you things better than you could have imagined —things that are worse than you could have imagined are

almost always products of your own thinking or perception of what they mean about you or your future.

24. Practice radical acceptance. Learn to tell the parts of your story you'd rather shove under the rug. You're allowed to say: "I don't love my body. I feel a little stuck right now. I am not happy in my relationship. I am in debt" without it being a condemning statement.

25. Realize that there are three layers of you: your identity, your shame, and your true self. Your identity is your outermost layer, it's the idea that you think other people have of you. Your shame is what's shielding you from expressing your true self, which is at your core. It is from your shame circle that irrational thoughts breed and thrive. Work on closing the gap between who the world thinks you are and who you know you are. Your mental health will change significantly.

26. Learn deep breathing exercises. This sounds kind of annoying if you've tried it and it hasn't worked before, but it's actually one of the most effective non-prescription solutions to a freak out.

27. Expand your perceptions. If you're uncomfortable, you're being pushed to think beyond what you've known. You're being called to see yourself in a new way. Open yourself to possibilities you normally wouldn't consider, or layers of yourself you've yet to see.

28. Practice rational thinking, and often. You shouldn't trust your mind to think healthfully on autopilot. You have to train it.

29. Part of that training will include knowing what to do when something irrational pops up—which is to evaluate it objectively, determine if it serves you, and laugh about it if not.

30. Irrational thoughts are sometimes products of intense, rational fears you've yet to fully acknowledge or deal with. When you're in a stable state of mind, sit down and be honest with yourself about what those are.

31. Differentiate the fine line between what you can and can't control. You can, for example, control how much effort you put into your work. You cannot control how other people respond to it. You can control what you wear each day. You cannot control how good other people think you look.

32. Stop pretending you know what other people are thinking.

33. Stop pretending you know what the future holds, indefinitely.

34. Understand that your sense of self is entirely a mental thing, and it's the foundation of your sanity. If you believe you're the kind of person who can bear pain or loss, you will be the kind of person who can bear pain or loss. If you believe you're worthy of love, you will experience love when it comes.

35. Work on redefining your sense of self by things that aren't material or shallow. Instead of thinking you are someone who is attractive and successful, learn to think of yourself as someone who is resilient, hungry for new experiences, capable of deeply loving others, and so on.

36. Learn to see each day from the perspective of your older self.

37. Think about who you were two years ago, or even five. Try to remember a random day in your life during those times. Notice how your focus immediately turns toward what you had to be grateful for. Learn to do that with today.

38. Sometimes, the best way to get over anything is just to work on forgetting about it. Not everything requires analysis.

39. The best way to forget is to fill your life with new, better things. Things you may not have expected, things you didn't know you didn't know about, things you never imagined you'd like.

40. Accept that irrational thoughts, much like anxiety, or sadness, or anything else, will always be a part of your life. They aren't going anywhere. Experiencing them isn't a sign that you've backtracked or that you're off-path or that something's desperately wrong, per se.

41. Recognize that there's a correlation between worry and creativity. It's the most basic aspect of human evolution—the more we fear something, the more creative we are in creating solutions to adapt to the alternative. See your fears as catalysts for bettering your life, not as you being condemned to suffering.

42. Remember that you can choose what you think about, and even when it feels like you can't, it's because again, you're choosing to believe that.

43. "Choose not to be harmed—and you won't feel harmed. Don't feel harmed—and you haven't been." —Marcus Aurelius

44. Go outside and look at the stars and drink a glass of wine.

45. Try bullet journaling. When you go back and re-read it, you'll begin to see what your patterns are, particularly your self-sabotaging ones.

46. Meditate and imagine speaking with your oldest, wisest, most optimal future self. What you're doing is tapping deep into your subconscious. Let your choices be guided by the person you hope to become.

47. Laugh.

48. When you ask other people for advice on whatever you're worrying about, first ask yourself what you hope they'll say. That's what you want to tell yourself.

49. Talk to other people and ask them to tell you about the silly things they worry irrationally about. You're in good company.

50. Work on developing your mental strength. Train your mind like you would your body. Work on focusing, thinking, imagining. This is the single best thing you can possibly do for your life.

51. Say thank you for the fact that you care enough about yourself to even feel panicked about something in the first place.

52. Remind yourself that what you fear is the shadow side to what you love. The more fear, the more love. Learn to start seeing what's right as much as you worry about what's not.

53. Give yourself permission to feel okay. This is why we love when other people love us. Nobody else can actually transmute the sensation of love—we crave it from others because it lets us flip the mental switch that gives us permission to be happy, proud, excited, or content. The trick, the whole work of "loving ourselves," is just learning to do it on our own.

54. Keep your spaces clean and clear.

55. Recite mantras or prayers or motivational speeches in the mirror, if you must. Anything that focuses your mind on something positive and hopeful.

56. Consume your mind with things that interest you—aside from your own problems.

57. If you cannot do this, it means you don't know yourself well enough yet. That's okay. The point is that you realize this now, and begin learning.

58. Practice happiness. External events don't create meaning or fulfillment or contentment; how we think about them does. If you're operating on a scarcity mindset, you'll always be unhappy, no matter what you have or get.

59. Do something unexpected. Book a trip, date someone wrong for you, get a tattoo, start looking for a new job in a field you didn't think you'd enjoy. Show yourself that you don't know what you don't know about your life or yourself. Not completely. Not yet.

60. Practice radical acceptance. Choose to love your home, and your body, and your work, even if you don't like it all the time. Choose to build your life from a place of gratitude and vision, rather than running from your own fears.

61. Be mindful of who you surround yourself with. Your most constant company will account for a lot of how you turn out

over the coming years. Pay attention.

62. Spend time on your own, especially when you feel like you don't want to. You are your first and last friend—you are with you until the end. If you don't want to be with you, how can you expect anyone else to, either?

63. Re-write your "success" narrative. Sometimes success is getting enough sleep. Sometimes it's doing what you know is right despite the fact that everyone else in your life is looking down on it. Sometimes it's just getting through the day or the month. Lower your expectations.

64. Write out your fears in explicit detail.

65. Listen to scary podcasts or watch horror movies. Expose yourself to things that are actually terrifying. (This will either make it better or worse, but hey, give it a try.)

66. Dream bigger. If you feel as though you're constantly running through the same issues in your mind, you've yet to visualize a future that is greater than your present. When you have something more important to work toward—or someone to be better for—the obsession with little, made-up problems will quickly dissolve.

67. Don't confuse a broken dream with a broken future.

68. Don't confuse a broken heart for a broken life.

69. Create a routine you love, one that involves enough sleep and down time, and a realistic degree of "stuff you know you should do" v. "stuff you actually want to do."

70. Validate yourself. Choose to believe that the life you have is more than enough.

71. Take an evening (or a few) to meditate on your past. Think of all the pain and sadness you shoved away. Let yourself feel those things. When you let them surface, they won't control you anymore.

72. Choose to do things because you want joy more than you choose to do them because you want to avoid pain.

73. Take an honest look at your life and evaluate how much you've constructed as a means to avoid pain, and decide whether or not those fears are even valid in the first place. Do you hold a lesser view of yourself so nobody else's opinion can hurt you? Do you choose relationships where you're unwanted so you don't have to open up to the vulnerability of love?

74. Make plans to build the life you want, not because you hate the one you have, but because you're in love with the person you know you want to become.

75. Be discerning about what you accept as truth, who you give your energy to, what you do when you procrastinate, and what you surround yourself with at home.

76. Connect with people. Connect with people. Connect with people.

77. Create vision boards. Or just use Pinterest more. Seeing the life you want is the first step to creating it.

78. Remember that you're not upset about what you lost—you're upset about what you never really had the chance to have in the first place. You'll regret what you didn't do, not what you've done.

79. Dedicate your time to helping someone else. Volunteer at a homeless shelter, donate your belongings, work with kids after school. Make your life about more than just your own wants.

80. Redefine "happiness" not as something you experience when you get what you want, but something you feel when you have something meaningful to work toward each day.

81. Focus on getting better, but let go of the end goal. You get better, not perfect.

82. Let yourself be loved as the person you are. You'll quickly see how the main person judging you is you.

83. Stop judging other people. See everyone with dignity, with a story, with reasons for why they are how they are and why they do what they do. The more you accept other people, the more you'll accept yourself, and vice versa.

84. Channel your overactive imagination into something creative. Write an insane novel. Write a short horror story. Make up songs and record them on your phone, just for yourself.

85. Or do what every wise person does, and use your overactive imagination to imagine the best possible outcomes rather than the worst, and then imagine how you can work toward getting there.

86. Let go of the idea that anything is "given" or "taken" from you. You create. You choose.

87. Ask for help when you actually need help. If you don't learn to do this, you will end up exacerbating a million other non-issues and seeking attention for those, because you don't actually have what you need, which is support in the moments that really matter.

88. Stop thinking that being sad or broken makes you unlovable or "bad." Your honest moments don't destroy relationships, they bond (as long as you're being genuine).

89. Thinking that there are starving kids on the other side of the world will not alleviate your pain, so stop trying to compare.

90. That said: There's a lot worse you could be going through, and if you think back on your life, you can probably remember instances in which you still were.

91. Read books that interest you, and read them often. Hearing a new voice in your mind will teach you how to think differently.

92. Take a nap. Seriously, wrap yourself in a blanket and go to sleep for 20 minutes. It's like hitting the "refresh" button on your brain.

93. Recognize that fear is an indicator that something is powerful and worthwhile. The deeper the fear, the deeper the love.

94. "The obstacle is the way."

95. Let what you dislike about your present be a guiding light toward what you want to love about your future.

96. Challenge yourself to think of possibilities you never imagined before, as often as you can. Let your mind explore itself and grow.

97. Nobody is thinking about you the way you are thinking about you. They're all thinking about themselves.

98. Recognize that when you're lost, you're also free. When you have to start over, you get to pick better. If you don't like yourself, you have a chance to fall in love with yourself. Don't stand in front of the road sign forever; map a new path.

99. "This too shall pass."

100. Fucking try. Honestly, seriously, try. Put your everything into the work you have. Be kind to people when they don't deserve it. You'll have a lot less energy to worry with when you're funneling it into things that are really worthwhile.

101. Learn how to relax. Work on learning how to happily do nothing.

102. Trust that things get better as time goes on. Not because time heals, but because you grow. You discover that you're capable. You realize that your fourth breakup doesn't hurt even nearly as bad as your first did. This isn't because life is easier, it's because you're smarter.

22

THE INHERENT
ZEN *of*
CREATIVITY

Being creative is as innate to being human as eating, talking, walking and thinking is. It has always been a process we naturally prioritize; our ancestors somehow found time to carve their images and stories on cave walls. But we've mistakenly grown to regard it as some form of luxury—you're lucky if you have the means to express yourself.

In reality, it is a manner of education, communication, and ultimately, introspection, and we are in constant manifestation of it. The mediums have shifted from rock particles to pixels, but we can all still see that there is something inherently human about wanting to imprint, impress, craft, mold, form, paint, write, and otherwise mold something abstract into that which is conceivable to someone else.

Unsurprisingly then, it seems that the most effective creative process is one that follows the art of Zen—meditation, mindfulness, intuition, non-resistance, non-judgment, etc.

I did not begin writing because it was something I liked. It was how I figured my way out of pain. It didn't take too long to realize that I didn't want to spend my life creating or exacerbating problems only to think and feel my way out for the sake of a job. I wanted to be able to write and create just because. Just because I'm alive and breathing and can.

I had to learn that my expression did not need to be justified—it is valid because I am a valid human being, the same as you and everybody else.

But in the meantime, I tried all the classic writing routines of the greats, the promised formulas for consistent, rhythmic creation. I tried to be structured, did anything to induce "flow," intentionally probed at the deep dark untouched corners of myself, was routine even when I didn't want to be, and found every bit of it to be dead-ended.

I was trying to create structure where structure need not be placed. It did little more than make the process stagnate.

The reason being, mostly, that we do not ebb and flow in and out of creation. It is an unseen constant, from the clothes we choose to the sentences we say to the way we arrange our desks at work.

It comes down to imagining writing (or painting, or singing, or whatever it is you do) as coming as naturally as breathing does: It's an effortless process, it draws upon what is outside you and transforms it as it goes through you, and it is tensed, stressed, ebbed, and made more difficult when we consciously try to do it.

In fact, anything creative tends to be most hampered by end goals. It is almost imperative that you are completely mindful of the moment, creating from a place of simply allowing whatever is going through you to flow out.

Because when you have a pre-prescribed path in mind, it means you are trying to align with somebody else's. It means that the inspiration you have found is you creating your own version of somebody's something else that made you tick and flow.

You'll seldom be inspired by work that is coming from a core truth, and that's because it shows you something about yourself. Not just something, the truest truth—that's what makes the process so goddamn unbearable.

And that's why we reach for structure, that's what makes us stopper the process. That's why we want inspiration and validation and external support.

In the true essence of real Zen, the most creativity can be fostered when you learn to do so without passing judgment, similar to how observing your thoughts and feelings objectively are the path to peace as well.

Some of what you write down you'll want to share or make consumable. Some you won't. That's okay, too. It's imperative to realize that even the greatest artists weren't consistently prolific, especially not publicly. But considering that "inactivity" a lack, loss, or failure is just attaching another ego-meaning to it all.

You cannot quantify your creativity, and though it is an extension and impression and expression of yourself, it does not define you.

You are free to keep the sacredness of your most inner self only within your own existence. The more you can express that and live that without judgment, and in the moment, the more you'll feel free to be honest, and open up to yourself. The more you feel comfortable with that core self, the more you'll feel able to create from a peaceful place. Just because. Whenever you want.

23

EVERYTHING
is here to
HELP YOU:
HOW INTRINSICALLY
MOTIVATED PEOPLE
become the
BEST VERSIONS
of THEMSELVES

The single most powerful, liberating thing any one of us can do is choose to believe that everything is here to help us.

If you want to understand why you perceive your life the way you do, ask yourself what you think the point of it is. This isn't a lofty, philosophical question that you can maybe entertain if you ever develop a penchant to do so. This is the underbelly of how you think and behave.

You either see yourself as a victim of what happens to you, or as someone given opportunity to change, grow, see differently, and expand. You either see uncomfortable feelings as suffering you have to deal with or signals you have to learn from. You either see the world as something makes you feel, or you see your interpretation of the world as a projection of your feelings.

When we think there is a purpose for our pain, the discomfort of it dissolves. It turns from an annoyance to an opportunity. Our suffering ceases.

The difference between this mindset (intrinsic) and the opposite (extrinsic) is whether or not we believe that we create our experience, or that our experiences are created for us (and imposed on us) from an external force. We spend most of our lives being taught that the latter is true—and there's a reason for this.

Society (likes to believe) it thrives when we are extrinsically motivated. At least, this is how capitalism runs, this is how people stay in power, this is how we are kept small. When people believe that they are victims, they forfeit their power.

They funnel their energy on other people's ideas, dreams, products.

Do we know for certain that there is some higher plan in which we confront obstacles in order to grow? Nope. But we never will. What we do know is that people who are able to create happy lives for themselves right here and right now are the ones who think that way.

Unbearable suffering awaits us all. A brief glimpse through history can confirm: None of us is guaranteed a happy life. If we want meaning we have to create it. If we want to find peace, we need to know there's a purpose for suffering.

You will either sit in discomfort for the rest of your life, or you will grow and be better for the things that are most difficult. It is very clear who does what.

24

HOW TO KNOW
when the only
THING IN THE WAY
of your
HAPPINESS
IS YOU

01. The only problem with your life is the way you think about it. Objectively, you have everything you could ever want or need, yet your unhappiness simply comes from a lack of appreciation (which is a cultivated trait, if not a practice).

02. The solution to most of your problems is just changing the way you think about them. For example, learning that people's opinions of you are largely projections of how they see themselves would solve your problem, which is evaluating your life through the idea of how other people could perceive it.

03. You're mentally lazy. You know you should be more present, but you won't put in the effort to practice it. You know you should meditate and learn to train your brain to focus so it doesn't become engulfed by negativity, but you head to the gym instead. You're lazy in the way it matters most, and that's your biggest problem.

04. You've accomplished things you thought would make you happy and immediately shifted them from "goals" to "notches on the belt." Once you achieved something, you immediately started to think of it as "another thing done" rather than "another thing in my life to enjoy."

05. You haven't practiced holding the emotion of happiness. We all have a tolerance for how "good" we'll let ourselves feel, our "upper limit." To go past it, we have to actually practice

letting ourselves feel—otherwise, we'll self-sabotage to bring ourselves back to our comfort zones.

06. You care more about comfort than you do about change. You'd rather remain moderately uncomfortable than deal with the uncertainty that is making a real change in your life.

07. You consciously choose to spend time with people who aren't "good" for you. Meaning: They don't really care about you, or they inspire you to behave in a way that is counter to what you're trying to achieve. In other words, they bring out the worst in you, yet you continue to see them anyway.

08. You won't let your idea of yourself evolve. You're stuck in only being comfortable thinking of yourself the way you were 3, 5, 10 years ago, because that's how other people are comfortable seeing you.

09. You choose what you think should be right rather than what actually is. You're more loyal to the ideas you have about things than the honest reality you know them to be.

10. You won't apologize. To yourself nor to others. You're not open to being wrong, and certainly not to taking the ego-hit that is admitting you didn't always do your best. Yet doing this is the first step in changing that.

11. You haven't fully taken responsibility for your life—you're still waiting for something to come and change how you feel. Often, people choose to suffer loudly because they believe it is a "cry to the universe," as in, if they are transparent enough about how bad things are, something or someone else will eventually have to fix or change them.

12. You've ascribed happiness to a level of accomplishment rather than a state of being. You think that only some people can be happy because their life circumstances are ideal, rather than choosing to seek happiness in the moment and realizing that has nothing to do with it.

13. You think that "happiness" is a sustained state of feeling "good," when it is really a higher "baseline" for perception.

You are better able to process every emotion, and because you do so healthfully, you return to your general state of contentment quickly.

14. You accept what you're taught even if it doesn't feel right. You're more trusting of dogma, teaching or religion simply because you knew it first, not because it resonates or helps you in a real way.

15. You have a good life, and you know you have a good life. At the end of the day, you know it's just about choosing to focus on it more.

25

THE PSYCHOLOGY
of getting
UNSTUCK
and the
3 STAGES OF
MAKING HABITS
AUTONOMOUS

Success is more a product of habit than it is skill. To excel at something, you must be able to do it prolifically. Many people write well. Few people write well and consistently. What separates experts from the rest of us is a blend of profound self-control, disciplined routine, and unwavering dedication.

While natural skill is more or less something you're born with, self-control is something you develop. Most people believe the opposite is true: that they can perfect their talent, but that the drive to do so will come easily.

Our minds have a limited means for self-control. This is to say, we are only capable of withholding ourselves from our impulses and desires for a period of time each day. With practice, we can extend that period, but it is finite regardless.

People who understand this use their time wisely: They eliminate unnecessary decision-making, reduce distractions, minimize what doesn't matter, and then they focus. Over time, it becomes second nature. In fact, in the 1960s, psychologists identified three specific stages[11] we must go through in order to acquire those new skills:

Cognitive: When we first intellectualize the task, make mistakes, and ultimately devise new strategies to perform better.

Associative: When effort is still required to complete the task, but it's less mentally strenuous than it was. Some aspects of the task are beginning to come naturally, mistakes are still being made.

Autonomous: We go into "autopilot," or in some cases, "flow." We can release ourselves from conscious focus and let our programming take over.

However, it is sometime between the last two phases that we get caught in a sort of plateau: We do the task often enough, but our expectation of how we should perform is still miles away from how we think it should be. It is what Ira Glass calls the "creative gap," the point at which most people give up.

"For the first couple years you make stuff, it's just not that good. It's trying to be good, it has potential, but it's not. But your taste, the thing that got you into the game, is still killer. And your taste is why your work disappoints you. A lot of people never get past this phase, they quit....If you are just starting out or you are still in this phase, you gotta know it's normal and the most important thing you can do is do a lot of work. Put yourself on a deadline so that every week you will finish one story. It is only by going through a volume of work that you will close that gap, and your work will be as good as your ambitions. And I took longer to figure out how to do this than anyone I've ever met. It's gonna take a while. It's normal to take a while. You've just gotta fight your way through."

The difference between the people who persevere to see that their work rises to their standard and the people who toss in the towel is not one of sheer, unprecedented talent. It's just a matter of having the (often uncomfortable) commitment to keep growing.

If you don't have the desire nor the ability to push past the plateau, then an exodus is a means of showing you that there's something else better suited for you. If you do, it means you must eliminate the unnecessary details, work with your current threshold for self-control, and keep going. Getting unstuck is realizing that you were never stuck in the first place; you only stopped to ask yourself, "Is this what I'm here for?"

---

11 Abdi, Hervé; Fayol, Michel; Lemaire, Patrick. "Associative Confusion Effect in Cognitive Arithmetic: Evidence For Partially Autonomous Processes." *European Bulletin of Cognitive Psychology.* 1991. Vol. 11. No. 5

26

THE ONE QUESTION
to ask yourself
IF YOU'RE TIRED
of fighting for
SOMEONE'S LOVE

We talk a lot about how to get love.

In fact, we talk about it incessantly. How to land a date, turn someone on, find a boyfriend, make yourself respected, admired, seen as successful. We talk about how to convince someone to commit, to get married, to take us out again. All of these things are the ways try to manipulate the love that people give us.

We talk a lot about how to get love, but we talk very little about how to give it.

We talk about getting love as though it's a precursor to giving it. As though giving if we aren't receiving makes us weak. As though no respectable person would keep being kind and loving to someone who didn't love them back. As though being loving is being devoted, rather than being strong and honest and true and sometimes walking away.

You cannot convince someone to love you if they don't.

This, above most else, is a rule. Love is not something you "get." It's not something someone else has and you must earn. It is not something that exists outside of you. When someone doesn't want to express affection and love and respect to you, you have two choices: You can try to change that fact (and keep yourself stuck) or you can keep giving love (which will let you move on).

The pain of not having love is the pain of your heart being closed.

The pain of losing love is the pain of your heart closing.

The pain of losing love is trying to change or manipulate someone into thinking or seeing you differently. It is not actually a loss of love, it is a step into delusion and denial. It is the adoption of the idea that you aren't lovable as you are.

Love is not something anybody can take away from you, though. (It's not something anybody can truly give you, either.) It's not something you "get"; it's something you experience—and that exchange requires an equal and honest and willing contribution on each side. It's not something that anybody is responsible to do for you, or owes you in a life.

If you go on living as though other people are required to give you love, you will never actually experience it.

If you go on living as though love is something that is always required of you, you will find it in everything. In every stranger on the subway, three-date-long relationship, six-year love affair that almost was "it," and everything else. All of these different loves become equally important. The pain of losing transmutes into the beauty of having discovered something more important than someone who can promise you forever.

Your life turns into a series of little love stories, all of which teach you how to love better, how to give more, how to be more of yourself, what you like and what you don't. How to walk away with grace, and respect yourself genuinely, and listen to your intuition.

When you want to pity yourself over how little love you're getting, I ask you to stop and consider: How much are you giving?

27

BE WHERE YOUR FEET ARE: MANTRAS
that will
REMIND YOU
that your life
IS HAPPENING IN THIS MOMENT

Presence is all we have, yet it often becomes a last priority. We know it's important to be in the moment, but if it were as simple as saying it, we'd have an easier time doing it. In a world that is constantly demanding more and more of our attention, we can't forget to give ourselves to what matters most: a glimpse at what's happening right now. Everything you've ever dreamed, wanted, worked for, wished for and are waiting for stems from this moment. What you do now is not just something, it's everything. Here, 15 little mantras that you can repeat to yourself when you need to re-ground and remember: Life happens in a series of moments, and any other ideas are just illusions that keep you from it.

01. All that exists is what's in front of me.

02. Potential unrealized becomes pain.

03. The only way to be extraordinary depends on what I do with the ordinary.

04. Little by little.

05. All we ever have is now.

06. If I had the life I wanted, what would today look like?

07. If I had the love I wanted, what would today look like?

08. Start where you are, use what you have, do what you can.

09. What are the most important things that must happen today?

10. My life consists of my days—what am I doing with this one?

11. What would my most fully realized self do with today?

12. Am I truly doing the best I can right now?

13. If I didn't feel tired, what would I do today?

14. Be where your feet are.

15. I am here.

28

16 QUESTIONS
that will show you
WHO YOU ARE
(and what you're meant to do)

Understanding who we are has less to do with discovery and more to do with remembrance than is typically understood. Have you ever had a realization that didn't precede a laundry list of examples, isolated moments, and meaningless experiences and random relationships that compile to reveal a pattern or truth? Probably not.

The real work of anything is simply becoming conscious of what is already true.

The essential point of a psychological guidance system (religious or not)—rather, the kinds that work—is not to supplant a mindset into you. Rather, it's to give you the tools for introspection, to figure out the answers yourself. To pose questions, to give examples, to have you reflect, and through that recognition connect to your inner guidance system, your intuition, and your essential self.

I say this with complete sincerity: The answers to these questions are some that have (literally) changed the course of my life. I'd be remiss not to have compiled and shared them. So here you go—the 16 most important questions you will ever ask yourself:

01. What, and who, is worth suffering for?

02. What would you stand for if you knew that nobody would judge you?

03. What would you do if you knew that nobody would judge you?

04. Based on your daily routines, where will you be in five years? Ten? Twenty?

05. Whom do you admire most, and why?

06. What do you not want anybody else to know about you?

07. What are a few things you thought you would never get over while you were going through them? Why did they seem so insurmountable? How did you?

08. What are your greatest accomplishments so far?

09. What would be too good to believe if someone were to sit down and tell you what's coming next in your life?

10. Who from your past are you still trying to earn the acceptance of?

11. If you didn't have to work anymore, what would you do with your days?

12. What are the five most common things in your daily routine aside from the basics such as eating and sleeping?

13. What do you wish those five most common things were instead?

14. If you really believed you didn't have control over something, you'd accept it as a matter of fact. What do you struggle to accept that you have "no control" over? What part of you makes you think or hope otherwise?

15. If you were to walk through your home and put your hand on every single thing you own, how many of them would make you sincerely feel happy or at peace? Why do you keep the rest?

16. What bothers you most about other people? What do you love most in other people? What bothers you most about yourself? What do you love most about yourself? (Dig until you see the correlation.)

29

HOW TO KNOW
YOU'VE EVOLVED
more than you
GIVE YOURSELF
CREDIT FOR

It's hard to see how far along the path you've come while you're so focused on taking each step—so to say. You've probably had the experience of a third party commenting on how much you've changed but barely being able to realize only because you're with yourself each day. This is normal but is also the product of focusing on how what's left to do rather than what you've already accomplished—which is why it's often hard to give yourself the credit you really deserve. Here, a few little signs you've evolved more than you realize:

01. You have something in your life that you would have previously considered impossible, or at least, a dream come true. Sobriety, a degree, a partner, a dream job...

02. You forget how much you've gone through simply because it doesn't cross your mind anymore. Your past seems like it happened "in a different life."

03. Your criteria for a romantic "type" are personality traits, not physical characteristics. Your idea of "love" has expanded beyond the feeling that sexual attraction gives you.

04. You have more than just your problems to talk about with friends. More interests you than just gossip—as you've learned that those conversations have very little to do with other people, and absolutely everything to do with you.

05. The worst happened, and then it passed. You lost the person you thought you couldn't live without and then you kept living.

You lost your job then found another one. You began to realize that "safety" isn't in certainty—but in faith that you can simply keep going.

06. You've created your own belief system, if not entirely and thoroughly questioned your existing one. You no longer subscribe to anything that doesn't resonate or make sense to you.

07. You're more discerning of who you spend your time with. You value your closest friends more than you do the idea of a "group."

08. You don't change any part of yourself—your personality, your opinions, even your clothes—based on whom you're going to be around that day.

09. You don't blame other people for your problems anymore. You don't choose to suffer because you assume if you complain loudly enough, the universe will have to fix it.

10. You don't relate to a lot of your old friends anymore, but you can still keep in touch and appreciate the role they had in your life.

11. You're not worried about fitting in anymore, you sincerely don't want to be "normal," and you sincerely do not care about being "cool," as you now see that the "cool kids" usually don't get very far past high school.

12. You can talk about the problems in your life that you thought you'd absolutely never get over—and you can also talk about exactly how you got over them.

13. You stop and enjoy life more often, rather than just sprinting from goal to goal.

14. You're highly skeptical of anything that's fed to you as being "just the way things are." You're always open to the idea that there could be a different, better, kinder, more enlightened way to live, and you're always willing to at least try for it.

15. If you were to tell your younger self about the life you have now, they sincerely wouldn't believe you.

108

30

SIGNS THE
ONLY PROBLEM
WITH YOUR LIFE
is the way
YOU THINK
ABOUT IT

01. You generally spend more time thinking about your life than you do actually living it.
    You spend more time dissecting problems than you do coming to solutions, more time daydreaming than you do asking yourself what those thoughts indicate is lacking or missing in your waking life, or coming up with new solutions as opposed to actually committing to the ones that are already in front of you. You've replaced "reflection" with "experience" and wonder why you feel unfulfilled.

02. You don't find wonder in the simple pleasures the way you once did.
    You think nature is boring and "play" is for children and there's nothing awe-inspiring about a shaft of light through the window or a stranger's smile or a spring day or your favorite book in bed. When you've lost sight of the magic of the little things, it's not because the magic has gone elsewhere, only that you've chosen to disregard it in favor of something else.

03. You have something you wanted in the past, but you don't enjoy it the way you thought you would, or you've replaced your desire for it with a desire for something else.
    Bring yourself back to the feeling of wanting what you have more than anything, the way you once did. Try to embody that. You're making yourself prouder than you realize.

04. If you were to tell your younger self what your life is like now, they'd be in disbelief.

You seriously could not have imagined that your life would turn out as well as it did—that the worst things became turning points, not endless black holes of emotion.

05. You think of money in terms of "obligation," not "opportunity."
Your mindset is: "I have to pay my bills" as opposed to "I get to pay my bills, which house me, clothe me, and feed me, and that I can pay for by myself." If you don't value money by appreciating what it does for you, you'll never feel as though you have enough.

06. You think you don't have enough friends.
You're measuring the connection in your life by a quantity, not a quality, assuming that the problem is not enough around you, when it's really that there's not enough inside you.

07. You're either over-reliant or under-attached to the friends you do have.
You either don't keep in touch enough or you get easily frustrated because you think that friends should make you feel "better" and "happy" in an unrealistic way. So you think that the only way to achieve that is to over-bond yourself to them or disregard them when they don't fulfill the role you've imposed on them. (Hence your feeling as though you don't have enough!)

08. You imagine your life as though someone else was seeing it.
Before you make a decision, you recite a storyline in your head. It goes something like this: "She went to college, she got this job, she married this guy after a terrible breakup, and all was well." This is what happens when your happiness starts to come from how other people feel about you, as opposed to how you feel about yourself.

09. Your goals are outcomes, not actions.
Your goals are to "be successful" or "see a certain number in the bank" as opposed to "enjoy what you do each day, no matter what you're doing" or "learn to love saving more than frivolously spending." Outcomes are just ideas. Actions are results.

10. You assume you have time.

    When it comes to doing what really matters to you—reconnecting with family, writing that book, finding a new job—you say "I'm only [such and such an age] I have a long time." If you assume you "have time" to do something, or that you'll do it later, you probably don't want it as much as you think you do. There isn't more time. You don't know. You could be dead tomorrow. It doesn't mean you have to get everything done today, but that there's rarely an excuse not to start.

11. A bad feeling becomes a bad day.

    You think that experiencing negative emotions is the result of something being wrong in your life, when in reality, it's usually just a part of being human. Anxiety serves us, pain serves us, depression does, too. These things are signals, communications, feedbacks, and precautions that literally keep us alive. Until you begin thinking this way, all you will perceive is that "good feelings mean keep going" and "bad feelings mean stop," and wonder why you're paralyzed.

12. You think that being uncomfortable and fearful means you shouldn't do something.

    Being uncomfortable and fearful means you definitely should. Being angry or indifferent means you definitely shouldn't.

13. You wait to feel motivated or inspired before you act.

    Losers wait to feel motivated. People who never get anything done wait to feel inspired. Motivation and inspiration are not sustaining forces. They crop up once in a while, and they're nice while they're present, but you can't expect to be able to summon them any given hour of the day. You must learn to work without them, to gather your strength from purpose, not passion.

14. You maladaptively daydream.

    Maladaptive daydreaming is when you imagine extensive fantasies of an alternative life that you don't have to replace human interaction or general function. Most people experiencing it while listening to music and/or moving (walking, riding in a car, pacing, swinging, etc.) Rather than cope with issues in life, you just daydream to give yourself a "high" that eliminates the uncomfortable feeling.

15. You're saving up your happiness for another day.

You're sitting on the train on the way to work, thinking how beautiful the sunrise looks, and how you'd like to read your favorite book, but you don't in favor of checking your email again. You begin to feel a sense of awe at something simple and beautiful and stop yourself, because your dissatisfaction fuels you. You're creating problems in one area of your life to balance out thriving in another, because your happiness is in a mental container.

31

DO YOU ARGUE INTELLIGENTLY?
from DEFENSIVENESS *to* REBUTTAL, THE 7 MAIN WAYS PEOPLE FIGHT

At its most basic level, argumentativeness is a reflex, not a choice. When we feel threatened in some way, we either respond by fleeing, freezing, or fighting. Eventually, most people begin to realize that unconsciously responding to random, external stimuli is exhausting at best and destructive at worst. We begin to censor our responses to things—these are the seeds of self-awareness.

However, this does not mean that arguing doesn't serve an important purpose. While it is often a product of grappling with our own threatened sense of identity, it is also how we can communicate feeling strongly about something important. When done intelligently, someone who knows how to argue well can be a master of their social surroundings—in business, love, and so on. The first step to doing so, however, is not sounding as though you're being argumentative.

Enter the hierarchy. To put it bluntly, there are a lot of idiotic ways that people try to argue with one another, and most of them do not work. They only leave both parties more frustrated, ultimately because they each avoid addressing the real issue in its entirety.

Name-calling.
You deflect from the issue at hand by proclaiming that someone is an "ass" or an "idiot" without any argument to back it up.

Ad hominem.
You attack the character or the authority of the person without addressing the actual substance of the argument. (If someone who

113

smokes says: "Smoking is bad," you respond: "Who are you to say?!" rather than seeing it as an objective truth.)

Responding to tone.
You criticize the tone or the diction of the person making the argument as a means of deflecting from actually addressing the argument itself.

Contradiction.
You state the opposing case with little or no evidence to back it up. You're arguing for the sake of it, you just inherently do not want to validate or agree with the person for some reason.

Counterargument.
You contradict the statement, then back it up with reasoning and/or supportive evidence.

Refutation.
You find the mistake in the argument and explain why it is a mistake using direct quotations or inferences from the person's original statement.

Refuting the central point.
You explicitly refute the central point of the argument, providing sound logic and reason (if not research, or personal experience) to back up your claim.

32

SIGNS YOUR
MENTAL BREAKDOWN
is actually
AN EMOTIONAL
BREAKTHROUGH

01. You're questioning everything.

    You're done believing that things are as they appear, or that what you were raised to believe about something is the right way to think overall. You're exploring new ideas of philosophy and spirituality and politics and thought, and you're coming to find that you didn't know what you didn't know.

02. You're realizing that there's a difference between happy thoughts and happy feelings.

    You've been trying to fill yourself up with "happy thoughts" forever, only to find that you get attached to a certain outcome (that doesn't become reality) and you're even unhappier in the first place. You're realizing that there's a difference between "a way of thinking that lets you enjoy the moment" and "a way of thinking that makes you happy about potentials, possibilities, and things that are everything but what's actually happening."

03. You're starting to see patterns.

    You're realizing that many of the things that keep resurfacing in your life—relationships, jobs, ideas, feelings—are products of what you believe they are or should be. They are patterns, and maybe if you could figure out how to change them, the way they emerge would change, too.

04. You feel irrationally angry.

    Anger is a good emotion; that is, when you finally figure out that you're not mad at the world—you're mad at yourself. This is usually what happens right before change is going to be made. Anger's younger siblings—dissatisfaction, resentment, irritation, self-pity, etc.—are unpleasant but not disturbing enough to make you act. Anger makes you act. It burns through you and delivers you somewhere new.

05. You're starting to question: "Is this all there is?"

You're starting to wonder whether or not you really were meant to just sleep, eat, work then die. You're starting to wonder if this is all that exists, or if it's a small aperture for a far greater reality.

06. You had the million-dollar idea, found The Relationship, got the big break, and all of a sudden, you're paralyzed.

We call this some good ol' resistance. When we perceive happiness, we perceive fear to an equal degree. It's not actually that you're resisting your new life, it's that you're very clearly identifying what you want (and experiencing a natural and balanced amount of fear about it).

07. It seems like your emotional state is unwarranted.

You shouldn't feel anxious and depressed, but you do. There's no reason for your irrational fears, but they're there. You can't quite make sense of what you're feeling, and you realize that's because you're in the process of developing that skill.

08. You're uncertain about who you really are.

You have come to terms with the fact that you've defined yourself based on either how people see you, or how you think you should be, and there's a bit of a discrepancy between what you think you want and what you actually want.

09. You're experiencing feelings and fears you had when you were a kid.

It's all coming back up to the surface, and what you're realizing is that it was never really gone in the first place. The thoughts, ideas, beliefs, and feelings you kept tucked away were silently guiding your life. You just didn't know.

10. You're terrified of loss right now.

Namely, you're terrified of losing one specific thing that you think in some way will "save" you (even just emotionally). This is what happens when you begin to realize that nothing can do that for you. You're not afraid of loss; you're afraid of being forced to accept that reality before you think you're ready.

11. You're giving up on the things you need to give up on.
    You're not giving up on your dreams. You're not giving up on your relationship. You are simply giving up on the idea that these things will be something more than what they are. You are giving up on what's not right for you. You're learning that "giving up" is such a negative term for something that's really healthy when necessary.

12. You've decided you're not going to be the victim of your own mind anymore.

People don't have breakdowns unless they are on the precipices of "breakthroughs." Breakdowns—or any kind of intense mental-emotional turmoil—are always a sign that things are in the process of changing. Otherwise, they'd just be "normal." You're done accepting your old "normal," and you're onto bigger, better, brighter, happier things.

HOW TO
STOP WORRYING
about how
YOUR LIFE LOOKS
and start
FOCUSING ON
HOW IT FEELS

Count how many times you've really been happy after you got something you thought you wanted. What happened after you got the relationship you were lusting after? What happened after you got that job? What happened when you made more money? Chances are, things were different, but proportionately good and bad.

Make a list of all the imperfect people you've known in your life who have had love. Who have had romantic partners and best friends and jobs you could only ever dream of. Make a list of all the people who are conventionally unattractive and spiritually adrift and imperfect and all the things each one of them had despite being that way. Make it your own personal proof that you do not need to be perfect to be good enough.

Ask yourself what you'd do if social media were no object and nobody would know. What would you do this Saturday, what would you do tonight? What would your career goals be, how many photos would you really take? Who would you hang out with, where would you live, if you weren't silently policing yourself through the lens of "what other people see"?

Ask yourself what you'd do if money were no object and you could do anything. This is a classic exercise that many people dismiss because of how impractical it is. Unfortunately, those people aren't thinking deeply enough to understand the real point. It's not to discover what you'd actually do if you didn't have to worry about money (that's not our reality), it's about the essence of what you'd do and how you can incorporate that into your everyday life. Would you vacation, would you keep your current job? It just goes to show you whether you value relaxation or accomplishments or whatever else, and understanding what you value is crucial to understanding who you are.

Take photos to remember happy moments, not prove that you looked good or did something cool. Make a special album on your phone just for "happy moments." When you feel good or are enjoying yourself or have some kind of revelation, just take a photo of whatever's in front of you (however unworthy of Instagram it is). When you look back at these seemingly random snapshots, you'll experience those feelings all over again. You'll see, by contrast, the emotional difference between capturing the moments that matter to you and creating moments to matter for other people.

Identify the "people" you always think are judging you. You know how people always say that? "People are judging me." "I'm worried about what people will think." Most of the time, those "people" are a faceless crowd that only exist in your mind. In other words, they're you, projected outward. It's what you're judging yourself for. The first step is realizing that the "people" you worry about don't really exist.

Think about what makes you feel the most jealous. The things that make us the most jealous and envious are usually the things that we feel we're not living up to within ourselves. We're jealous of the beautiful girl not because we want to be beautiful like her, but because we're lacking something so much more important, which is love for ourselves. We're jealous of the successful writer not because we also want to be lauded, but because we know we're not doing the work to get there.

Don't clean before someone comes over. Save for people who, you know, aren't hygienic, don't worry about setting up a stage when someone else visits. I'm not talking about straightening up or putting personal items away, but actually trying to construct an appearance that is the physical equivalent of bleached-blonde hair dye. Let people into your life in a true way. Let them enter a moment in your life just as it's happening. It's the only way you truly bond.

Rethink how you celebrate the most important days of the year. Most people do it with relatives they see only on holidays, who they don't have genuine relationships with otherwise, and who they are

119

vaguely unhappy to have to see. These days are meant to be spent treating the people who love you all year 'round to parties and meals and gifts. Not the people who you feel morally obligated (but emotionally repressed) into stomaching.

Get rid of things that aren't purposeful or meaningful. The reason why this is so important is because things are defining, especially when we buy them with the intention of making us "different." Our things construct our experiences. They create what we see and by extension how we feel. They are the means through which we put ourselves together each day. It's not about having as little as possible, it's about having only things that serve purpose or hold meaning. Do it. It will transform your life. (And that's no small claim to make.)

Ask yourself: "If I knew nobody would judge me, what would I stand for?" What do you inherently agree with once you're past all the self-imposed social filters? People think being conscious of their hidden thoughts and feelings and prejudices = being unaware and ignorant, but the opposite is true. It's being unaware that's a problem.

Ask yourself: "If I could tell every single person in the world just one thing, one sentence, what would it be?" Would you say: "It's going to be okay?" "Don't worry so much?" "Seek the best in others?" "Follow me on Twitter?" What you think you'd want to say to everyone out there is actually a projection of what you most need to hear. That's what you most want to tell you.

Decide that to be worthy of something is just to be grateful to have it. You choose what your self-esteem is measured by. You decide what your worth is based on. You decide whether or not you're good enough for something, and because that is the case, you decide that the people who are worthy of what they have are the ones who are grateful to have it. Nothing more, nothing less.

Realize that you are not only as accomplished as you are over your biggest hurdle. You're not only as "good" as you are "perfect"; you're not only as "good" as you are better than someone else, either. In the words of Oprah (who else?) you can have everything, just not at the same time. Be grateful for this: It means you have the opportunity to appreciate what's in front of you, and you always have something else to work toward and look forward to.

Assume that all things are for the best. When people care most about how their lives look is when they're most closed to how their lives feel. When they're most closed to how their lives feel is when they don't want to feel pain. Being truly at peace requires realizing that everything is for the best. Everything in your life does one of three things: shows you to yourself, heals a part of yourself, or lets you enjoy a part of yourself. If you adopt that perspective, there's nothing left to fear.

Ask yourself: "If the whole world were blind, how many people would I impress?" Truly imagine a life in which you could not see things. In which all that exists is how you feel and how you make others feel. In this kind of world, what kind of person are you, and is it for those reasons that, perhaps, creating a life that looks good to earn other people's love has supplemented having your own?

34

WHY YOU
shouldn't
SEEK
COMFORT

01. Your brain can't differentiate "good" from "bad"; it only knows "comfortable" and "uncomfortable." This is a pretty raw example, but it's the reason why criminals never think their actions are "wrong," they think they're justifiable. It's why we do things we objectively know are bad for us and confuse them for "feeling good."

02. You don't want what you want; you want what you've known. We are literally incapable of predicting an outcome that is out of the realm of what we've known previously. So rather than trying to seek "better," we seek "the best of what we've known," even if "the best" is really just the solution to a problem we didn't need to create again.

03. "Familiar discomfort" feels the same as "comfort." Which is why so many people are stuck in "ruts" or absolutely do not want to change even though they know it's what would be best for them.

04. There's no such thing as true security. We seek comfort believing that it makes us safe, but we live in a world in which there is no such thing as true security. Our bodies were made to evolve, our physical items are temporary and can be lost and broken, etc. To combat this, we seek comfort rather than accepting the transitory nature of life.

05. The only way you grow is by stepping into the unknown. It's why so many people have "breakdown before breakthrough" moments. Often, their lives are leading them to better possibilities than they thought possible; they just didn't know it was "good" at the time.

06. Most people don't change until not changing is the less comfortable option. But there's usually a long period of time of increasing discomfort before "not changing" is the worst-case scenario. The universe whispers until it screams, and happy people listen while the call is still quiet.

07. There are two mindsets people tend to have: explorer or settler. Our society has a "settler" mindset, our end goals are "finalizing" (home, marriage, career, etc.) in a world that was made for evolution, in selves that do nothing but grow and expand and change. People with "explorer" mindsets are able to actually enjoy what they have and experience it fully because they are inherently unattached.

08. There's no such thing as real comfort; there's only the idea of what's safe. This is a big one to swallow, but there's really no such thing as "comfort," which is why comfortable things don't last, and why the best adjusted people are most "comfortable" in "discomfort." Comfortable is just an idea. You choose what you want to base yours on.

09. Life isn't about being "certain," it's about trying anyway. Comfort is, essentially, certainty. You can either choose to be certain about what you've known or certain that you'll make the best of whatever happens. (Guess who has a better time?) Because nobody is ever really certain. The people who have lives they love try anyway.

35

THE 6 PILLARS
OF SELF-ESTEEM:
why it is not
HOW YOU FEEL,
but what you think
YOU'RE CAPABLE OF

We tend to think of self-esteem as a static thing, a state in which your mind naturally fuels you with positive, supportive thoughts, never being too deeply influenced by any doubts or dislikes. This, however, is where the fine line between self-esteem and self-aggrandizement blurs.

In the words of Anna Deavere Smith, self-esteem is what really gives us a feeling of well-being. It's the very inherent sense that everything's going to be all right, because we are capable of making it all right. "[Self-esteem is knowing] that we can determine our own course and that we can travel that course. It's not that we travel the course alone, but we need the feeling of agency—that if everything were to fall apart, we could find a way to put things back together again."

Self-esteem is not how much confidence you have in how well people perceive you, but how much confidence you have in whether or not you can manage your life.

What's interesting about having real self-esteem is that it eliminates the need to focus on how we're superior to others. When we don't feel we're actually in control of our lives (or aren't happy with how things are going so far) we often focus on "how much better things are than someone else" to placate the feeling of failure.

Nathaniel Branden outlined what exactly it takes to build a healthy sense of self[12]. He notes, particularly, that people either take the "feel good" approach (I am beautiful, I am rich, I am successful) which is merely a substitute for the real thing, or they build it in a genuine way.

125

He says that the two fundamental elements self-esteem boils down to are self-efficacy, which is "a sense of basic confidence in the face of life's challenges," and self-respect, "a sense of being worthy of happiness."

"[Self-esteem] is not an emotion which fluctuates from moment to moment, but a continuing disposition to experience a sense of efficacy and respect for oneself. Thus, it is something which is built over a long period of time, not just wished into existence. It is reality-based; undeserved praise, whether it comes from oneself or others, will not provide it."

Here are the six practices, or "pillars," on which Branden argues self-esteem can be built. They prove that it is not just a choice to feel confident in yourself, but it many choices, made continuously, and with as much effort as possible.

Living consciously.
To live consciously is to not be controlled by your subconscious biases and desires. Your "shadow selves," as they're called, are out in the light. You understand what's going on around you, and you can make informed choices based on that inherent understanding.

Self-acceptance.
You aren't aggrandizing your looks or your intelligence or being willfully ignorant of the natural balance of traits and characteristics every person possesses. This is true self-acceptance. It is seeing your whole self without judging or condemning parts of it.

Self-responsibility.
You hold yourself accountable for your own happiness. You understand the phrase "it may not be your fault, but it is still your problem." You are in control of your life because you are not letting other things do it for you.

Self-assertiveness.
You can stand up for yourself without being defensive. Defensiveness is born of fear; assertiveness is born of confidence.

Living purposefully.
You live mindfully and intentionally. You recognize that your "purpose" is just to be where you are, doing whatever you're doing.

In this, you infuse your days with a sense of purposefulness, as it is something you choose, not wait to find or have created for you.

Personal integrity.
You hold yourself to a certain standard of morals and ethics and accountability. You develop a code of conduct for yourself, rather than just abiding by the one that you were conditioned to. You are able to look at choices objectively, even when the circumstances are difficult. You realize the importance of the phrase "the road to hell was paved with good intentions..."

---

12 Branden, Nathaniel. *The Psychology of Self-Esteem*. 2001. Jossey-Bass.

36

WHY YOU SHOULD
THANK THE PEOPLE
who have
HURT YOU
MOST IN LIFE

01. The people who were able to hurt you most were also the people whom you were able to love the most. We aren't profoundly affected by people who aren't already deeply within our hearts. For someone to have that much importance in your life is sacred, even when it goes askew. It's a gift to know someone who was able to truly affect you, even if at first it didn't seem like it was for the best.

02. Difficult relationships often push you to change your behavior for the better. In feeling helpless, you learn to take care of yourself. In feeling used, you recognize your worth. In being abused, you develop compassion. In feeling like you're stuck, you realize there is always a choice. In accepting what was done to you, you realize that nobody has control at the end of the day, but in surrendering the need for something we'll never have, we can find peace, which is what we were actually seeking in the first place.

03. What you learn and who you become is more important than how you temporarily feel. That relationship may have seemed almost unbearable at the time, but the feeling is transitory. The wisdom and grace and knowledge that you carried with you afterwards aren't. They set a foundation for the rest of your life. The ends far outweigh the means, and to be grateful for what you've been through is to completely acknowledge that.

04. You don't come across these people by accident; they were your teachers and catalysts. In the words of C. Joybell C.,

we're all stars that think they're dying until we realize we're collapsing into supernovas—to become more beautiful than ever before. It often takes the contrast of pain to completely appreciate what we have, and it often takes hate to incite self-recognition. Sometimes the way light enters us is, in fact, through the wound.

05. Even if it wasn't your fault, it is your problem, and you get to choose what you do in the aftermath. You have every right to rage and rant and hate every iota of someone's being, but you also have the right to choose to be at peace. To thank them is to forgive them, and to forgive them is to choose to realize that the other side of resentment is wisdom. To find wisdom in pain is to realize that the people who become "supernovas" are the ones who acknowledge their pain and then channel it into something better, not people who just acknowledge it and then leave it to stagnate and remain.

06. The people who have been through a lot are often the ones who are wiser and kinder and happier overall. This is because they've been "through" it, not "past" it or "over" it. They've completely acknowledged their feelings and they've learned and they've grown. They develop compassion and self-awareness. They are more conscious of who they let into their lives. They take a more active role in creating their lives, in being grateful for what they have and in finding reasons for what they don't.

07. It showed you what you do deserve. Those relationships didn't actually hurt you; they showed you an unhealed part of yourself, a part that was preventing you from being truly loved. That's what happens when we finally get past hurtful experiences and terrible relationships: We realize we are worth more, and so we choose more. We realize how we blindly or naively said "yes" to someone or gave them our mind and heart space when we didn't have to. We realize our role in choosing what we want in our lives, and by experiencing what seems like the worst, we finally

acknowledge that it feels so wrong because we deserve so much more.

08. Truly coming to peace with anything is being able to say: "Thank you for that experience." To fully move on from anything, you must be able to recognize what purpose it served and how it made you better. Until that moment, you'll only be ruminating over how it made things worse, which means you're not to the other side yet. To fully accept your life—the highs, lows, good, bad—is to be grateful for all of it, and to know that the "good" teaches you well, but the "bad" teaches you better.

37

TRYING TO
MAKE SENSE
of your life
IS WHAT'S ACTUALLY
HOLDING YOU BACK

You should try to make sense of your feelings. You should trace the lines of your thinking, find the genesis of your innermost beliefs, and make sure they're really yours. You should make lists of the things you do and don't value, you should ask yourself what you most feel you are lacking, then look at how little you're giving them.

But you should stop trying to make sense of your life. Doing so is trying to make sense of the trajectory, as though it's something that controls you, not the opposite way around. Doing so is applying the life you have to the person you were.

Using logic and being mindful are not the same thing as "trying to make sense." The former is methodical: It uses a grounded awareness to enact your true desires, while the latter is looking at the product of those actions and wondering how they got that way.

There are questions to which answers may not exist. There are answers that just create more questions, solutions that can only be made from having lived something out, seen it through, tried.

The best things will not make sense—not initially, at least.

Love is not logical. Grace and joy and beauty rarely are, either. That doesn't mean you cannot use logic to work with them, just that to fully see them, you need to use a different point of understanding.

All things in their purest state are confusingly, singularly standing. They are magical because they are mysterious. They have unknown origins and palpable endings and there is nothing to do but to live them and to see.

People who waste their lives search for reasons to love rather than ways to love. They try to create avenues through which they can justify their happiness, rather than just letting themselves feel it for anything. They try to wield misguided logic to hold back from their happiness rather than facilitate it.

There will be things you understand immediately, effects for which the causes are entirely, consciously yours. There will be things that happen in your life that you know you've chosen, and then others that seem to be the opposite of what you'd want. Those things are just as important, if not more so.

There are things that have reasons that will reveal themselves to you immediately. There are things that you won't understand for years and years to come. There are things you'll look back on and say: "I never understood why that was."

And yet that will not make it any less so.

Sometimes the point is to experience not knowing and confusion. What is born of your uncertainty is sometimes more important than not having been certain in the first place.

You may never know whether or not you're "meant" to be in the city you live in, but you will live there anyway, because you have chosen to. You won't know whether or not you're meant to be with someone until you try. You will keep seeking comfort in the things that hurt you because you've yet to step into the discomfort of something new. Something better. Something unknown and foreign and not aligned with what you once thought you wanted.

That does not make it wrong or bad; it just means you didn't anticipate it. You didn't know well enough to have chosen it.

Trying to make sense of your life is trying to see if the old story checks out, if the person you once were would be happy with the life they lead today. You're looking for answers in people that don't exist.

Clarity comes from doing, not thinking about doing.

A good life comes from choosing to work with what you have, accepting that you don't always choose what you work with, but knowing you're always given what you need to use, especially when you don't realize you need to use it.

38

HOW TO
DETOX YOUR MIND
*(without having
to go completely
off the grid)*

Though we have miles to go in terms of learning what it means to take care of our bodies, we're even further behind on how to take care of our minds. Our brains construct our experiences, and there are so many factors that alter and shift our perspectives that are completely in our control but totally out of our awareness. Here, a few things you can do to detox your mind, deprogram, and wipe the slate clean now and again.

01. Travel to assimilate to culture. Alter your base-point concept of "normal." What it will show you is how many behaviors/values/beliefs you've unconsciously adopted from your surroundings (and ways you can change them).

02. Create physical solutions for emotional problems. People default on the idea that one emotion will cancel out or fix another. If you're upset, seek a high to eliminate it. But negative emotions are just calls to action that are being ignored through a little mental gymnastics and a lot of justification. Detoxing your mind is letting go of emotional highs in place of creating actual solutions.

03. Know that emotional toxicity is born of mental resistance. Instead of trying to create a certain emotional experience for yourself (if I do this and this, I will feel this way), try to practice complete acceptance of whatever you feel in the moment. Mental resistance keeps you in your emotional discomfort, even if it numbs it for a minute.

04. Identify your tethers. The problems that are in front of you are actually behind you; they are cracks in your foundation that are holding you back. Stop trying to dismantle symptoms; go back and identify the causes.

05. Go for a long drive and let yourself get lost. Drive through neighborhoods you never would have known existed. See how other people live. See them come home from work and what their living rooms look like from the outside. It will comfort you in that you'll realize how small you are in a more practical way than just staring at the ocean. You don't know what you don't know.

06. Rearrange your furniture. Your brain constructs your experience through props and signals that those props fire off. You are continually, subconsciously triggering negative or stagnant associations because of how your brain processes your surroundings—change them, change how you think, change what you feel.

07. Do a mental purge. Just write down whatever weird thoughts continually cross your mind or the little incoherent bits that are clogging your head. Just getting them out will give you relief.

08. Restructure your digital life. It's not realistic (or desirable to a lot of people) to be forever disconnected, but it's also not realistic to keep things that don't serve you positively in your social feeds and expect it not to affect you. Instead of just unfollowing what you don't want to see, follow positive accounts/groups/organizations/publications that you do.

09. Notice your unconscious movements. Notice your feet walking and how you are not deciding to lift each one up and forward and yet because your mind said, "Okay, self, let's get to this point today," you began to go. Consider your morning intentions similarly.

10. Cleanse your space emotionally: Consider the emotional attachment you have to the things you keep around you. Did you buy those clothes to be someone you're not? Do you

have decor around your apartment that you got during a particularly crappy time in your life? Let those things go, but decide what to let go by thinking about what they make you feel.

11. Place yourself. Make a chart with three columns and on the left write everything you feel you've accomplished in your life and in the middle write down what your daily life entails and then on the right put what those consistent habits will lead to/what you hope to do in the future. It helps you focus on the big picture; getting lost in minutiae usually causes people anxiety.

12. Shift your physical position every time you start falling back into toxic thought cycles. This basically creates a new experience for your body and refocuses you in the moment (and it's simple enough to do at your desk at work).

13. Stretch your brain. Pick up a book on something that interests you and learn more about it. Look at research on something you have a theory about. Learn to love learning through actively engaging with things that naturally interest you. If nothing else, it will make you a bit more aware of the world.

14. Reevaluate the extent of your connected disconnectedness. If the bulk of your relationships happen digitally (that aren't long-distance) and you haven't had a conversation in person without being interrupted by a phone in a long enough time, evaluate how much you're prioritizing people in your life, and realize that screens > people is basically the best way to create an extremely anxious lifestyle for yourself.

15. Identify what your addictions are keeping you distracted from. Most things people struggle with are addictions in some form: a thing you keep doing though you don't really want to. Understand that addiction is a disconnection from yourself, and a disconnection from yourself is born of something present that you (think) you can't face.

16. Learn to let "good enough" not be the opposite of perfect. If there is one thing that will give you the most mental-emotional

relief it is in letting good enough be good enough.

17. Dismantle the parts of your life that are solely performative. The thing is that most of what clogs our minds is all the unnecessary effort we put into constructing a life that seems a little more palatable, a little more noble, a little better than someone else's (so therefore good enough). But it accomplishes the opposite of what we intend: We place ourselves further from a genuinely happy experience (which is in accepting that life is small and simple and more than enough) through grandiose ideas and attachments that end up making us into characters, not people.

18. Write down what you hate about other people. This is what you need to change about yourself/your life (but are resisting too much to actually do something about). Know that it's often not a surface level issue: You don't hate your annoying neighbor because she always bothers you for lunch and you secretly bother other people for lunch, you hate her because she acts as though she's desperate for love and you feel that way too but avoid it because you think it's embarrassing. This is a cheat sheet to seeing what's actually wrong in your life. It's important because completely understanding the problem is the same thing as knowing the solution. If you don't know what to do, you don't know what's wrong. If you don't know what's wrong, it's because some part of you is resisting seeing it.

39

12 SIGNS
THE ONLY PROBLEM
WITH YOUR LIFE
is that you
THINK ABOUT IT
more than
YOU LIVE IT

Anxiety is usually bred out of inaction. We were born to actualize our potential, not just analyze it. Binge thinking is what happens when introspection becomes a means of avoiding a problem. Critically evaluating your life is supposed to facilitate living it, not the other way around. Here, all the things that happen when you let your life exist more in your brain than in reality.

01. Your goals are perfect outcomes, not perfect actions. You're more in love with ideas than you are with work and processes required to make them reality. When you dream up your perfect life, you think about how you're seen, rather than what your daily tasks include.

02. You're a maladaptive daydreamer. Maladaptive daydreaming is when you imagine extensive fantasies to replace human interaction or general function. Many people experience it while listening to music or doing some kind of rocking motion (walking, pacing, swinging, etc.). Rather than cope with issues in life, you just daydream about grandiose alternatives that give you a "high" to eliminate the uncomfortable feeling.

03. Your purpose in life is abstract. You know that you want to help people, or teach, or give a voice to the voiceless, but you don't know how to do it, and you certainly don't focus on embodying it in your present life, in the situations you're

already in, with people you come across in day-to-day interactions.

04. The solution to most of your problems would just be to make some small change but you absolutely refuse to. This is the classic sign that you're using overthinking as a means of deflection. It's easy to do, as picking apart a problem is a noble-seeming distraction, but it's only useful until you have the answer—then you actually have to act on it.

05. You're always busy, yet never productive enough. Your work never seems to be done, you lose hours and don't know where they've gone, you're always stressed and frizzling-out your brain, as though you're perpetually in the middle of a high-intensity task that never sees completion.

06. You tend to resist what you want the most. Rather than putting forth genuine effort, opening up to it bit-by-bit, you've convinced yourself that you're not worth it, or that it's impossible, or that to have what you want means you could also lose what you want (so better not to have it ever than have it for a little bit).

07. You're one of those people who only bonds over what you hate. All this really means is that you: a) aren't doing enough to have something else/more interesting to talk about, or b) are so deeply insecure you thrive off of recognizing that someone else is on your level (judgment = a need to be superior, which = feeling incredibly inferior).

08. Most of your problems come back down to a fear of judgment, or exclusion. If this fear is present in your life to any significant degree it's usually because you've already constructed a lot of what you think you like or do based on what other people think. It's for this reason that you don't naturally take action—you think about it, change what you want to do in some way, and then (maybe) act (still fearful) that people will not like the façade, either.

09. If you stopped and thought about it, you could come up with 10 things you are grateful for. Your "problems" aren't so much

"not having" as they are not recognizing what you do have. Gratitude incites more doing, more reciprocation. Positive feelings never leave you stagnating and over-thinking them.

10. You want to change something about your life, but your focus is on dismantling the old rather than building something new that renders it obsolete. In other words, you're one of those people who tries to find comfort in overanalyzing old things to make more sense of them, when in reality, complexity is a product of insecurity, and insecurity a product of being unable to accept the simple reality of the situation.

11. You look for quick solutions more than you focus on restructuring the questions. When you try and fail at something, you spend too long focusing on why you failed, rather than learning what you need to then moving on and trying something new. You keep yourself stuck between knowing what's not right and not being willing to figure out what might be.

12. You're always imagining what you want to do, yet never really doing it. You've convinced yourself that life begins when all the pieces are in place, but in reality, life is the act of doing just that.

40

WHY LOGICAL
PEOPLE LEAD
BETTER LIVES
*(in a generation where
"passion" is at a premium)*

Our generation believes that passion is the answer—the solution to a life joyously, successfully, happily lived. We were the kids who were told, "You can be anything" and heard "You can succeed at everything." There are a lot of people much smarter than me who have argued this beautifully.

It's not about following passion; it's about following purpose passionately. Passion is a manner of traveling, not a means to determine a destination. Passion is the spark that lights the fire; purpose is the kindling that keeps it burning all night. (I've said this before.) This is to say: The opposite of passion isn't settling for a lukewarm life, it's marrying it to logic that will actually get you where you want to go.

The ability to objectively look at our lives and interpret emotions and events and decisions with a grounded frame of mind is not only positive, it's essential to functioning. The head and heart must be separate entities that you figure out how to merge together. Here's why:

01. Passion tells you that you should go after what you most want in life, but it's never about "what you want," it's about what you want most. It's about which of your (often conflicting) desires you let win.

    The only reason people don't do what they claim to want most is because there is something else they want a little bit more. They ultimately don't get what they want done because they're trying to follow their most intense desire rather than prioritizing them.

I'd like to have another day off but I'd also like to work on my retirement fund and build my business some more. Right now, I'm choosing the latter so it can facilitate the former later on down the road. See that? Choosing which desire I let win.

When people try to build their lives solely on emotions, they're incapable of choosing which desire they're going to follow, so they choose the one that elicits the most extreme high, which is fallible because it's impermanent and it can come at the cost of innumerable consequences that are ultimately counterproductive to what they had intended in the first place.

02. Passion bases relationships on the high; logic bases relationships on the purpose.

The "purpose" being love (not attachment or not wanting to be alone or money or ego, as some people unfortunately do). We're usually taught that love is just a "good feeling" or a "verb." But there are a lot of "good feelings" you can have that are not rooted in love and things you can do out of what you perceive to be love when you're with someone important to you.

It's the commitment to ground your relationship in something more than just a transitory feeling that will ultimately make it work. When you believe that passion is love—no more, no less—you'll want to end a relationship as soon as you're not getting that hormonal high from your partner; or worse, you'll blame them for it and seek out what they're lacking and why.

The way this usually manifests is in people being very indecisive and uncertain about "whether or not they love someone," whether or not they should let go or try harder or wait it out or accept that love isn't always a fever dream.

I have personally have spent years trying to figure out whether or not I really loved different people, and about half that time flip-flopping in and out of relationship(s), only to eventually figure out that I confused passion for love (and they aren't the same thing).

03. Logic allows you to see objectively; passion is subjective and consuming.

The thing about the things people are most passionate about is that it's a scream that takes all their might and echoes out into the void. There's no practice or reason, it's just a flush of emotion and when it collides (or contradicts) someone else's, it can feel like a personal affront.

No matter how fierce your feeling or belief, it exists next to a variety of others, not all of which will overlap or align. This does not mean you or anybody else is wrong, just that passion does not allow you to acknowledge coexisting truths: It is singular, and it is destructive when it can't be placed in reality.

04. Logic helps you make decisions for the person you hope to be; passion helps you make decisions for the person you are or were.

What makes a sense of passion so intense is that, essentially, it answers a question you didn't know you were asking. It is a solution to something you've struggled with all along. It is something that proves a point you didn't know you had to make. It is self-evident to you. It is some kind of liberation or transcendence. Something about it gives you a high, which means that it's familiar, and it's serving as an antidote.

The one true sign that you're moving ahead with your life is that you don't know where you're going. If you knew what you were doing, you'd be circling the same path again. The one true sign that you're living in the past is if you feel that reckless "high." (You're proving something to someone or to yourself.)

05. The passion narrative says you should strive for a life that maxes out your wildest dreams; the logic narrative says you should strive for a life that maxes out your potential.

The passion narrative, therefore, keeps you in a place of assuming your life is "less than" because you're not doing what you think is ideal. The logic narrative, however, tells you to evaluate why you want those things and eventually brings you to the conclusion that most of the time, you don't. Rather than maxing out your dreams, logic tells you to max out your potential, which ultimately gets you to the same place that passion could only have you (keep) dreaming of.

06. Passion is born of attachment; logic counteracts it.
Passion is an attachment to an idea, or more often, a particular feeling. It is the desire to keep experiencing that one feeling and to do what it takes to facilitate that feeling no matter what. When people imagine a passionate life, they imagine doing things and being with people that make them feel a specific way. Not only is that unrealistic, it's ultimately impossible. Logic tells you that even at a job you adore, there will be hard days. Being in a relationship with the love of your life doesn't necessarily make it easy (though that's what people assume and yearn for). When you go in with the "I will do what it takes, even when it's hard" attitude, you end up building the foundations, skills, and abilities to cope so well that after a period of time, the initial difficulty ironically dissolves.

07. Gratitude is born of logic; a happy life is born of gratitude.
The reason people "practice gratitude" or make a commitment to reflect on what they are grateful for is that, unfortunately, few people naturally sense it in their lives, and no matter what your current situation, anybody can find a reason to.

Cultivating a sense of gratitude—which is not waiting for a feeling of being happy with your life but choosing it by actively focusing on what you're fortunate, grateful, and proud to have —is essential to ever feeling satisfied with your life, because it puts you in a mindset to seek more to be grateful for. As anybody can tell you: What you seek, you ultimately find.

08. Logic dismantles emotion. Passion tries to use emotion to dismantle other emotions.
Logic can dismantle irrational, illogical, or painful emotions and bring you to a higher state of awareness by evaluating their roots/determining their causes, deciphering whether or

143

not they are useful, or by actually listening to them and acting accordingly if that's what's best.

Passion tries to use emotions to dismantle others. A high to negate a low, a new feeling to replace an old one. It's like trying to grab at water with your hands thinking you'll ever get enough to drink.

It is a strong, clear, guided mind that undoes the irrational stress of what Buddhists call the "monkey mind" (the irrational, unprompted series of thoughts that cross everyone's mind each day, which, ultimately, affect if not construct your emotional state). Logic can tell you how the mind and heart correspond; passion thinks they're one in the same.

09. A lot of people who want to "pursue passion" and find "passionate relationships" are seeking out of a place of lack.

Things that are soulful, genuine, and loving are rarely, if ever, hysterical or highly emotional. They're peaceful and desirable and beautiful and sometimes powerful, but the manic desire to do anything is usually an attempt to fill a hole, run from a problem, avoid a truth.

The obsessive desire for a passionate relationship is usually a reflection of a lack of love for oneself. The manic need to pursue a passionate career is rooted in an intense unhappiness with present reality. They are a series of soothing thoughts and deflection methods and escape routes: The monster everyone's running from, of course, is themselves.

10. Nobody ever got anything from wanting it badly enough.

I really don't care how passionate you claim to be about something, it doesn't mean you're right for the job. Or the relationship. Or the promotion or apartment or whatever the case may be.

But people tend to claim "being passionate" as a qualifying factor, when at the end of the day, the person who gets the job is the one who is most technically capable, both parties need to be convinced the relationship is "the right one" for it to ever be, the promotion will go to the person who worked the hardest and the apartment to the person with the best credit score. Often people focus, and communicate, how badly they want something to suffice for the actual reason(s) they aren't right/qualified/good enough to get it.

11. It's doing, not thinking about doing, that creates a life well lived.

If you want your life to be different, do differently. A lot of our concept of what makes for a happy existence is rooted in the abstract: Think clearly, have a positive frame of reference, be surrounded by people you care about, have a sense of purpose in your work. But these things don't work unless they are genuine, and too many people try to fake it as though they can even convince themselves it's real.

The alternative is doing the work. It's the nitty-gritty, ass-on-the-ground, nose-to-the-grindstone hard work that people avoid because they don't want to be responsible for their own failures. (Can't fail if you haven't tried, eh?)

Confidence is built from what you do, a positive mindset is rooted in what you do, loving relationships are sustained from what you do, purposeful work is cultivated by doing it, not thinking about why you should (and believing that's the same thing).

12. Passion is the easy way out.

Take $150K in loans to study something you "love" for 5+ years, but not be able to move out/travel/get married/have kids/work a job you actually like because you're drowning in debt for the next 30. That's what passion does.

Marry the person you're consumed by, whose neglect and abuse fuels you in its recreation of your childhood issues. Be so torn apart when they leave you that you convince yourself that they are the only one for you. (How could you ever be so broken over anything but true love?) Base your relationship on how far from reality you stretch when you're together. Lose friends and work and a sense of self. That's what passion does.

Or rather, that's what passion does when it's not married to logic. That's what unbridled feelings will do when they aren't stopped by thought and understanding. That's what happens when you believe your emotions rather than questioning their origins. It's what happens when you try to avoid the inevitable suffering of the human condition with a surge of emotion that you think will be the antidote.

Passion is the easy way, the cut corner, the half-assed route to the life you want to live. As with all things passion is born of, it can only sustain an idea, not a reality.

41

THINGS YOU NEED
to know about
YOURSELF BEFORE
you'll have the
LIFE YOU WANT

As C.G. Jung once said, "Until you make the unconscious conscious, it will direct your life and you will call it fate." When it comes to building the lives we want to lead, we're taught to start constructing from how we imagine we want things to look. Titles rather than roles, images rather than realities, concepts rather than day-in-and-day-out tasks and duties and practices. It's time to dismantle the ego-frenzied Western obsession with a Big Life and break down what it takes to actually exist in a way we desire. Here, all the things you must know about yourself so you can choose the life you actually want, not the one you think you do.

What do you want your daily tasks to be?

We're instructed to choose the life we want based on what we think we want to be, but we're only capable of determining that insofar as we are able to think of what it would mean to have the title of a role. We rarely consider the nitty-gritty daily practice that is required for a peaceful, meaningful existence. Instead of "I want to help people each day," start asking yourself if the way you really want to do that is by caring for people physically, doing the tasks that actually requires. It all sounds flowery and noble when you think of what you want your life to be about, but you must consider the reality. When you go in choosing what you want each day of your life to consist of —how much paperwork, how much time at the computer, how many hours of leisure—you're able to actually build the existence you want from the ground up.

What kind of person do you want to be? (As opposed to: What titles do you want to have?)

147

It's not about choosing what kind of adjective you'd like as a preface to your job title, but what kind of person you want to be doing it. It ultimately doesn't matter whether you're a teacher, or student, or editor, or construction worker. It matters what kind of person you want to be while you do those jobs. Are you someone who is kind and understanding? Who spends the better portion of their day conversing with loved ones? Someone who is busy from daybreak to day's end? Someone who is distracted? Attentive? Hard-working? You ultimately are defined not by what you do, but how you do it.

What do you want to be remembered for?

What do you want them to say at your funeral? That you wore a small pant size and had a successful job that prevented you from actually developing relationships? Or that you were loving, and kind, and cared about your work, but cared about people more? Your impermanence is a thing you should meditate on every day: There is nothing more sobering, nor scary, nor a faster-way-to-cut-the-negative-bullshit than to remember that you do not have forever. What defines your life, when it's all said and done, is how much you influence other people's lives, oftentimes just through your daily interactions and the courage with which you live your own. That's what people remember. That's what you will be known for when you're no longer around to define yourself.

What comes most effortlessly to you?

We tend to believe—and induce—a kind of difficulty with tasks we determine to be meaningful or profound or important. If the things we love, and especially get paid for, are also effortless, it seems as though they are unmerited. We believe we have to suffer for the things we have and love, when we, in fact, do not. It's just as worthwhile—if not maybe more so—to figure out what you effortlessly, naturally do, and learn to capitalize on it while not feigning effortlessness, but just allowing it.

What do you (even unconsciously) believe that your existence is about? Is it random? The act of a higher power?

It doesn't matter who is right or wrong or totally nuts—we may never know for sure—but it is about developing a personal dogma that serves you. This is the singular most telling belief about a person, because it essentially defines how you approach everything

148

else. If you believe that your fate is yours to choose, you will. If you don't, you'll stay victimized, self-pitying, waiting and begging on your knees until some external circumstance shifts and it's deemed the random work of a higher power. If that's how you want to exist, that's your prerogative, but I find that most people don't. Most people want to reclaim their power and choose for themselves. But that liberation begins with one question: What do you think you're here for? What's the point of it all? Explore what you most inherently believe, and then determine how you can live that out to the best of your ability.

Why do you do what you do each day?

Is it to feel a high? For money? For livelihood? There's no right or wrong answer here; the point is simply just to know what most strongly motivates you. Even if it's just making a living, you can fuel a passion project with the desire to more comfortably pay bills each month. Longer-term goals and simple survivalist needs are often the most grounding and constant desires to base yourself in. They should be balanced out with meaningful work and a sense of purpose, but if they are ultimately why you do what you do; don't fight it for some morally superior alternative. Use it to fuel something emotionally-mentally-spiritually positive.

In your fantasy daydreams, who and what are you, and how do other people regard you?

The recurring thematics of your daily daydreaming represent what you're actually seeking from others in various areas of your life. This is your subconsciously motivating factor, because it's the thing you have yet to give yourself. Whatever it is, it's a projection of the thing you most feel you lack—and, therefore, subconsciously seek from others. Is it that people admire you for your beauty? Your creativity? Your talent? Your success? Your money? Figure out what you crave, and figure out how to feed that need yourself.

What do you dislike most about other people?

What you most dislike in others is, in some variation, true of you: You just haven't been able to acknowledge it yet. The more angrily and fiercely you respond "no" to that idea, the more intensely you are trying to avoid it. Anger = recognition. You don't lash back at things you don't, in some way, regard as being real.

So figure out what you most need to heal within yourself by seeing what you most want to change in others. Doing so will free you in a way you can't imagine. Doing so is a necessary piece of the life-you-want puzzle, because all the energy you're using trying to avoid, deflect, delude your way into not acknowledging what you need to heal/change/deal is being wasted, at best, and is actually actively keeping you from the life you want, at worst.

What is worth suffering for?

Everything is hard in some way. It's hard to be in the wrong relationship. It's hard to be in the right one. It's hard to be broke and miserable, it's hard to achieve your dreams. It's hard to be stuck in the middle, not really feeling anything at all. Everything is hard, but you choose your hard. You choose what's worth it. You don't choose whether or not you'll suffer, but you do choose what you want to suffer for.

What owns you in this life?

Is it your desire for happiness? The past? The relationship that almost-was-but-ultimately-didn't? Your body hang-up? Your fear? Your loneliness? Your lack of self-worth? Everybody has one thing that ultimately owns them, drives them, controls them at some visceral level. It's the pattern that everything else is rooted in; it's the issue that crops up again and again. It's what you insatiably seek, then run away from, only to find you ran right into it. What owns you in this life makes up the majority of what you do, so you need to know what it is. It's usually not about freeing yourself from these ties that bind you, but learning to wield them for a greater purpose. Finding the shard of empathy and hope and understanding, tucked deeply within your existential suffering. There is a purpose to all things. Your job is not to understand why, but just to find it in the first place.

42

THINGS
EMOTIONALLY
HEALTHY PEOPLE
know how
TO DO

Of all the health concerns our culture claims to be concerned about, it is perhaps our emotional health that is most severely neglected. (It's not the same thing as mental health.)

We're comfortable talking about our recurring headaches, as we don't feel their presence makes a statement about us. They're disassociated from who we believe ourselves to be. But we know our emotions are a result of who and how we are, and in a desperate plight to preserve the sanctity of our self-idea, we hide. Ironically, that's where the trouble comes in: It's the parts of us we suppress and ignore that are the parts that become silent, insidious, controlling monsters. (It's referred to in psychology as "shadow selves.")

Talking about how one gets from there to here, at the place of emotional health, is another topic altogether (and would require books worth of writing to fully flesh out) so in the meantime, I gathered the 10 elements of an emotionally healthy person. This hypothetical hybrid of positivity probably doesn't exist, but these are, nonetheless, worth considering (and maybe striving for).

01. Emotionally healthy people know how to listen to their pain. Emotional stress and discomfort is a signal that there's a better way, that something's misaligned. It's always directing us toward something better, more aligned with who we are and want to be. The only challenge is getting past whatever made us ignore it in the first place.

02. They know to observe thoughts objectively and not identify with them.

You are not your thoughts. You are not your feelings. You are the being that observes, reacts, uses, generates, and experiences those things. This is to say: You can't control them, but they don't control you. You choose what you think about. You choose what you allow to pass. (And when you can't allow yourself to let things go, you're trying to tell or show yourself something. Pay attention.)

03. They can see within them the things they dislike in others.
One more time for the people in the back: You love in others what you love in yourself. You hate in others what you cannot see in yourself. When you practice self-identifying every time you find yourself frustrated or inexplicably annoyed with someone or their behavior, you tap into an ultimate tool for growth and the fastest route to creating a more peaceful existence for yourself. You're no longer at the whim of other people's behaviors, because ultimately, you were never angered by them...it always existed in you.

04. They're able to differentiate loving something v. loving the idea of it; to be conscious of why they desire something, not just that they desire it.
Ideas solve problems we make up in our heads. If we believe that we're unworthy of love, we need the idea of a loving, doting partner who affirms how perfect we are to correct it. Without understanding that we want that love to fix something in us, we just think we desperately want love because we're romantic, or because happy lives do not exist without it. But the people who are conscious of why they desire something are able to choose wants that are not based in solving a problem, but in something more genuine and healthy.

05. They know when it's time to break up with a friend.
It's often difficult to determine the line between "being committed to a relationship even when it isn't sunshine and happiness" and "knowing when it's time to step away from something that's no longer a positive force in your life." Often we feel almost guilted into remaining close with people to whom we don't actually feel obligation, and that is a recipe for

emotional disaster. Emotionally healthy people can identify the people who are spiteful, jealous, or too wrapped in their own issues to not project them onto everybody else. Do these people need love and companionship, too? Certainly. But sometimes walking away is the best way to do that. Most of the time, it's the healthiest choice.

06. They live minimally, but realistically.
Emotionally healthy people know that no physical acquisition can shock them into feeling what they desire—not for more than a moment, anyway. So they forgo the rat race and learn to be grounded in the simplicity of life. They want not and waste not, keep in their space only things that are meaningful or useful. They are mindful and intentional, grateful and wise with what they consume and keep.

07. They can be alone.
What you find in solitude is perspective. When you're not in the presence of people with whom you must monitor your reactions and choose your sentences wisely, you can let yourself just be. It's why we find it most profoundly relaxing and why emotionally healthy people practice it often. When there's nobody else around for whom you must tailor your emotions, you can experience them fully.

08. They let themselves feel.
The core of every emotional issue is the belief that it's not okay. It's not the presence of it that's harmful; it's the resistance to it that ultimately screws us up. Emotionally healthy people know how to do one thing profoundly better than anybody else: let themselves feel anything and everything they're going through. They know it won't kill them. They know to set aside time to process. They know that contrary to common belief, doing so is not a loss of control, but rather the route to being grounded and resolved enough to actually be fully present and centered...which is as "in control" as a human can be.

09. They do not attach to any one outcome being "good" or "right."

The moment you decide one outcome is the right outcome, you are also deciding that another outcome is the wrong one. Beyond this, some things work out the way we intend for them to, others don't. This is a gift, too.

10. They see the value and purpose of each and every experience.

The point of anything is not what you get from having done it; it's who you become from having gone through it. It's all about growth at the end of the day. The bad things grow you and the good things do, too. (And in reality, "bad" is only what you're taught or come to believe isn't "right.") The point is: It's not about how much you get right, it's how much you get better, and every experience—the good, bad, terrible, wonderful, confusing, messy, great—does just that. In the words of Johanna de Silento, "The only way to fail is to abstain."

43

HOW TO
measure
A GOOD LIFE

We measure a "good life" based on how well we adhere to trajectories. How closely what happens is aligned with our temporary, subjective past thoughts about it. The measure of a life well lived is a cultural, social concept, and it's changed over time. The governing belief of what will make for a worthwhile existence right now, for us, is individual accomplishment (at other times in history it was religious obedience, or procreation, and so on.)

We're not made to be self-serving in an existential way. In fact, we classify doing so as all but a mental disorder. Everything, even our most rote daily tasks, only seem comfortable if they add up to something in the end.

But we set out to maximize our pleasure regardless. To aggrandize individuality in lieu of community and wholeness, and in the process, we find that instead of our passions compounding into a spectacular life, we're empty and stressed and exhausted and twisted in mental circles trying to make sense of why things don't feel the way they appear.

Nothing looks the way we think it will. Nobody reflects on their lives and concludes with, "Yes, this is exactly how I thought it would go." The point is not to get reality to align with ideas about it or to manipulate those ideas about the uncontrollable so we feel in power of them.

Yet the measuring stick for a good life does just that, as it's still rooted in our most basic operating system: our survivalist instincts, which want sex and pleasure and fame and recognition and ego-augmenting attention. It's the hit and go, get and chase, want and strive and ruthlessly steal. We're able to dress these things up to seem civilized, when the people acting on them are in offices and grocery stores and our Tinder accounts.

Animals don't actualize what it means to have gotten their prey or not. They don't consider the psychological implications of a potential mate walking away. They don't piece together their lives or reach for "more." Their instinctive existence works because they don't inherently desire to transcend it.

Animals have no need to evaluate whether or not they've had a "good life," so they don't strive to be more than they are. But we do.

Yet by measuring how much "good" we've done by images, ideas, and clean storylines, we sorely miss the point. We always fall short.

We were not built to be more than we are. Our desire to be more isn't a matter of being beyond our humanness, but wanting to be comfortably in it. Sages teach that we're designed for the messiness and simplicity of everyday life—that desiring an external "more" is a mechanism of the ego. It's not transcendence, it's avoidance.

The way to measure a good life is by how much you still want to change it, which is proportionate to how much you inherently know it can be better. You measure a good life by your capacity to feel discomfort. The extent to which you've questioned yourself. How many times you've changed your mind. The series of dogmas you've adopted and left. The family you chose for yourself.

The number of coffee cups over which you've had funny and serious and hurtful and beautiful talks. The depth to which your empathy extends. The number of long walks you've taken by yourself and journal pages you've filled with the incoherent thoughts. The evolution of the way you philosophize your existence. The evolution of the way you perceive other people.

The days you've soberly worked despite the shards of passion having dissolved. A good life isn't passionate, it's purposeful. Passion is the spark that lights the fire; purpose is the kindling that keeps the flame burning all night.

The number of relationships you've had the courage to end. The easy way out is to stay. The comforting idea is to settle. The liberation is how many times you reach for something more even though you can't conceive of what that could be. That unnamable feeling is the mark of a good life.

You measure a good life by the time you sincerely felt the sunlight across your bed sheets in the morning was awe-inspiringly divine.

The ways you can count you were a better person than before. The ways you can count you'd like to be better in the future.

The number of things that you lost and learned how to not attach to anymore. The number of moments in which you were almost at the end of your capacity, only to find that there was another ocean's worth once you were pushed beyond the surface.

A good life is not measured by what you do, it's about what you are. Not how many people you loved, but how much. It has nothing to do with how well things turn out or how seamlessly the plan is followed. It's about the bits of magic you stumble upon when you dive off path. It's not about the things that didn't work out; it's about what you learn when they don't. Those bits and pieces, awakenings and knowledge, are what build and make you able to perceive things greater than you can currently imagine. A good life is not how it adds up in the end, but what you're counting along the way.

44

THERE IS
A VOICE THAT
doesn't use
WORDS;
this is how you
LISTEN TO IT

The voice you have to listen to will rarely make sense. It won't use words. It won't use logic. It won't fit within the neat trajectory of the storyline that you imagined. It will be subtle, and it will speak to you without you ever knowing that it is.

The feelings your inner voice gives you will be unjustifiable. You won't have reasons for them. You'll know you love someone not because they're attractive and smart and interesting, but just because you do. You'll want to live somewhere or do something not because it's "cool" or everybody says you should, but just because you do.

The unjustifiable things, the illogical things, the things that are genuinely unexplainable, that's where the magic is. The "right" stuff always just is, it's the illusions and fears and things we force that have to be justified and made sense of in our minds.

If you are making a choice that you can only feel good about when you back up with a list of "because," you're not really listening to what you want.

This is probably the biggest secret (and most important fact) of all: If your little, inner voice were telling you that you weren't interested, or you were on the "wrong path," it wouldn't say anything at all... you'd just let it go.

Consider the people you aren't romantically interested in. The career paths you know don't call you. Do you sit around and belabor whether or not they're right? Nope, you don't. You just don't acknowledge them at all. (The opposite of love is indifference, eh?)

There's no difference between the things that pain you and the things that please you—they are both intended to teach you something. You have brought them into your experience because you want to learn from them.

Illusions have to be justified. Half-truths have to be made sense of. The genuine things, the best things, the "most right" things, truly just are. If it's in your life, there's something to be learned from it. The process of unlearning the reasons to justify the illusions is how you reacquaint yourself with the voice that doesn't use words.

It's ultimately why you choose to get lost in the first place.

45

EXPERIENCES
we don't have
ENGLISH WORDS
FOR YET

01. When sunlight shines through the trees, the interplay between light and leaves.

02. When you're with your friends and decide "who is who" in a show or movie you all watch and then laugh hysterically about how "them" that character is behaving. (2a.) The running joke that develops around you characterizing the members of your social circle based on some cultural stencil. (Think: *Sex and the City*.)

03. The feeling of your skin on someone else's.

04. The temporary, beautiful high of deciding you're going to change your life in some aesthetic, easy way. (4a.) The conviction that this will change anything or everything else.

05. The inability to grasp the fact that we can't grasp what we don't know yet.

06. Hearing something a dozen times and then finally understanding what it means only when it becomes the answer to a problem you have.

07. When physical, human age has no bearing on connectedness, intelligence, ability.

08. The parenting style that consists of trying to punish, embarrass, scold, and oppress children into being functional, kind, successful members of society.

09. Wanting to have a spiritual-sexual experience with someone, sex that is more than just a grinding race to orgasm.

10. The mental preparation that occurs before you step into a social situation in which you have to play a "role" for the sake of maintaining a relationship: i.e., rehearsing your conversations with yourself by yourself.

11. The feeling of absolute peacefulness right before you fall asleep.

12. Not just assuming we know what other people are thinking and feeling, but acting on that "knowing," judging them for that knowing, and really in a lot of ways capping off their potential with what we think we know of them.

13. The feeling of lightness in your whole body.

14. The love you know has an expiration date.

15. The love you know you're eventually "meant" for.

16. People who are funny without being mean.

17. People who are deep without being negative.

18. The frustration you feel when somebody is mad or upset over completely false things that they've made up in their mind, a complete lack of understanding on a situation.

19. The random, weird, scary, embarrassing thoughts that cross your mind and sometimes freak you out that you think you're alone in having because everybody else is scared and embarrassed by them, too.

20. The art of trying to figure out someone's intentions by piecing together a bunch of random bits of "evidence."

21. The kind of stuck feeling of knowing something isn't quite right, but you're not yet aware of what the alternative would be.

22. The comfort that comes with arriving at small, safe conclusions now and again.

23. The real peace of dissolving those illusions.

24. The feeling of realizing that your "purpose" won't usually feel like a "purpose" as you have to do the work regardless and so

the whole act of "finding it" was just a mechanism of the ego in the first place.

25. How we define periods of our lives and personal development beyond years or grades or segments of schooling.

26. The space between raindrops.

27. A course of study that teaches you the art of the non-traditionally-academic things that take up the majority of our lives: love, relationships, doubt, faith, parenting, work, friendship, self-image, etc.

28. Being in love with someone who you only used to know, and at some level still feel as though you do.

29. The happy tired feeling you get after you eat a big meal.

30. The sensation of looking back on something far more fondly than when it was actually happening; the idea that maybe this kind of enjoyment is not to be fought or transcended, but just appreciated for what it is.

31. The feeling of feeling a feeling.

32. A person or thing that also feels like "home" (a non-house home).

33. The idea that is "all is as it should be."

46

HOW TO
become your own
WORST ENEMY
(without ever realizing it)

Let yourself be governed by the illusion of separateness. Believe that you are always in competition with those around you, that you are only as good as you are better than someone else. Believe your conditioning is the only one, the right one. Drown your desire for connection by manically scrolling through feed after feed, day after day. Live your life waiting, waiting, waiting for someone else to make you feel love. Put it all in their hands. Condemn them when they don't perform. Believe you're not enough on your own, that there's something in this world that will save you, and can, and should.

Believe that marriage licenses mean love, job titles success, religion goodness, money contentment. Trust fully in the powers that be; let them teach you how to let your fear control you.

Do not let yourself feel anything other than what other people say it's okay to feel. If your life looks good from the outside, don't take the liberty to say it doesn't feel good on the inside. Act only in accordance with what will make sense to other people. Make the most important facet of your existence being palatable to anyone and everyone else. Trick yourself into thinking that kind of numb safety is happiness.

Hate yourself for still caring about the person you aren't supposed to care about anymore. Shame yourself until you're completely suppressing everything you feel. Spend days and months and years checking their status updates and new pictures in search of something, anything, that justifies the feelings you just want to kill off. Tie yourself in mental knots trying to get your head and heart to coexist. Make caring a bad thing. Make loving worse.

Assume that the line between "good" and "bad" runs between religions, or races, or creeds, or nations, rather than in each human heart. Disregard our universal capacity to drown in our denseness.

Fail to recognize the sameness and beauty in the people you've condemned because they were born with genetics or practices or perceptions that are different than yours...because they were conditioned the opposite way to which you were.

Never realize that you were conditioned at all.

Believe that you are your thoughts, that you are your emotions, rather than the being observing those things. Never realize the constant stream of conversation you hold with yourself. Never realize that two-thirds of the statements you make and ideas you have are not organically yours. Disregard that they don't lead you to contentment or kindness or hope, and accept them anyway.

Pick and choose the people to whom you afford humanness. Decide who is worthy and not. Sift through the traits and habits of others, categorize them into what's acceptable and not. Don't let someone be worthy of love and respect just because they are alive; doing this will ensure you never give the same kindness to yourself.

Be your worst enemy so nobody else can be. Assume the worst so nobody can surprise you with it. Call it being realistic. Accept the life someone else thinks you deserve. Don't believe that change is real. Don't believe in anything other than what you can immediately sense and see. Suffocate the chance of possibility. Sustain yourself on temporary highs, the kind that come from other people and their attention. Let your past experiences quantify your self-hatred. Create your past in your present.

Let other people wash away the good parts of you. Call this being strong. Settle because you are afraid to choose. Call this being smart. Fight others so you don't have to face yourself. Resist and reject until it seems like everyone and everything is seeping under your skin and torturing you. Never realize your mind does the wielding. Never realize that bit by bit, you created the life you never really wanted with the pieces you never really chose.

47

IF WE SAW
SOULS
instead of
BODIES

If we could see souls instead of bodies, what would be beautiful?

What is the first thing people would know about you? What would you be most afraid of them seeing? Who would you impress? Who would you love?

What would you adjust as you walked past the mirror? What kind of work would you be in? What would your goals be, how would you strive to be better if what you collected in the bank or put on your body or attached next to your name on a business card no longer affected what people saw?

Would you spend your time in gyms and stores or in libraries and temples? Who would you let yourself fall in love with? What would your "type" be? Tall, dark, and handsome or creative, kind, and self-aware?

Whom would we idolize, and what? How much of our governing body would be fit to lead? Whom would we make famous? Whom would we celebrate?

Would we restructure our value system to prioritize the things that bring us true peace and desire, not just better than the norm? What would we do with all that money if we weren't spending it on decorating and changing and convincing everybody else that we are a way we really aren't?

How would we define success? As who gathers the most shit around their souls or who is transformed the most and shines the brightest? What would it be like if our priority was to just become lightness? What kindness and joy and healing and rawness would come of the journey there?

What would happen if we could see people not as "bad," but as... blocked? If we could see the ways they've packed away their pain, or how they hold a belief that keeps them away from being kind to others? How they are unaware that those issues even exist?

What if we weren't afraid of the ways people are different than us?

What would happen if we realized our bodies never wanted anything more than to feel connected, and acted out on nothing more than their false ideas of being separate, different, exiled, the odd one out, the almost-but-not-good-enough?

What would happen if we embraced our desire to play out and finagle with our individualism, but eventually returned to the knowing that we are all just energy fields? And where would we be if we realized that we were all from the same one? What would happen if we realized we really weren't that different at all?

48

16 REASONS WHY
you still don't
HAVE THE LOVE
YOU WANT

01. You want someone else to do the work of unearthing, creating, activating, and then convincing you of the love in your life.

    You want someone else to do what you were taught that you couldn't do for yourself. Every time you think, wish, imagine, or hope for someone else to give you something, dream of the day when they will, belabor and obsess over why they aren't, realize that thing is what you are not giving yourself.

02. Historically, it has not looked the way you thought it would, and that's because it never looks the way we think it will or comes the way we think it should.

    When we hold an idea of what love should look like, we attach to something that often just quells an insecurity, saves us from a reality, or helps us prove ourselves to someone else. Love never looks the way we think it will...because it's not supposed to look any certain way. Because the look of it won't actually give us the experience of it, but the pursuit of that will distract us from actually finding something genuine.

03. You think that love is just a good feeling, when love is really a consistent state of being in communion with body, mind, and soul.

    It is a daily commitment to learn what it means to love someone else in small, practical, mindful ways. You can be more or less attracted to someone, more or less compatible, but choosing to love and appreciate someone regardless of those variables is a constant that you can choose (and it's the belief that you can't because love must give you what you cannot give yourself, that leads to so many breakups, divorces, etc.).

04. You are unaware of the fact that love is nothing but an enhancement.

It magnifies and brings clarity to whatever is most present in your life. So if the things that are most present are self-doubt, lostness, insecurity, etc., you will only have more and more of that. Love is not your life; it is the avenue through which you share your life (and more palpably, see yourself).

05. You believe that love will "blossom" when the circumstances are correct, as though you must place two reactive chemicals together and assume that an instantaneous physical/emotional response should equate to lifelong, sincere love.

Hormones are reactive. Expectations are reactive. Love is cultivated from and because of those things, but more effectively, because of a mutual appreciation and respect for one another.

06. You are caught up in trying to make yourself objectively appealing to the opposite (or same) sex, as opposed to really finding who you are and then attracting someone who appreciates that person, too.

I am so saddened by how many young girls (and boys, for that matter) are instructed to present themselves a certain way, because that's just "what's attractive." It's so silly to think generalizing what "every" person likes is helpful, because more insidiously, it keeps you trapped in avoidance of your true self, as you assume that person isn't "good enough" to elicit the approval of the masses.

...and then we sit around crying and cursing the stars over why we can't find somebody who loves us for who we really are...

07. You aren't clear on your intentions about what you want, and that's because you're still trying to edit and enhance them to appease, impress, or elicit someone else's approval.

In other words, you can't be honest about what you want because you aren't comfortable with the truth of who you are. So long as you are functioning from that mindset, you are filtering your life, and whether or not you see the love in it, through how well it fits the "image."

08. You blame others because you don't realize that every relationship you have is with yourself.

Love does not suck. People do not suck. You suck. Relationships are the ultimate teaching tools, the most intense healing opportunities, the most explosively beautiful chances for us to really see what is unresolved within us. You run into the same problems, you find the same faults, the same relationships, the same pain, because it is all in you.

09. Likewise, you do not realize that negative emotions are calls to heal, not to change or drown or ignore because you don't want to "feel bad" anymore.

Our feelings are how we communicate with ourselves. Healing is, essentially, reopening to seeing good, to being hopeful, sustaining and then creating more love. Our "negative emotions" are not signals of what other people are doing wrong, they are meant to show us how we are mis-navigating, misunderstanding, or being controlled by past experiences and fear-based beliefs.

10. You don't know how to use your heart and mind in tandem— the heart as the map and the mind as the compass.

We're given two opposing sets of commandments: Follow your heart regardless of logic, and don't do anything stupid and illogical when it comes to who you choose to share your life with. The reality is that so long as you are polarized in the utilization of the most important guiding tools you have (or worse, you don't realize you have them), you will be lost as hell. That's a technical term, by the way.

A quick cheat sheet for you: The heart will tell you what; the mind will tell you how. Let them stay in their corners of expertise.

11. You have yet to honor the child inside you.

If you want to know who you really are, imagine speaking to yourself as a child. What would you say and do to make them feel happy? That expression is reflective of what you really need to give yourself and is very, very helpful for people who are seeking love. Because learning to love yourself is, as odd as it may sound, learning to honor, respect, love and acknowledge the child in you, or in other words, your most essential self.

12. You want love to change your life.

You want it to provide for you what you think you cannot give yourself: stability, security, hope, happiness. So long as you function on this belief, you place "love" as being something that is outside of you when the reality is that you cannot see, create, or experience on the outside what you are not already on the inside. Speaking of:

13. You don't realize that what you love most about others…is what you love most about yourself.

The more you are open to your own joy, the more you appreciate others. The more you are healed of your own anxiety, the less you have to cast blame and try to fight others into fixing you. Loving someone else comes down to being able to see what you appreciate about them, as it is similar to what you appreciate about yourself.

14. You not only think that somebody else is responsible for fixing you, but that there is something wrong with them if they don't.

And so you want to change, fix, or condemn them for how they've wronged you. You want to blame them for not being good enough. (You want to impose on them a whole lot of what you're really feeling about yourself.)

15. You've forgotten kindness, when kindness is the fabric of love.

I don't think there are people crueler to one another more than people who really, really love each other. They see so much of themselves in one another that they simply cannot stand it, and retaliate in all the same ways they are rejecting themselves! The foundation of a happy relationship (and life, really) is unconditional kindness. It's synonymous with love, and maybe even more effective, because it shows you the action as opposed to the feeling or expectation.

16. You are looking for the answer outside of the question.

For the tenth time, say it with me now: The love you really want is your own. What you're seeking in someone else is what you aren't giving to yourself. What angers you is what you aren't accepting and healing; what gives you joy and hope is what you already have within you. Finding a relationship to be that great enhancer, to have someone to share everything with, begins with you. It's as though we were taught to "love ourselves first" without ever being told that "loving yourself" is giving yourself what you want someone else to.

49

HOW TO
(actually)
CHANGE
YOUR LIFE
THIS YEAR

People want to change their lives. They want to change their relationships, their bodies, their income, their brokerage accounts, their statuses, their homes. It's so easy to identify what's wrong on the outside and blame it for the feelings on the inside. Never is this so painfully clear as when the calendars reset and we think we're offered a fresh slate and blank page. It's easy to think a different year is a different life away.

But we carry ourselves—and our baggage, and our energies, and our hang-ups and insecurities and hopes and mindsets—into that glimmering hopeful fresh-start blank-page new life. Our "resolutions" don't stick because you can't change the outside and expect a different inside.

People want to change their lives. They want to change other people's lives, too. They want to change the injustices they see. They want to change the whole damn world.

But they do not want to change themselves. (Not their image. Not their appearance. Not their worldly success. Themselves.)

Which is, as it turns out, the one thing they can change. The one thing that must change first.

We walk around with the cripplingly false idea that we must adjust how things are, as opposed to adjusting how we are and how we see them. This world might as well be a damn hall of mirrors. Rather than trying to break them all to distort and rearrange how you see the image, you have to let go of the idea that your image is all that exists.

The things that torture us and the negative patterns that follow us and the reason we have to keep making the same resolutions year after year is that we are not making the shift, we are trying to shift other things.

And the most hilariously, wonderfully, sadly unknown part of this is that when you do so, you end up with what you set out to achieve in the first place. The love and contentment and "success." Only this time, your worth doesn't depend on it. You aren't a failure if you lose it one day. This all stems from self. ('Tis not the mountain man conquers, but himself.)

So here is what you need to know.

Whenever there is a problem in your life, there is a problem with how you are thinking, reacting, or responding. Whatever you feel you are not receiving is a direct reflection of what you are not giving. Whatever you are angered by is what you aren't willing to see in yourself.

So where you feel you are lacking, you must give. Where there is tension, you must unpack. If you want more recognition, recognize others. If you want love, be more loving. Give exactly what you want to get.

If you want to let go of something, build something new. If you don't understand, ask. If you don't like something, say so. If you want to change, start small. If you want something, ask for it. If you love someone, tell them. If you want to attract something, become it. If you enjoy something, let yourself feel it.

If you do anything compulsively, ask yourself why. Stop trying to curb your spending or change your diet or avoid that one person or lash out at innocent people you love. Look for the cause of the feeling (not just the feeling itself), and you'll fix the problem for good.

If you miss somebody, call them. It is silly to suffer in silence. It is noble and humbling to tell someone that they matter to you, regardless of whether or not you matter to them.

If your life is missing something you cannot place back into it, restructure. You will get nowhere dismantling the pieces with nothing to take their place. You'll end up reassembling the parts of the old life you are trying to do away with. Step away and build anew. Anything new. You cannot expect to carry on with the same life you had without someone and not have that gaping hole torture you. Give yourself permission to build something beautiful. Something true.

173

If you want to be understood, explain. There is nothing we need more than people who are willing to kindly, gently, wholly, patiently explain to others.

If you want to be happy, choose it. Choose to be consciously, consistently grateful for something. Choose to immerse yourself in something beautiful and peaceful and joyous. If you can't choose this, choose to start working on figuring out what blocks you—be it health or circumstance or mindset. Get help. Ask for it. Saying you can't choose is giving up for good. (Don't do that.)

Choose change. Your routine, your job, your city, your habits, your mindset. Never sit and fester in frustration. It does not matter whether or not you're in the absolute worst-case scenario, complaining, worrying or being negative will never help. Anything. At all. Ever.

Everything you do, see, and feel is a reflection of not who you are, but how you are.

You create what you believe.

You see what you want.

You'll have what you give.

50

HOW WE
LOSE OUR MINDS
to other
PEOPLE'S GODS

People allow accountants to map the blueprints of their lives.

Not their essential desires, their favorite philosophers, the ideas that induce visceral reactions and become beliefs. These things don't provide a measure of what it takes to survive, a gauge on the things that have been pressed on us to seem enjoyable, so they are considered secondary.

An accountant can tell you how you can live and where. What opportunities will be open and not. How comfortably you can buy holiday gifts and fund your child's education. We gauge our quality of life not by what or how much we do, but how we appear and what we earn from that doing.

We're not quite at fault for this. Present-day monoculture, the governing pattern, the master narrative, the beliefs we accept without ever having consciously accepted them, tells us that if wealth and attractiveness and worldly possessions don't make us feel high and alive, we just don't have enough of them.

It makes sense on an initial level, but as anybody can tell you, acquiring another 0 at the end of the balance on your bank statement, or a variety of new things (that really just represent your perceived worth or lack thereof) only changes how much you have surrounding you, not how deeply or sincerely you can appreciate them, feel them, enjoy them, want them, be happy because of them.

If it takes more than the slightest bit of personal experience to attest to this, pluck from the endless, proverbial pile of research.

External acquisition does not yield internal contentment.

And yet we trek on. We are still enslaved to the things we are taught are ultimate "goods." We justify our faith in the system by flawed and influenced logic. We continue to believe that something external can change our internal ability to be aware, to appreciate, to live, to feel.

Once we are initially convinced that not just money, but an idea of morality, education, and yes, general wealth, parlay into contentment, we become rats on a spinning wheel and we'll spend the rest of our lives there if we aren't careful.

If you've never heard of it before, we all seem to be suffering from a sort of Diderot Effect. Denis Diderot was a philosopher during the Enlightenment, author of the fictional essay "Regrets On Parting With My Old Dressing Gown." As the story goes, he lived a very simple life and was happy until a friend gave him a gift, a gorgeous scarlet dressing gown. The more he wore his gown around his small apartment, the more the simplicity of his life seemed...out of place.

He then desired new furnishings, as one with a dressing gown as beautiful as his shouldn't be living in a lowly home. He then wanted to replace his other clothes, his wall hangings, and so on. He wound up in debt and toiling his life away trying to maintain the glamour of his surroundings—an elusive, endless task.

Because modern, daily life keeps us consistently dipping our toes and dousing our senses in ads and "success stories" that are born of luxury and married to materialism, it is almost impossible to take a step back and see the system objectively. So most don't.

I don't know about you, but I have never seen a god so worshipped and adored as a dollar bill. Never so much faith put into systems designed to maintain power and serve the ego. The most insidiously effective governors are the ones that do not tell you they are controlling you, and they are the ones who have programmed your need to keep running on the wheel, staring at the illusory screen, thinking you're heading to that end goal. Behind the cage, what you cannot see is that the wheel you are running on endlessly powers their monopoly.

And because of this predisposed, collective mindset (that is very evidently not serving us) we believe in a variety of "goods." Be educated. Be a "good person." Have money. Be attractive. Work out. Have a great job. Buy a house. And onward.

It ignites the interest of our senses, our base instincts, our egoic selves. But how often do we question the "good" that has been imposed on us, how often do we really stop and question how much faith we have in a system that has us convinced our natural state, our simple lives, our inner joys... are not good enough?

The next time you make a choice because you are trying to be a "good person," I implore you to consider that those who commit suicide terrorism believe they are being "good people"—martyrs for their god.

The next time you equate a degree to an education, consider the state of really any aspect of our society—we are absolutely starved for knowledge, and yet the premium on education these days seems to be limitless. There is no amount of debt, disinterest, or complete disregard for actual learning that will stand in the way of people getting degrees and believing their education is complete for their lifetime.

I often look around at older people and wonder how we've confused "respecting your elders" with allowing them to believe it's okay to stop learning after age 23 and let them sit and fester in the prejudices of the generation in which they were raised.

So we're handing out empty degrees like candy—degrees that promise success at a steep, suffocating cost—and placating bias and prejudice with a laugh and sigh, because that's what we're instructed is "right."

I'm not saying there's no value in education; I'm saying it's the only thing of real value, and we're falling cripplingly short of actually giving that to the masses. I dream of a day that college grads leave school not believing that their education is only the leg-power to latch themselves on a corporate treadmill for the better parts of their lives, but rather something that has given them the context, the history, the perspective, and the opportunity to learn what makes them tick and flow, how to question everything and discuss anything objectively, to choose the life they want, not adhere to the life that was chosen for them.

Neither Hobbes nor Plato nor Spinoza nor Hume nor Locke nor Nietzsche nor Jobs nor Wintour nor Descartes nor Beethoven nor Zuckerberg nor Lincoln nor Rockefeller nor Edison nor Disney nor countless other game-changing, culture-shifting, brilliant-minded individuals were academics. The pattern is enough of a trend to make you wonder whether or not a component of their (exceptional) success was that they were never conditioned to believe one thing was "good." Their ideas were never edited or tailored to the liking of someone else's. They never had to quell their real opinions in lieu of a grade, and they never compiled other people's ideas for years and called it "research."

In Plato's *The Republic*, he tells an (oft-cited) allegory of men chained together in a cave, with their backs to a flame, believing that the masterfully crafted shadows that those behind them were holding up were reality. Seeing that light, metaphorically or not, is the truest education, mostly because we need not lay eyes on it to understand it. We need only piece together the illusions we perceive to make sense of what is behind us.

And really, at the end of the day, it is not our own illusions that are dangerous, it's other people's—especially when we accept them not only as integral, unmoving parts of our (ultimately dissatisfying) lives, but when we believe them to be good. Unquestioningly. Unfailingly.

Nobody ever gave someone permission to be enlightened. No new line of thinking or creative genius was born of what was already acceptable. We associate "acceptable" with "good," when really, "acceptable" is, mostly, "staying within the lines someone else uses to control you by" (for better and for worse).

Our lives are not measured by other people's gods, not their dollars or illusions or business plans. Not their beauty standards or declarations of what's right and wrong and good and bad and whom we should be on any given day.

It seems the task of the generation (century, maybe) will be radically accepting ourselves in a society that feeds on the opposite. Seeing illusions for what they are, even, and maybe especially, when they are other people's. Making kindness cool and humility humor. Forgiving the way things are, knowing the only way to reinvent anything is not to destroy what's present but to create a new, more efficient model, one that renders the other obsolete.

178

Dear reader: Someday you will stand before God. It could be today. Are you ready?

If God says to you at that final judgment: "I do not know you," what will you say in your defense?

You may say: "But all religions are the same, it doesn't matter what we believe." The Bible says salvation is found in no one but Jesus. (Acts 4:10-12)

You may say: "But I am not a sinner." The Bible says that all have sinned and are unable to stand in the presence of God. (Romans 3:23)

But I figured there was plenty of time.

You may say: "But I figured there was plenty of time. I always believed I would live to see old age." The Bible says that NOW is the time of salvation and we must seek the Lord urgently. (2 Corinthians 6:2; Isaiah 55:6)

You may say: "But the church is full of hypocrites and I was offended by their behavior." The Bible says someday every one of us will give an account of himself to God. (Romans 14:12)

51

HOW YOU FALL
OUT OF LOVE
with the idea
OF SOMEONE

There are two ways things turn out:

You lose a thing, you replace it with something else, it's better than what you lost, you're happy.

You lose a thing, it doesn't disappear when it's replaced, not having it becomes as much of a presence as having it was.

You're told the things you can't forget about are meant to be in your mind—the simple aftermath of having loved somebody so deeply: You hold onto a someone and someday that was supposed to be yours.

We are told to believe that not being able to let go of the things we lose does nothing but prove how much we loved them in the first place, and I don't think this is true.

Living with a ghost, crafting an idea that you need to hold onto—to fill a space or insecurity with—is using the idea of someone to fix something about yourself.

We love heartbreak, and we love putting it on ourselves. We're more nostalgic for things that never happened than we are grateful and present in the things that are. We start missing things we never had, that we just created in our minds, in this false, alter-reality.

The things that are easily replaced are usually the ones that you haven't attached existential meaning to. That is to say: They're the things you don't rely on to give you a sense of self.

The things that don't leave your head are not the ones that show you what's "meant to be"; they're the things that show you what you're still not okay with on your own.

You know what unconditional love is? Unconditional love is loving someone even if they don't unconditionally love you in return—that's

179

affection without pretense. That's what we claim we're after, and yet we can barely grasp the idea.

Most people we enjoy because they're contact highs. The idea of types and standards are proof that we're just looking for somebody to play a role. Heartbreak is the aftermath of when somebody steps out of the very specific notion you had of them. Suddenly, they're not doing what you think they should be doing and so they are wrong. The inability to detach is holding onto the fact that the package looked so perfect, the pieces seemed to fit, and yet. But still.

Being in love with somebody that you only used to know is like falling in love with a book (which sounds like a dumb example but people really do fall in love with them). The point is: You can love it all you want, but it's a story that runs parallel to yours. At the end of the day it's static. It's memory. It's a sentence and you can't change it. It ends how it ends. It says what it says.

A friend once told me that the secret to finding love was not to actually look for it, but to heal the things that were preventing you from seeing and receiving it. I think the biggest one of all is, "What will having this love fix?"

What will having this person next to me make me feel better about? What do I need them to tell me? What do I need them to prove? Who do I need them to look great in front of? What purpose do they serve for my ego?

This is true of many things, not just of love: We confuse genuine affection and real love with the light, happy, free feeling we experience for a few seconds/days/months when we have fed our egos.

That's why it doesn't last. That's why we hold onto ideas of things that were and things we need to be: The idea of someone saves something about ourselves. And the more we hold onto those fragments of a person, those soundbite dreams that distract us from the moment, we end up with a few distilled memories that we've turned into life-sustaining hopes, and we piece it all together and place it on the shoulders of the person who we thought loved us enough to make us love ourselves.

And if you're not careful, that person will become a part of you. They will become the good part, the whole part, the love of your life.

52

WHY WE
SUBCONSCIOUSLY
love to create
PROBLEMS
FOR OURSELVES

I think most people could objectively look at their lives and see how frequently the problems they had were of their own making, their suffering self-inflicted. We absolutely love to make problems for ourselves, and we do it all the time.

We worry needlessly, we choose immobility, we resist acceptance, we externalize our power, we surrender our ability to choose, when really it's up to us to decide how we react, when we change, what we entertain our minds with. It's yet another symptom of our own masochism to say that we don't have a choice in the matter.

And we do it because we love it. There's something...fun...in making problems for ourselves. There is something we keep returning to. Whether it be because we feel we deserve it, that it gives our lives meaning, that it gives us human credibility for having been through something—anything—we want to create our own problems.

Because when we are the ones who make them, we are the ones who can overcome them.

It seems we almost stage accomplishments in our minds. We subconsciously know that we're going to get through it, but we choose to entertain the suffering only to feel that sense of "ah, I've done something, I've proven my own strength." We make things difficult so they seem warranted of feeling good when they aren't anymore. The more we suffer, the more something is worthwhile.

We craft our victories subconsciously. We know there's no point in fretting or worrying about anything: If something can be solved, solve it. If it cannot, worrying and fretting will not suddenly change that. In either scenario, it is pointless, needless noise.

But the point is that we like worrying and fretting. If we didn't like it so much, we probably wouldn't do it incessantly. It feeds some human part of us that modernization has robbed us of. What are we surviving? What is the point? Why, why, why?

Well, because when everything has an answer, what is there to do? If everything has a solution, what is there to consider, or work toward, or feel excited about accomplishing? Or rather, really, why do we need to work toward something? Why do we need to feel excited about accomplishments rather than what we already have? What exists within us that is so unsettled that we cannot be at peace?

I think we create our own problems to address the things we know would otherwise become issues outside of our control. We make them in ways that allow us to heal, address, fix, cope, and acknowledge whatever we want to get to before some other heartbreaking, external circumstance does it for us.

We create our own problems in the scope of knowing we eventually have the solutions, so we can safely (albeit painfully) deal with them. So really, it's not a matter of not making issues for ourselves, but being aware enough to understand what they are...and that we're asking ourselves to heal them.

53

WHY DOES
a soul want
A BODY?

Yesterday I took a shortcut while walking home and ended up crossing through a small graveyard in the back of a city church. I stopped and I looked at the names and the dates and the veterans and the three-year-olds and loving wives and fathers and sisters and husbands the immortalized bits of what their lives were summed up to be and I thought to myself,

Why would a soul want a body?

What can a body do that a soul can't? Why would it want an impermanent, gross, heavy, hurting thing?

I was standing in front of a husband and wife that died in the late 1800s. I looked at their final resting places, a few inches away from one another, and realized,

A soul can't touch.

Assuming the idea that a soul is an energy field, that our spirits do indeed exceed the speck of life our bodies provide in the span of infinity, a soul can't touch. It can't see the light; it is the light.

It doesn't know the need for human skin. It can't run its fingers over someone else's hand and neck and back and it can't feel crippling desire and ecstatic passion. Those are symptoms of a madness we call love, but it's human love. It's often shallow and wild and manic and the equivalent of smoking crack cocaine. It melts into an appreciation of something deeper, or it burns brightly and then it goes out.

Souls can't experience a beginning or an end, nor an array and spectrum of emotions. They can't be surprised because they were never confused or unknowing. They don't know physical-emotional warmth or what it's like to hold and kiss a new baby on the forehead or the jilt you get in your chest when you smell the person you love.

Your soul can't feel the cadence of reading your favorite book or the sensation when your mind puts someone else's story into your life, or how your fingers flip through the broken binding for the trillionth time and how lovely that book smell is, especially when it's your favorite one.

It doesn't know that crisp and comforting coolness of fall or the heat of the sun on your back in the summer. It doesn't know that deep feeling you get when you spread your fingers out and run your hand through water. It can't wear your favorite T-shirt or eat cookie dough or sweat or breathe or cry or dance. It doesn't know the lifetime comfort of your mother or your lover wrapping their arm around you matter-of-factly.

A body is responsible for the most amazing part of anything—physically finding or creating. Once we have something, we don't want it anymore. What we really want is to make and fight and become.

A soul doesn't have to pay the bills or go food shopping or cook dinner or schedule a checkup or do the dishes or make plans for Friday to keep up with a relationship. It doesn't have to take hot baths to relax or organize the house or run errands or take walks to think. A body can learn. A body can feel the magic of realization. It can piece the pieces together and understand. It can get lost so it can be "found." It can suffer so it can heal.

What if the series of rote tasks we want our lives to be better than aren't better than us at all? What if they're what we're scheduled to do? What if there is no greater meaning than just simply doing them? What if what we feel in those little moments we want to escape and place in the context of a greater meaning is the meaning itself?

If healing is just acknowledging pain, then maybe living is just acknowledging life.

There are so many anxieties and frustrations and terrible things that cease instantly when we just say them out loud. The point of learning to grieve and mourn and be present is only so we can just be aware. Recognition is the remedy. It's the only thing we're really supposed to do.

And the real suffering, the inescapable kind, comes from avoiding what's in front of us. It follows and haunts us until we acknowledge it and are okay with it, even if it doesn't make us happy. Even if we're anything but.

184

A soul wants a body so it can experience things, and that body will fight itself until it makes itself aware. Until it does what it was programmed to do. Until it takes what it needs to take and feels what it wants to feel, no matter how dark that seems.

We're not supposed to be better than our humanness. Doing so is overlooking the point of the body in the first place. We can choose happiness, but we choose the full spectrum of experience instead.

Maybe instead of believing things are linear and the road only goes upward and toward happiness, we allow ourselves what we choose. We pay bills and do dishes and cook dinner and wonder why. Maybe there's no point to feeling other than to feel it. Maybe it just persists because we pretend there is.

54

THE IMPORTANCE
OF STILLNESS:
why it's
IMPERATIVE TO
make time to
DO NOTHING

We're conditioned to associate stillness with inactivity and inactivity with failure. We're trained to be overworked and to believe that if, at any point, we aren't doing something that contributes to our goals, we're not doing anything.

It makes us unable to just be with ourselves—our purpose only legitimate if it's serving someone or something else.

In fact, we are so opposed to being with ourselves, in a study[13] done by the University of Virginia, over 700 people were asked to just sit in a room alone with their thoughts for 6-15 minutes alongside a shock button that they could press if ever they wanted out. 67% of men and 25% of women chose to shock themselves rather than sit quietly and think.

Stillness is psychologically imperative, though. We are not built to be running all the time, and doing so leads to absolutely detrimental effects, the least of which I will touch on here. When overworking is our identity, we lose track of who we actually are, and in the process, we stop living actual lives.

01. What we call doing "nothing" is actually crucial for our physiological selves and is essential to maintain a happy, peaceful, balanced lifestyle.
    The idea that we must always be doing something is completely cultural (and completely unhealthy). Notice how we only feel we are doing "something" when that "something" can be externally measured... by other people?

02. In the "do nothing" state, the brain is super-powering itself: It's completing unconscious tasks or integrating and processing conscious experiences.

In the resting state, neural networks can process experiences, consolidate memories, reinforce learning, regular attention and emotions, and in turn keep us more productive and effective in our day-to-day work.

03. Human beings are not designed to be continually expending energy whilst conscious, and it has a massive effect on the very thing they're trying to put their energy toward: their work. Tony Schwartz cited a study in his piece[14] on productivity and restfulness in *The New York Times* which proved that not getting enough sleep, or "do nothing" time, was the highest predictor of on-the-job burnout. (Another Harvard study he cited estimated that sleep deprivation costs American companies $63.2 billion a year in lost productivity.)

04. When you do not sit and allow yourself to reflect, reconcile, and acknowledge what you feel, you actively give said feelings more power.

Stephanie Brown argues: "There's this widespread belief that thinking and feeling will only slow you down and get in your way but it's the opposite...most psychotherapists would contend that suppressing negative feelings only gives them more power, leading to intrusive thoughts, which can prompt people to be even busier to avoid them."

05. Creativity thrives in stillness and nothingness; creativity is fostered in the state of stepping away from the project, task, or issue at hand, and distracting oneself with other day-to-day tasks.

Countless studies show that people who are deeply creative on a consistent basis, who develop the most innovative and unique ideas, are the ones who free themselves from structure and allow their minds to wander, rather than focus on various tasks at hand. Einstein called this initiating the "sacred intuitive mind" (as opposed to the rational mind, which he sees as its "servant").

06. You're more likely to actually achieve what you set out to do if you work on it intermittently, and you'll maintain a healthier, happier lifestyle in the process.

Keeping your mind in a consistent state of focus leads to life-shortening (and quality-depleting) stress, and while you're in the process of neglecting the things that also matter (your health, your family, your state of mind), you're more likely to reach your saturation point and simply give up on what you were devoting all of your time and energy to in the first place.

07. It helps you become more mindful (more aware of the present moment).

Cultivating mindfulness aids in reducing general stress, improving memory, decreasing emotional reactivity, more relationship satisfaction, cognitive flexibility, empathy, compassion, general decrease of anxiety and depression/increase of overall quality of life, and on and on.

08. It's not taking a "break" or time "away" from what you are actually "supposed to be doing," it's what human beings are designed for.

Tim Kreider argues[15]: "Idleness is not just a vacation, an indulgence or a vice; it is as indispensable to the brain as vitamin D is to the body, and deprived of it we suffer a mental affliction as disfiguring as rickets....The space and quiet that idleness provides is a necessary condition for standing back from life and seeing it whole, for making unexpected connections and waiting for the wild summer lightning strikes of inspiration—it is, paradoxically, necessary to getting any work done."

---

13 Samarrai, Fariss. "Doing Something Is Better Than Doing Nothing For Most People, Study Shows." 2014. University of Virginia.
14 Schwartz, Tony. "Relax! You'll Be More Productive." 2013. *The New York Times*.
15 Kreider, Tim. "The 'Busy' Trap." *The New York Times.* 2012.

55

WHY YOU'RE
STRUGGLING
in your
RELATIONSHIPS,
based on your
ATTACHMENT
STYLE

It's common knowledge that most of our beliefs about the world are shaped in childhood, and most issues that people experience as adults have something to do with what was experienced in the earliest phases of life. Never is this more true than with romantic relationships. They are, after all, extensions of the bonds we build and things we come to understand about men, women, and how they interact through our parents. Many people spend their lives re-creating their first familial relationships, often to their own detriment. Here, the four types of attachment styles children develop, and how understanding your own can help you stop struggling so much in your relationships now.

Secure

If you are someone who attaches securely, one or both of your parents were completely attuned to your needs during early childhood. You learned to trust people, and objectively struggle the least with relationships, as you don't over-respond to the idea being rejected or dismissed. You just don't fear it as much.

However, if you are struggling in your relationships, it's likely because of your complacency. You're willing to stay in the wrong relationships for too long, because they're "good enough," but at the same time, you're more hesitant to commit to the "right" relationships when they come along because there's more risk involved. You are comfortable and prefer to stay that way, possibly at the detriment of your heart's true desires. What you need to do is open up to the reality that love is scary, especially the kind of love that's worthwhile. Take your time, but don't choose the easy way out.

Avoidant

If you are someone with avoidant attachment, you were likely the child of parents who were emotionally unavailable and insensitive to your genuine needs. You became a "little adult" at a young age, avoided (and still avoid) expressing true pain or need for help (especially to parents/caretakers), and highly value your independence, almost to a fault. You are self-contained and most comfortable alone. Your parents likely punished you for feeling anything other than "happy," or at least shamed you for crying or expressing your feelings in any way that wasn't convenient for them. This likely has lead to intimacy issues, as you struggle to be your whole self around someone else.

If you're struggling in your relationships, it's because you've grown to associate "imperfections" with dismissal. You think that opening up completely and genuinely will inevitably lead to you being unloved or rejected, because you learned at a young age that expressing genuine feelings could be dangerous. You are probably overly accepting of other people's flaws, but absolutely cannot tolerate any of your own. What you need to do is practice opening up to other people in a genuine way (start with friends, maybe) and see that you won't be disowned for being who you are. Once you develop a more trusting attitude with others, it will become easier and easier to be intimate.

Anxious

If you've developed an anxious attachment, it's because your parents were inconsistently attuned to your needs. At times you were nurtured and loved, but at others they were overly intrusive and insensitive. You likely struggle with indecisiveness and fear of the unknown, as you never know what kind of treatment to expect from people. You have a hard time trusting others, but at the same time, are easily overly attached and clingy, even just to the idea of a person. This is because you are afraid of anything you haven't grown to known as "safe," and want to hang on to people rather than face your fear of the unknown.

If you're struggling in your relationships, it's because you are spending too much time mind-reading, assuming, projecting, predicting, and anticipating outcomes in an effort to "shield" yourself from pain, or because you refuse to let go out of fear that you'll never find anybody else. Either way, you're more in your head than in your heart, and you're letting your life be guided by what you're trying to avoid, as opposed to what you're trying to achieve. Being better in your relationships will likely be the product of learning that the anxiety and urgency you feel is in your head. You need to work on refocusing your thoughts, differentiating reality from your fears, and surrounding yourself with trustworthy, caring people.

Disorganized

If you formed a disorganized attachment in childhood, it is because your parents or caretakers were abusive, frightening, or even life-threatening. You wanted to escape, yet your livelihood depended on the very people who were hurting you most. You may not have been fully able to escape until adulthood. Your attachment figure was your main source of distress, and to survive, you were forced to begin disassociating from yourself.

If you're struggling in your relationships, it's because you haven't learned to listen to your emotional navigation system yet. You aren't choosing partners you genuinely care about, or are ignoring your instincts because you grew up being forced not to trust yourself. Sure, you were in pain, but if you wanted to survive, you had to ignore that pain and convince yourself everything was all right. What you need to do is some very serious mental/emotional work that likely involves recalling your past trauma, and rewriting your narrative of what happened in your life. You will need to reassociate with your inner guidance system and learn to trust it more than you do your thoughts or ideas.

191

56

16 WAYS
SUPPRESSED
EMOTIONS
are appearing
IN YOUR LIFE

Many people will agree that suppression is the least effective emotional regulation strategy available, and yet it's the most common go-to coping technique. In a sense, emotional suppression is simply just ignoring your feelings, or invalidating them by believing they're "wrong." This is dangerous because your emotions are responses that are designed to keep you alive and well. This problem is created, of course, from basic emotional intelligence not being common knowledge. Rather than face the scary unknown, we just avoid it.

In 1988, Daniel Wenger conducted a groundbreaking study[16] that showed just how insidious emotional suppression can be. The results of his research were the ability to identify the "rebound effect of thought suppression." Essentially, the group in the study that was instructed to push away thoughts of a white bear had more thoughts about the white bear than the other group, which was allowed to think about anything (including a white bear). Ever heard the phrase "What we resist, persists?"

Long story short: You can't avoid your emotions. You can't deny them, invalidate them, or suppress them. You can only try to ignore them, but for reasons more powerful than your conscious mind can grasp, they will make themselves known in many other ways. Here are a few ways suppressed emotions resurface in life/signs you may be experiencing this, too:

01. Your self-image is polarized: You either think you're the greatest person on Earth or a worthless piece of garbage, with little in between.

02. You become anxious when anticipating social situations, as you feel you cannot just show up as you are, so you will have to "perform" or be subject to judgment from whoever is there.

03. You catastrophize. One bad remark from a colleague is cause for an existential breakdown about your self-worth; one argument with a partner is cause to rethink the whole relationship, and so on.

04. You exist in comparison to others. You feel you are only as attractive as you are more attractive than someone else, or the most attractive person in the room, and so on.

05. You cannot tolerate being wrong, as you associate making a mistake with being invalidated as a person.

06. You have random, almost completely unprecedented bursts of anger over very small, unimportant things.

07. You complain constantly—about things that don't even really warrant complaint. (It's a subconscious desire for other people to see and acknowledge your pain.)

08. You're indecisive. You don't trust that your thoughts or opinions or choices will be "good" or "right" the first time, so you overthink.

09. You procrastinate, which is just another way to say you are fairly regularly in a state of "dis-ease" with yourself. (You can't simply allow flow, which is a product of suppression.)

10. You'd rather feel superior to other people than connected to them.

11. When someone you know is successful, your immediate response it to pick out their faults rather than express admiration or acknowledgement.

12. Your relationships end for similar reasons, you feel anxiety over similar things, and even though you assume time will diminish these feelings or responses, the patterns persist.

13. You're resentful of whomever you think is responsible for your pain, or your lack of success, or your inability to choose.

14. You feel as though you can't really open your heart to someone.

15. You suffer a "spotlight complex," in which you feel that everyone is watching you and is invested in how your life turns out. (They aren't. They're not.)

16. You're afraid to move on, even though you want to. You may be ready to move on mentally, but until you completely process the accompanying feelings, you'll remain exactly where you are.

---

16 Wenger, Daniel. "Suppressing the White Bears." 1987. *Journal of Personality and Social Psychology*. Vol. 53. No. 1.

194

57

50 PEOPLE
on the most
LIBERATING
thought they've
EVER HAD

Your life unfolds in a succession of revelations.

It's when you set down the book and stare ahead and repeat the sentence in your mind again and again, apply it to every little thing you twist to make applicable. You answer questions you didn't know you were asking, tie ends you left off years ago.

The key to a completely liberating thought is that it's self-evident. It's proven itself in your experience. It doesn't have to solve the problem; it has to help you understand why you had it in the first place.

Every conscious thought you have either circles you back into the mental cycle you're in, or it liberates you from it.

Some cycles are healthy; some are not. Some you want to maintain; some you don't. Some you want to change and you know you want to change them. Some you want to change and you don't know you want to change them. Some you need to change and you don't know how.

I think your life improves in direct proportion to how often you are put in situations in which you have no choice but to seek a greater truth. That is something I think. People who are comfortable don't have to keep reading, or searching, or seeking. They don't grow because they don't have to. (A sad but important thing to know about humans is that they don't change until not changing is the less comfortable option.)

I know that my success has been directly proportionate to my suffering. That is something I know. That is the experience to which I have arrived at the aforementioned theory.

At this point, the most liberating thought I have ever had is that I would not change a thing. Everything in my life served a purpose, the darkest and shittiest and terrible and most self-destructive among them. They all brought me here.

I was never crazy. I was the product of my circumstances. (That one took a long time to completely acknowledge.) But it's true: I responded and reacted and behaved the way any normal, healthy, functioning person would and should.

I wasn't supposed to be happy. Had I responded well or complacently, I would have ended up where I was headed. I would have lived the life other people imposed on me. I would have actually constituted for being mentally ill.

It was crucial that I didn't have it together or consistently feel good.

I grew out of my suffering by being able to perceive what was wrong and uncomfortable, really without knowing any differently. How incredible is that? That we can know when something is wrong even if we aren't entirely sure what the opposite would be?

There's not a good thing in the world that was not built of a thousand tiny revolutions, and people are no exception. I wanted to compile a series of not only the most liberating thoughts—the revelations that have changed and shaped and created me—but also other people's. Here, 49 strangers shared theirs (one is mine), in hopes that maybe some of them can be yours as well.

01. "I get to choose what I think about."

02. "I don't owe anybody an apology for disagreeing with them."

03. "You can have everything you want, just not at the same time, and if you think that's unfortunate, consider that if you had everything at once, you wouldn't really experience or enjoy it completely."

04. "You can choose your family. You can choose your religion. You can choose who you are every day and it doesn't have to be the same person you were yesterday. You do not have to become only what other people are comfortable with or can understand."

05. "My life does not define me, I define my life. This moment is not my life, this is a moment in my life."

06. "Everything I perceive is a projection of who I am. If I want to change my life, I change myself."

07. "I don't have to accept anything. I don't have to change everything."

08. "Freedom is a state of mind."

09. "There is nothing you can have forever, but there are many things you'll miss experiencing if you're too busy trying to keep them rather than love them while you have them."

10. "There are so many kinds of love worth pursuing, other than romantic love. There are so many experiences to have, other than just happiness. Anything other than ideal is not failure. It's life. It's what we're made for and meant for."

11. "I am a person of value. I deserve happiness. I deserve to be kind to myself. I deserve love."

12. "I will get over what I am struggling with in the very same way I got over the other things I thought I never could. That's the most comforting thought, in my opinion: comparing what you're going through to what you've been through, and knowing you have what it takes to get through it."

13. "You don't remember years, you remember moments."

14. "I'm not supposed to be anything other than what I am."

15. "Nothing is permanent, not even the worst feelings."

16. "I can change my experience just by deciding to see things differently. I may not be in control of what happens around and toward me, but I am always in control of how I see it, how I respond, and how I react. At the end of the day, that is all I am responsible for."

17. "Nobody cries at a funeral because the world will be missing out on another pretty face. They cry because the world is missing another heart, another soul, another person. Don't

wait until it's too late to focus on what will actually matter: creating something that lasts far beyond your body."

18. "People do not love you based on a flowchart on which they compare you to other people. People who are the prettiest and thinnest and best-off financially are not the most loved! They do not live the best lives! I have to remind myself that every time I start worrying more about what I look like than what I am."

19. "The moment is all that exists. The cliché that tells you to live in it is overdone, but there's no other option, really. It's whether or not you're paying attention that's the problem."

20. "The way to get through anything is to embrace the fact that whatever comes, comes with reason, whatever stays, stays with reason, whatever hurts, hurts with reason. Ignoring or fighting the effect will not fix the cause."

21. "What you focus on expands."

22. "This, too, shall pass."

23. "I've always been compelled to act when I was meant to. I never had to think too hard about the things that were meant to be. I only had to be open to them."

24. "What I went through made me who I am; what I'm going through will make me what I will be. What I choose to put my energy toward now will create that person. I decide. My circumstances don't."

25. "Never forget that you are not in the world; the world is in you. When anything happens to you, take the experience inward. Creation is set up to bring you constant hints and clues about your role as co-creator. Your soul is metabolizing experience as surely as your body is metabolizing food. (This is a quote from Deepak Chopra.)"

26. "There is always a way...even when it least feels like it. There is always a way. There are different jobs, new ideas, apartments opening up across the country, flights leaving in the next hour to the places I've always wanted to go. There is

a way to find the money, get the gig, find the love…there is always a way! I am never stuck, I am only in the mindset that I am."

27. "There is no grand moment in life. You don't wake up and say, 'Aha! I've made it!' Happiness is all in details, the joy is all in the journey. Always has been, always will be."

28. "The purpose of being here is growth. Growth means being able to experience and see more because you are aware of it. The purpose of being here, then, is expanding awareness."

29. "The worst things to happen to me were the things that had to teach me what nothing else could, to prepare me for things so wonderful, I couldn't imagine them, let alone know I had to get ready for them."

30. "You haven't failed until you've stopped trying."

31. "I do not have to adopt other people's problems as my own to help them."

32. "You do not have to be loved by everybody to be worthy of love."

33. "The present is the only time. If you don't start living in it, you don't really live at all."

34. "You teach people how to treat you. You get in life what you have the courage to ask for."

35. "My only regret, in my entire life, is just that I didn't enjoy it more."

36. "The things I'm meant to have will simply come to me. All I am responsible for is making sure I'm ready."

37. "Don't take anything too seriously. Nobody gets out alive anyway."

38. "I cannot change those around me. Real change happens one by one, each person doing the only thing they can: seeing where they can stand to improve as opposed to pointing fingers at the injustices they see in others."

39. "Wisdom is knowing that you don't and will never really know anything. We used to believe the Earth was flat. A discovery changed that. You don't know that we won't discover we're all robots in some matrix simulation, or I don't know...the point is, wisdom is just being, not making sense of."

40. "I once bought a train ticket for myself, and was on a trip that I completely funded, and realized that I can support myself, and I don't have to answer or please anybody else. I work hard so I can live the way I want."

41. "I am infinite. People always say: What would you do if you could live forever? Well, I'm here to say: If you believe your soul is eternal, you can...what are you doing with it now?"

42. "Even if you abandon faith, hope, and love, they don't leave you."

43. "I am made of love and light. That is who I essentially am. Everything else is simply a disconnect. I am not one thing that has to be transformed into another...I am love and light, and I choose whether or not I remember that, or I decide to be blocked out of fear."

44. "When you step into a library, all the knowledge in the world is before you. When you wake up each day, all the possibility in the world is, too. You choose whether or not you just see books. You choose whether or not you just see another day."

45. "I am always one choice away from changing everything."

46. "If I choose not to be upset, not to spend time feeling a certain way, then I do not feel upset. If I do not feel upset, then I have not been harmed. Marcus Aurelius said something similar, but I prefer it in my own words."

47. "There is immeasurable joy in the small things. In a great book, fresh vegetables, a warm bed, the arms of someone you love. These things, in our twisted world, are rarely valued, but in the end, they're probably the most joy we're going to have."

48. "We take our lives way too seriously...in a few hundred years, most people will be completely forgotten about. That's not depressing, that is liberating. Do what you can and make it hella good. Give love and do what you most genuinely want to. It won't matter anyway, so make it matter now."

49. "I do not have to be what other people see me as. I do not have to assume they know best."

50. "You're going to be okay. Not because I said so, but because 'okay' is where we all end up, even if we fuck up entirely along the way." (This is a Cheryl Strayed quote.)

58

YOU'RE ONLY
IN YOUR 20s
—IT'S NOT
too late to
COMPLETELY
START OVER

I know it seems like your 20s are designed for the build—a steady progression of acquiring better and more. I know it seems like the most important thing in the world is to build a picture of mind's eye comforts—the ways you have it "together," the things the world would look at and approve of. The things you can think about to soothe yourself out of a panic attack. But your 20s are about unlearning, too. Stripping away lukewarm loves and work you don't thrive doing and friends you've outgrown and limiting ideas you've been leaning on to guide you. You're making room for your actual life to begin.

Most people stumble in their 20s because they've spent their lives anticipating them. They've lived for this point—when happiness can ensue. But the most unhappy people are often the ones with the pretty nice apartments and the decent amount of friends and the good-enough job in fields they're at least somewhat interested in, because they've spent their lives building ideas rather than learning how to feel.

Your 20s are about undoing as much as they are anything else. Choosing new. Deciding otherwise. Shedding layers that have muddied your idea of who you think you are. This is the kind of scary magic you want. The kind that leads you into the beautiful unknown. You are becoming the person you are going to be for the rest of your life. How genuinely are you going to live? How afraid are you going to be? For how many more years are you going to let your demons conquer you?

You are only in your 20s. It is not too late to start over.

In fact, I hope you start over all the time. Not by burning bridges or ditching town or closing yourself to what you have, but by no longer fearing what you don't. I hope you spend your free afternoons working on the skills you need to have the job you want someday. I hope you accept that you're not supposed to look the way you did in high school, or really want the same things. I hope you ask yourself: "What do I want now?" every time it occurs to you to do so. I hope you learn that there is only one way to guide your life, and it is by consistently focusing on the next right step.

Genuinely unhappy people are never upset by their circumstances; they are upset because they have externalized their power. They put their faith in finding the right person as opposed to being able to attract and choose the right person. They put their faith in finding the right job, in the right economy, as opposed to honing their skills to the point that a company would be remiss to overlook them.

If you want to genuinely start over, clear the slate of everything you ever thought about how to get your life together. Don't predict, project, mind-read, assume. Don't imagine a better elevator speech. Don't only think of what it makes sense to do. Think of what it feels right to do. Not what your impulses say, not what your laziness says, not what your fear says. Those things have probably gotten you where you are. But a layer beneath them is a more resolute voice, and it will tell you which way to go. You only have to get quiet, listen, and act.

Learn to live your life more than you're inclined to sit around wondering about it. You can't reflect your way into a new existence, but you can think yourself into paralysis. If you know, at your core, that you must start over, it's not a matter of whether or not you will—it's whether you'll do it later, or whether you'll do it now.

59

17 IDEAS
you're keeping
ABOUT YOUR LIFE
that are only
HOLDING
YOU BACK

01. If you work hard enough, success is a guarantee. Most people are rarely "successful" in the way they first set out to be. Rather than work toward an end goal, work toward liking the process of getting there. Whether success is a product of chance or fate, all you can control is how much work you put in (not exactly what comes out).

02. Wanting something badly enough qualifies you to have it. Nobody ever got anything from just wanting it badly enough. You have to want it badly enough to sacrifice, and to work hard, become qualified, keep your head up through tons of rejection and doubt, and then rinse/repeat for as long as it takes.

03. You'll be the exception to everything, so you don't have to wear sunscreen or save money, or worry about your retirement plan or treat people respectfully, because your circumstances are just different than everyone else's.

04. You're a celebrity in your own mind—everyone is watching you and judging your choices. The "spotlight complex" is undoubtedly linked to social media, but regardless, nobody is thinking about you the way you are thinking about you, nor nearly as much. Nobody cares if you wear an unflattering shirt out to the pharmacy. Nobody really cares what you do with your life, so stop making choices as though they do.

05. If you're doing something right, results will be instantaneous. If you're doing something right, the results will take a very long time to build up and produce an outcome you're happy with.

06. "Busyness" is a good thing. Being busy is what happens when people are ill equipped to manage their stress. People who actually have a lot to do focus on getting it done simply because they don't have another choice.

07. There's a "right time" to create. Or get married, or have a child, or start pursuing the life you feel called to. If you're looking for an excuse as to why it's not the right time, you'll always find one.

08. Adulthood is "hard." There are lots of things that are challenging and heartbreaking and trying in life, but learning how to perform basic functions is not one of them.

09. Your purpose is something existentially profound. Your purpose is just to be here and to do whatever job you find yourself doing. You don't have to be consciously changing the world to fulfill it.

10. Everybody can have a job they love if they work hard enough. Everybody can find a way to enjoy their job—regardless of the inevitable challenges that come with any job—but nobody is entitled to do work that happens to fit precisely within their realm of interest and comfort.

11. You're not responsible for that which you do unintentionally. Accidentally hurting someone's feelings doesn't really hurt them; time you don't realize wasting isn't wasted; money spent on "necessities" isn't money spent. Essentially, if you aren't conscious of the repercussions of something, they don't count.

12. Your life partner is responsible for making you feel one very specific way. And you use that singular feeling to determine whether or not your relationship is "good" or worthwhile.

13. To accept something, you must be happy about it, or at least okay with it. You can accept your circumstances (acknowledge they are real) while still disliking them strongly. You don't have to like everything, but if you want to preserve your sanity, you have to accept whatever comes into your life before you can change it.

14. People are ruminating on the embarrassing stuff you did five years ago. They're busy ruminating on their own stuff the same way you are. (Are you thinking about things other people did over the years to any significant degree? It's unlikely.)

15. You must be "right" to be a valid, intelligent human being. Really the most intelligent people are more open to being wrong than anyone (that's how they learn) but regardless, you do not need to be consistently right or exceedingly smart or stunningly beautiful or anything else to be worthwhile and lovable.

16. You are your struggles. You say, "I am an anxious person" rather than "I sometimes feel anxiety." You identify with your problems, which is likely a huge reason why you can't overcome them.

17. You can only be as happy as your circumstances allow. You will only be as happy as you choose to focus on what's positive, reconcile and problem-solve what's negative, build the relationships that matter, validate yourself, and develop your mindset. You cannot choose a feeling, but you can always choose what you think about. Rejecting the idea that you can do so is to submit and doom yourself to a life in which you are never truly happy at all.

HOW TO BECOME
the kind of person who
DESERVES
THE LIFE
YOU WANT

We're conditioned to believe that there is only so much happiness to go around.

Beginning at a young age, we're almost pitted against one other in the race for superiority. That mindset still seeps into our daily interactions and is certainly a pillar of the me-centric media culture we've created. We're taught that there are winners, there are losers. There are people who make it, there are people who don't, and you need to be someone who does. There are only so many positions, so many success stories, so many opportunities to make the life you want. You need to choose from the human catalog of physical success and fight for a limited-edition lifestyle.

We settle ourselves into the idea that happiness and success are things that somebody else bestows upon us—bosses give jobs, lovers commit to "forever." No wonder we constantly feel out of control. No wonder we suffer so much at the hand of what we assumed we wanted.

Wanting is the ugliest thing you can do. It keeps your experience in a state of "not having." It keeps good things at a distance. You get what you most want when you don't want it anymore. When you shift your mindset and your experience to that of "already having," you naturally create and attract things that align with your idea of yourself. Acceptance is the root of abundance.

The things you genuinely want rarely have to be thought out. Putting labels and words and ideas to them is creating an image of something that's pure and essentially yourself. The way we get the most tripped-up is when our ideas don't evolve as our beings do, and we create what we want while still being attached to an old idea.

This is how you let go of those ideas. These are the things nobody will teach you about doing so.

These are the ways you carry yourself out of the life somebody else constructed for you, how you stop fighting and tearing apart old ideas, and start creating new ones. These are the things you need to know to become the person who deserves the life you most genuinely want—not the life that somebody else wants for you.

There are ways to pay the rent. There is no way to make somebody love you if they don't. Creating the moment-to-moment, day-to-day life you want, with the people you want, happens one job and month of rent and load of laundry and sink of dishes and electric bill at a time.

Adults don't do these things just to do them. These things are freedom. They are holding your own roof above your head. They are reducing yourself to the single notion that nothing matters more than your peace of mind.

Leave if you have to leave. There is rarely an excuse to remain with people who don't love or accept you. There are ways to survive. There are second jobs and extra hours and rooms that kind people are willing to rent or share. But these things are reserved for the people who place their mental well-being over immediate convenience. These are reserved for the people who deserve them and who know they deserve a space or room or home or apartment in which they decide what is and is not acceptable for their lives.

You are not supposed to always be happy and certain and stable. If you were, it wouldn't be such a struggle. Transcending the pain of humanness is one thing and one thing only: allowing yourself to be it. The struggle is trying to escape that which is inevitable.

Surrendering to it is not accepting defeat; it's being honest. It's being real and messy and gorgeous and tortured and darkly nuanced and glimmeringly hopeful. That's what we're meant to be. The only thing we really want to transcend is the inability to be what we are, as we are it.

There is just as much value in the negative space. Not every second of your life has to be filled. A packed agenda is not success. Living to work as opposed to working to live is not a quality of life. Things are not split into "times in which you're doing something that other people can quantify" and "times you're doing nothing." It's all important.

Your deepest revelations happen in silent moments with yourself. Being crowded with people and appointments and ideas and creative outpourings wouldn't be so profound and stunning if there weren't also moments of aloneness and nothingness and mental drought. The context of things matters just as much as they do. The focal point of a piece of art wouldn't exist without the negative space to frame it.

Unfortunately, nothing and nobody can hand you your happiness. Fortunately, nothing and nobody can take it away. You'd want to write that one off as the oldest mind trick in the book, and yet. But still. We're still seeking, even though we know better. We're fighting our nature to grow and expand and enlighten and seek and create in place of the idea that it's just meant to come to us. It's as though we apply the ideas of "wanting" and "trying" in completely wrong directions.

Time is not linear in the way we perceive it; everything is happening at once. You call into your experience that which you need and that which you are. You're never with and you're never without. You'll never receive and you'll never lose. You always were, you always are. That knowing is the foundation on which the real magic occurs.

Happy is boring. Beautiful is boring. People aren't interested or attracted to just "happy" and "beautiful." They're interested in people who are interested in things. Who are different-looking. Who have stories, and ideas, and mindsets that mirror and complement their own. Nobody wants a person who gets mad if they convolutedly believe somebody insinuated that they're "fat." They want a person who says: "Fat is not a thing you are, it is a thing you have, and even if that weren't the case...even if I were fat, who gives a fuck?" Love is more than pretending you look and behave and live a certain way.

The universe whispers until it screams. Your body whispers until it screams. "Bad" feelings are not meant to be staved off. They are not meant to be inconveniencing. They are you, or something greater than you, telling yourself: Something is not right.

Your gut voice will never go ignored. It will project out and eventually turn into big, loud external voices that demand you pay attention.

Learn to listen while it's little.

The most hilariously ironic thing of life is that you have the most success doing what feels right. Following our genuine happiness, our internal peace, is our only real responsibility. The people who love what they do are always, always more successful than the people who "work hard" or claim to. There's an X factor you can't mimic when you do something you're genuinely passionate about. You tap into an otherwise untouchable energy.

Your identity does not have to be cohesive. Your story doesn't have to flow. You don't have to be neatly packaged in a way that other people understand.

You have to stop living for your synopsis, the summary we try to piece together in our minds when we imagine people explaining us or evaluating who we are. It doesn't have to make sense. You're allowed to be great at a lot of things that don't necessarily relate to one another. You're not limited to just one purpose, one talent, one love. You can have a variety of jobs, each of them meaningful at the time you have them. You can be good at a lot of things without lacking in others. You do not have to be a novel; you can be a book of stories. You don't have to merge your coexisting truths and dull your shine just so it makes sense to a small-minded person who wants you to fit into a narrow understanding of what they're comfortable with.

You do not have to only be what other people are comfortable with.

You often do not know what's best for your life. Predicting your future does not make it more guaranteed to happen. It just closes you off. It gets you attached to an idea that you only want to be reality because you're attached to it. The content of our attachments matters little in comparison to just wanting to be correct, to be in control, to feel as though we know what's best and we're succeeding by virtue of living out that which we just knew would happen.

Nobody in the history of the world looks back on their life and says, "Yes, this is exactly what I thought would happen." But many, many people look around one day and say: "Yeah, I knew this is what I was meant for, but the details always surprised me."

Things will work out better than you could have chosen or designed them. In your unknowingness, however, it will seem as though everything's been shot to shit. In the moments before you realize something better than you can fathom is coming to fruition, it will seem like every plan you made and hope you had has been completely disregarded by whatever higher power you do or don't believe in. Have faith that you'll get more than you think you deserve.

You have to become the kind of person who deserves the life you want. Nobody ever got what they wanted by wanting it badly enough. Your life will unfold in direct proportion to how much you believe you deserve. Not how much you think you should have. How much you believe you deserve.

211

61

THINGS WE
EXPECT OF OTHERS
*(but rarely consider
changing ourselves)*

01. We expect other people to be honest and open with their intentions (especially romantically), but how many people are we keeping on the back burner? How many people do we leave lingering and wondering and waiting just because it's more convenient for us?

02. We get angry at people who aren't unconditionally kind. We try to teach children to be kind by punishing them when they're not. We demand that other people are open-minded and loving, often in very closed-minded and unloving ways.

03. We expect that if somebody is interested in us, they should have to make the first move. Nobody wants to be sitting around waiting for someone to ask them out or sweep them off their feet, but nobody wants to do the asking or sweeping, either. When's the last time you leaped out of your comfort zone to tell somebody you care about them? When's the last time you definitively asked somebody on a date—not just to hang out? When's the last time you did what you want others to do for you?

04. We don't understand when people aren't compelled by the cause(s) we feel most strongly about, but we complain the second somebody else's passions inconvenience us in the form of too many ALS bucket challenge videos on our Facebook feed or "annoying" political opinions that we don't want to have to see or hear about each day.

05. We expect people to trust us right off the bat, but the reasons we don't trust others are always justifiable.

06. When someone isn't there for us unconditionally or doesn't know that we need them without us having to say so, we find it rude and selfish. But how often do we go out of our way to try to psychoanalyze and predict the actions and desires and intentions of the people in our lives?

07. We call people small-minded for making judgments about parts of our lives that they don't know the whole of, but how often do we do that to strangers and coworkers and friends as a matter of daily conversation? We know that if people really knew us—really knew our whole story—they'd understand...and yet we run around judging others for things that we don't understand, stories we don't know the entirety of.

08. A common source of frustration is when people don't take care of their relationship issues in a way that seems obvious to us—leave if the person isn't perfect, "get over" the things you can't change...but how often is that the case in our lives? We don't allow others to be messy, but we expect them to lend a comforting shoulder when we're in pieces.

09. In theory, we expect people to be accepting of all religions, yet if someone doesn't understand our dogma or belief system or religious background, we consider them just "not at the level" to understand it. We can claim that every path is valid, but many people don't realize they believe theirs is just a little more effective.

10. We think people who judge others over petty things are terrible, but we're judging them...for judging...

11. We expect people to not make jokes at our expense, despite the fact that often the cheapest shot at humor is in tearing other people down, and at the end of the day, we're quick to go for the lazy (and mean) jibe that gets a laugh when we need to feel a little lifted.

12. We expect that people value themselves, and stop disparaging themselves but we also expect them to lift us up

213

when we do it ourselves (or we even think our constant self-deprecation is endearing).

13. We expect people to change overnight, whether it's eating better and taking control of their health, getting out of a toxic relationship or job—whatever it is, when other people self-sabotage, we think a pep talk will do the trick. That's rarely the case—we need only to look at our own detrimental habits to see that.

14. We roll our eyes and shoot dirty looks at people who don't behave the way we think is considerate and appropriate—who are too loud in public, who are late or messy or in some way unkempt, yet when we're tired and stressed and behind schedule, we don't care if we loudly take a work call while on line for coffee, or hold up a waitress or cashier to accommodate a random need. It's fine when we're loudly laughing and talking over brunch because we're excited, but it's annoying when someone else does the same thing. It's only not a nuisance if we're doing it.

15. We expect complete honesty from others, and yet when that "honesty" is something we don't want to hear, it's "mean," and when it's our turn to tell the truth, we avoid doing so until there's no other choice.

16. We expect unconditional love from the people who are closest to us, as if that will be enough to make up for the fact that we do not love ourselves.

62

YOU DON'T
have to
"LOVE YOURSELF"
PERFECTLY
in order to
BE WORTHY OF
SOMEONE
ELSE'S LOVE

When people say that you need to "love yourself" before you can love someone else, what they mean is that if you are subconsciously seeking a relationship to fix your life, give you direction, or make you feel better, you will perpetually choose the wrong person, and you'll never really have the kind of relationship you want. Unfortunately, what gets communicated is that you have to wait until you love yourself—and every aspect of your life—before you can be worthy of finding and committing to the right person.

What it sounds like is if you don't have love, it's your own damn fault. It's because you aren't good enough yet, because you haven't mastered enough, because you haven't done enough to earn it. What it sounds like is that you shouldn't accept love until you think you're ready for it, and that we are only meant to evolve autonomously, and once we're in a relationship, we can stop.

But you are not going to be ready for the love of your life when they show up. Nobody is. And if you deny yourself that relationship because you think you need to do more work beforehand, what you're really doing is missing out on the most effective growing tool there is.

Love is a grand magnifier: It shows you what you love and what you dislike about yourself and your life. The right relationship will encourage you to address that fully and work on it. The right

215

relationship will help you learn to love yourself. It is meant to change everything, and it always does.

So learn to thrive in the meantime. Use the days you have on your own to be your own person, and do what you can only do on your own time, and by yourself. But never confuse that for the idea that you cannot be loved before you are completely loving, that other people are only obligated to be as kind as you are to yourself, that you'll be ready for love when it comes.

Yes, the way you treat yourself will dictate and determine how other people treat you, but the work of being a whole, evolved, complete, loved and loving human being is not how well you can thrive in isolation and solitude, it's how you can stand up for yourself, demand respect, choose love, and learn to keep moving and evolving even when the person you've always been looking for is finally standing right beside you.

Loving yourself is letting yourself be loved, too.

63

30 QUESTIONS
you need to
ASK YOURSELF
if you still
HAVEN'T FOUND
THE RELATIONSHIP
YOU WANT

01. Do you think of relationships as something you earn for being "good enough" or something you develop when you're strong enough to open your heart?

02. What does "love" mean to you? Is it just a good feeling? Is it companionship? Is it comfort? Is it direction for the future?

03. How could you possibly get those things in your life if not through the company and proclamation of undying intimacy from someone you probably don't even know yet?

04. If the love of your life would reflect all of your unhealed issues, mirror your flaws, and bring your deepest insecurities to light, would you be ready to be in a relationship with them?

05. Do you try to relate to other human beings, or do you try to exert superiority over them? Do you want to connect or do you want to seem impressive? Do you engage in discussion to learn, or to sell someone on your way of thinking so you feel supported and "correct?"

06. Are you thinking about your love life more than you're actually living it? Have you developed a plan to find the kind of love you think you are so desperately missing?

07. If you were to develop a plan to find that kind of love, what would it look like? What would you need to do? What could you try? Where could you go?

08. Is the prospect of online dating, being set up by friends, and generally putting yourself out there less comfortable than the idea that you could possibly spend the next few years (or longer) by yourself?

09. Are you open about the fact that you're looking for love? If you're trying to play it like you're cool being single, you're going to miss out on a lot of opportunities to meet friends of friends, simply because they don't know you're willing.

10. What makes you happy, aside from affection from other people?

11. If you decided to take control of your relationship destiny today, as opposed to just waiting for it to "happen" when it's "meant" to, what would you start doing differently?

12. Do you think a great relationship is something you find, or something you develop and strengthen over time?

13. Do you believe that people who are more beautiful, successful, smart, talented, or in other ways superior have more love than you ever could?

14. Have you ever taken an honest look at the people around you who have love, and evaluated them on that same scale of attractiveness and intelligence and superiority?

15. If you did that, what would you find?

16. Would it blow your mind to learn that relationships aren't just nice, they are the stitching that keeps the patchwork of this entire damn world together, and that spending as much time and energy on them as you would anything else that matters would not only be essential, but crucial to you fulfilling your highest purpose as a human being?

17. Would it blow your mind to learn that even people who are surrounded by friends, in seemingly "happy" relationships, with families to return to every holiday and then some are sometimes still cripplingly lonely, because it's a matter of how you connect, not who you have around?

18. Are you aware of what your needs are in a long-term relationship?

19. Are you willing to advocate for those needs if they aren't being met, or would you forgo doing so for the sake of seeming more likable to your partner?

20. If you find the relationship you've been dreaming of, and then it doesn't work out, what would your game plan be?

21. Would it surprise you to know that the most overlooked key to a happy, healthy relationship is the belief that even if said relationship dissolved, you could still carry on as a functioning, thriving human being?

22. Could it be possible that you're not alone right now because you're broken or unlovable, but because there is something profound and divine that you must discover, and it is only knowable through solitude?

23. If you knew that the love of your life was on their way, and that this time in your life was only temporary, what would you do with the nights you have alone? What would you invest your efforts in? Writing your book or scrolling through Facebook? Developing relationships with friends or envying people who have love? Learning to meditate or taking a swig of wine every time you feel the slightest bit uncomfortable?

24. Do you assume other people are doing you a favor by giving you love and spending time with you?

25. Do you ever think about the fact that they likely are just as hungry for love?

26. Do you ever think about what you can *give* to a relationship, as opposed to what you want to take?

27. Are you committed to a lifetime of growing with, and alongside, another human being, or is your mental image of love something that allows, and supports, unconditional acceptance that is, in reality, complacency?

28. Are you willing, or ready, to let go of every preconceived notion you had about how love would come, what it would look like, and what your partner would be like? (You need to.)

29. What are you willing to suffer for in this life? You suffer over your fears, your thoughts, your work...what about the one thing that's actually worth it? Are you willing to give it your all, fail a few times, and then reach the end (love, commitment) only to find that dating was the walk before the run, the beginning of the real work?

30. Are you ready to let it gut you and help make you the person you were intended to be?

64

THE MOST TABOO
thing in our
CULTURE IS
RADICAL HONESTY,
and that's exactly
THE PROBLEM

We are being suffocated by a culture—and a people—that, out of an irreverence for honesty, has grown an inability to coexist.

We call opinions that aren't immediately harmonious with ours "offensive" and use that word to make it wrong to see or hear them. (Not to mention, we're more "offended" by a woman's nipple and a swear word than we are half of the global atrocities of famine and war and the destruction of the environment.) We police people into only saying and doing things that make sense to us. We grew up in a culture that taught us to put ourselves last, even when "putting other people first" is fake and disingenuous and rooted in resentment and dishonesty. We are all dying of some untouched, unrealized internal loneliness, grasping onto the bits of writing and music that speak in the way we otherwise cannot. We're suffering from anxiety and depression and loneliness and uncertainty and fear and failure mostly because we have to continue to paint an outward picture of the opposite. The inability to realize those natural, crucial parts of life are what make them "bad." Nobody is honest and so nobody is finding anybody who loves them for them, because they aren't being who they are. There are only finding people who love their shells, which, as we all know, easily break.

So many of our relationships hinge on whether or not we continually fulfill a set of expectations that we often know about but sometimes do not. Our fear of honesty and change is rooted in no longer being acceptable or wanted or held in high regard by the people who claim to love us.

We associate "doing what we want" and "putting ourselves first" with being selfish and with not considering others. We're taught that what we should want is what makes others happy. But do you want people in your life who secretly don't want to be there? Is it really surprising that we're all lost and scrambling and disconnected from ourselves when we're taught not to follow our instincts and truths for the sake of someone else's ego? (No.)

It's not "mean" to tell the truth; we're just not used to hearing anything other than what we want to hear. We've chalked anything that isn't coddling and placating and aligned with our most delusional and comforting thoughts to be "wrong." "Truthfulness" and "meanness" have become synonymous because so long as people aren't doing and saying what we want to see and hear, they're wrong, and they're hurting our feelings by, subconsciously or not, making us feel unaccepted, unwanted, and invalidated (because we're only finding those things externally).

What you have to keep in mind is that the people who shout the loudest about needing to behave a certain way are, undoubtedly, the very people who have most deeply and profoundly had their lives shaped by doing what other people wanted. They listened to the people who shouted loudly at them, and for that, they got emptiness. The very emptiness that their words are echoing through and out of.

At our core, there is only light. I guarantee there is not one person you wouldn't love if you knew their true story, their whole story, if you lived a day or a year or a lifetime in their shoes. We can't expect equality when we're holding up façades of inequality through dishonesty. How can we expect people to treat all others as equals if they're constantly feeling beneath someone else?

The root of equality, and understanding equality of the human condition, is being honest about it.

The only way to change the course of our society, to enlighten the closed minds, to shift the way we perceive gender and race and humanity itself is first and foremost by getting it all on the table. We are talking in circles and affirming only with people who inherently agree with us, rather than trying to understand where the people who don't are coming from. This is not change. This is ego-steroids. There's so much value placed around "helping others" and "being selfless" and forcing people to volunteer when they don't genuinely want to.

The only kindness we grow and support is that which we force on other people, the sort we perceive as correct.

Fake kindness is not worth it. It makes the world worse. It is the root of resentment and ill will and self-hatred and bigotry and prejudice.

Often the kindest things we experience in life are the moments in which someone cared more about who we were than how our feelings would be hurt to tell us the truth that saved us or showed us some otherwise invisible reality. Often the way we are kindest to ourselves is by saying "no." Often the things we are most grateful for are the ones that were (and are) the most trying, the most deeply compelling, the most wholly changing, even if, at first, they aren't necessarily comfortable.

So you should say no when you want to say no. You should speak precisely and kindly and with understanding but directness when you see a friend struggling to make a simple choice that will have a profound effect on their entire quality of life, instead of walking away and discussing with everybody else but them. You should leave your house if in it; you're not wanted. There are ways to pay the rent; there is no way to make somebody love you when they don't. You should say how you feel before it stays in the darkness so long that it becomes the foundation on which the rest of your life is built—and then collapses through. You should tell the people you love that you love them. You should tell the people you don't that you don't, and let them find people who really do. You should dig deep into the untouched abyss of yourself and see what you come out with. First, it will be the unhealed wounds you didn't know you had. Second, it will be the light and love and passion under which they rest. Third, it will be the desire to take those things and run with them and build something remarkable. You should evaluate your choices not in light of how other people will perceive them, but how in line with your deepest, truest self they are.

You should rise and say, "This is who I am, even if you'll crucify me for it" in the very way so many religious and political and social idols and icons have, even if their fans and followers are the very ones who will do the crucifying.

You should give to others what you most need. Which, more often than not, is to say the following: You are not loved by everybody, but that does not mean you are not loved at all. You are not the most beautiful, but being the most beautiful is not what matters most. You are bound by nothing but your own fear, so you will not find freedom anywhere but within yourself. Everybody suffers. Not everybody comes out on the other end shimmering and ready to let that light reverberate through the dense and otherwise impermeable darkness. Not everybody has the guts to be truthful, but everybody has the capacity to. And the greatest irony, the most profoundly cunning thing of all, is that the very love and passion and acceptance we are seeking resides nowhere else but within our own unbridled honesty. So go to it, and let it finally breathe.

65

7 REASONS WHY
HEARTBREAK IS
often crucial
FOR HUMAN GROWTH

There have been so many poets and thinkers and philosophers who have spoken to this idea: the purpose of suffering. The wound through which Rumi claims the light enters. The beautiful people Elisabeth Kübler-Ross says had to know defeat and suffering and struggle to know appreciation and sensitivity and understanding. The pain Khalil Gibran believes sears the most incredible characters' hearts. The suffering through which Fyodor Dostoyevsky claims a large intelligence and deep heart can be born. The people C. Joybell C. sees as stars: dying until they realize they are collapsing into supernovas, to become more beautiful than ever before.

Heartbreak may not be responsible for fundamental, biological human growth, but rather the kind that we also know: in our minds and of our hearts and throughout our souls. If the philosophers couldn't speak to it well enough, surely you've experienced something of the same strain in your own life: the pain that was crucial to the process, the things that were lost to prepare for those that would be gained, the excruciating experiences that made you who you are now.

It's a phenomenon so many people talk about but most can never quite define: the catalyst that breaks you open, the rock bottom on which you build the rest of your beautiful life. The suffering that was somehow so crucial, you're grateful for it when all is said and done. It's the human equivalent of metamorphosis, the darkness against which we can finally see light.

It's my belief that if we could understand why our pain is necessary, we could bear it with more grace, or at least learn to listen to it before it forces us to. Here, the 7 reasons why heartbreak is often necessary for human growth...

01. Suffering is only necessary until we realize it isn't, but it usually takes something to make us realize that.

Pain and suffering are not the same thing; I'm sure you've heard this before. We love pain. We make the same expression during an orgasm as we do while being tortured. Crying is cathartic, the physiological sensation of pain ultimately keeps us alive. It's suffering that we don't like. Suffering is a resistance to pain, and it's in resistance that we suffer. We don't choose what pains us, and that's a good thing. We do choose what we suffer for, and that's even better. It was always only of our own volition.

02. Human beings think they are seeking happiness, but they are seeking comfort and familiarity above all else.

People are incapable of predicting what will make them happy. This is because all we know is what we've known. Our culture, however, is big on "planning" for the future, choosing our happiness, and chasing it. In an effort to do this, we just choose something we knew from the past, even when, objectively, it wasn't happiness at all. It was something we desire more: comfort. Until our loyalty to our comfort zones becomes too uncomfortable to bear, we won't be forced to seek something genuinely greater than whatever it is we once thought was best.

03. Suffering teaches us that trying to change the external world to be happy is like trying to change the projection on the screen rather than the projector that's playing it.

Byron Katie speaks to this beautifully: "Once we realize where the lint is, we can clear the lens itself. This is the end of suffering, and the beginning of a little joy in paradise." She is referring, of course, to our minds, and the fact that we don't realize to turn inward until we dig ourselves deep enough into a dark hole of trying to change what's outward. Your mind is the lens through which you perceive the world. You must adjust its focus to change your life, not the opposite way around.

226

04. Often "suffering" comes to us in the form of a breakdown, which is really just a breakthrough that we haven't seen the other side of yet.

Through learning that sometimes (...oftentimes) we don't know what's best for us, and yet somehow, our subconscious, instinctive selves do. I'm not claiming to know that there's necessarily a divine intervention responsible, but I am claiming to know that many times even in my own life, I somehow knew when it was time to break my own heart for the sake of something greater, even though I didn't know what that greater thing was at the time.

05. A capacity to feel joy must be balanced by a capacity to know pain.

Our world is born of, and exists because of, duality. This is a fundament of our natural world, but it's also important to see in our own lives. The truth is that the greater capacity you have for darkness is as much contrast through which you can see light. The yin/yang of our emotional selves is always in balance; it truly just depends on what perspective we choose to view things through—both are equally available to us, the choice is always, ultimately, ours.

06. Pain is a signal that something's wrong, suffering is what happens when we don't heed it.

Physiologically, of course this is true, but it's even more true emotionally and mentally. We almost like to create problems for ourselves out of a very deep belief that we deserve pain (the bad kind) out of retribution for how terrible we (wrongfully) believe ourselves to be. It's only through grappling with that pain that we realize it was always self-induced and served mostly just to help us unlearn our need to create it, to realize why we don't deserve it, and in the process of doing so reconnect with who we truly are, not just what the rest of the world sees us to be.

07. The universe whispers until it screams.

There is no traumatic experience that is ever a completely singular event. There is no heartbreak that is ever just the cause of one thing. It's the pattern. It's what the loss compounds on. It's the final hit that breaks us open, the moment when we realize that we knew what was true all along, though something prevented us from heeding the calls early on. That is what we break through when we break open. How beautiful, to live in a body and world that allows you to explore the darkness, but pains you when it's time to come back. How wild that nobody tells us about this until we're in it, or already almost too far gone.

66

WHY WE HOLD
ON TIGHTEST
to the things
THAT AREN'T
MEANT FOR US

I used to wonder how you let go of the things that are killing you, when it feels like it would kill you to let go. How you decide between "if things are meant to be, they will be" and "if you want it, you have to go get it."

I think we hold on tightest to the things that aren't meant for us because at some level, we know they aren't really ours. We're always seeking the love we know we don't have. We're always trying to prove the things that are not entirely self-evident.

We know that when we stop thinking and talking and racking through the details again and again, it will really be over. When all that exists is an idea, holding on is the only way to keep it.

Because letting go has little to do with giving somebody permission to leave our lives, or declare that they don't love us anymore, or walk away for good, and everything to do with accepting that they already have.

I don't know about fate. But I do know the things that are ours don't require us to mentally and emotionally latch onto them to remain. That the best things are never forced, are never created out of ultimatums, never leave us reeling and questioning them for months or years at a time.

I do know that you cannot prove how much you love by how much you're pained over loss. That you do not prove your character by how well you can convince other people you're doing the right thing.

And I do know that it's never the love that hurts you, it's the attachment to the idea of what it's supposed to be. I do know that we will never be able to find real love unless we learn to detach from what it should be. I do know that we're never going to find true happiness until we do the same. I do know that nothing here lasts, and the idea that it does is an illusion—we eventually lose everything, every last thing we have and are and own.

So the point isn't what we lose, but what we had in the first place. We aren't meant to attain things like bullet points on a resume; we're supposed to go through them and let them go through us.

Some love teaches us what it has to teach us in a month. Some a lifetime. Neither is more important than the other.

The things that are meant for us are the things that force us to stop seeking an external light, but to start becoming it. The things that are meant for us are trying and joyous and beautiful and excruciating. They're the things we don't think about.

The things we don't have to hold on tightly to make happen.

67

THINGS
YOUR 20s
are too
SHORT FOR

01. Letting anybody convince you that because you're young, you're incapable.

    Plato began his career in politics before he was 20 and has stated that he faced ridicule in his coming-of-age for that reason. Some of the greatest cultural tycoons of this century were in their 20s when their first huge contributions were made: Jobs, Zuckerberg, etc. Imagine where we'd be if they listened to the people who said, "What do you know?"

02. Arguing with people whose intentions are not to understand you, only to prove themselves right.

    You do not owe it to anybody to carry on a conversation that is only serving the ego, but you do owe it to yourself to step out of the inevitable frustration and self-doubt of interacting with people who don't listen to understand, but to respond; who don't speak to be heard, but to defend.

03. Wasting your energy placating the habits of people who don't take the initiative to actually get their shit together.

    Often the most frustrating thing about dealing with someone who is going through a tough time is that they aren't willing to listen to reason or logic, or even simply your opinion. You end up having to pretend. You nod along with whatever they're saying because you don't want your every interaction to turn into a fight. The resentment will build and the relationship will crumble anyway.

04. Justifying your choices to people who only care about how you look within the context of their lives.

The people who will squawk the loudest about what you should and shouldn't do or how you're on the wrong path or whatever else they couldn't possibly have the grounds to know are usually the ones most concerned with how it makes them look and how they're going to explain you to friends or cousins or sisters or family or coworkers. Remember that while you're deciding who matters, and while we're on the topic...

05. Remaining in contact with people you don't like because you "should," because it's more convenient, because you'll feel guilty if you don't, because you're too afraid of what someone will think if you're finally honest with yourself and other people.

    You do not have to waste your life bending over backwards to make people happy when they don't—and wouldn't—do the same for you.

06. Holding onto love that's already run its course because you fear the best has passed you or you won't find anybody who makes you feel the same way.

    The purpose of most great love is to gut you open, teach you what you need to know, and send you on your way to bigger, better, even happier things. Don't let your irrational fears talk you out of letting yourself find that.

07. Eating food you don't like, keeping plans you don't want, staying digitally connected with people who annoy you, hoarding clothes for a "someday" that never comes and putting your life on hold for someone who does not—and will never—want to commit.

    The amount of life we waste gathering and holding onto the things that will never really serve us does one thing and one thing only: keeps us away from the things that matter, that bring us joy and purpose and meaning, for that much longer.

08. Not taking time to figure out what you want, even if it's to be okay with knowing you're not sure and don't need to be. Don't let the fear of not finding something definitive keep you from finding anything at all.

You'll be running around in the circles somebody else drew for you so long as you don't take the time to reflect and evaluate and really connect with that core, inner knowing that screams when you come across something you know is what you're meant to do or be or become—even if it's just for a day, an hour, a year.

09. Not taking the time to heal the wounds of your childhood.
The things that have molded you will be constructs that you—and only you—will have to dismantle for yourself. The time to do this will either be now, while you're still adaptable and developing, or later, when your unhealed walls are forcibly knocked down by powers greater than your own self-control. (The choice is yours; it always will be.)

10. Judging people for things that seem "wrong." Every single thing serves a purpose. The goal is not to create a seamless image, it's to go through the experiences that need to grow and teach and change us.
You don't know that a completely wrong and illogical marriage is what someone really needs. You don't know that there's no element of fate or destiny involved in the birth of a child that seems young and for which the parents seem ill prepared. You don't know that the people who seem to be doing nothing with their lives are gathering the knowledge and experience that will one day write the next great American novel, uncover the next great philosophic idea, etc. As hard as it may be to grasp, all things are good, because all things serve us in the way of growth and development.

11. Never taking the initiative to learn how to live within your means—whatever your means might be.
It doesn't matter how much or how little money you are making, how many investments you have or savings accounts that are stacked or absolutely empty, it doesn't matter how much or little debt you still have to pay off, if you are not already in the mindset and lifestyle of living within the means you have, the same financial problems will follow you no matter where you go or what you achieve.

12. Putting the things you want most off until it's more "convenient."

If you're looking for a reason not to, you'll always find a reason not to. If you're looking for a way how, you'll always find a way how.

13. Burning bridges over minor frustrations—bridges that could have led to jobs or relationships you didn't know you'd want or need.

While you're in this weird period of infinite opportunity and inevitable, uncanny irony and serendipity, you're in no place to assume that you're not going to need every last contact you've got. If you must walk out of something, learn to do so gracefully, so the door won't be locked if you need to walk back in.

14. Staying at a job where you're miserable.

I'm not saying it will happen tomorrow. I'm not saying you'll find your dream job in a week or even a month or three or six. I'm saying that anybody who has accomplished anything they've really wanted at a young age had one thing in common: They were at the right place at the right time because they were consistently putting themselves out there. To create your own luck, up your chances and have faith that some greater, destined force will do the rest for you. (It sounds like a loose argument, but please, trust me.)

15. Staying in a relationship in which you secretly get the sense that you're settling because there's nobody else around.

Similar to how terrible, temporary jobs become a terrible 10 years at that same job before you do anything about it, relationships you settle for become marriages you settle for, etc.

16. Not experimenting with your appearance because you're afraid any one change will define you as a whole.

There are two things it would benefit you to do here, and those are to get really goddamn comfortable with the body you're stuck with and get really goddamn comfortable with that body changing, because it's only going to do so from

234

here on out. Some of that change will be within your control; most will not. Don't let yourself be so attached to one way of appearing that you make your inevitable growth and aging even harder for yourself.

17. Never learning to say "sorry" or "thank you"—not for the sake of how it will make you look, but because you are able to recognize the ways in which you could have done better and the things for which you're humbled.
    To your parents. To your exes. To your teachers. To strangers, friends, family, the people you once knew. But most importantly, to yourself.

18. Not ordering pizza at 4 a.m.
    Or eating cake for breakfast at least once, or kissing a stranger, or giving the person you've been eyeing across the bar or café your phone number, or taking a road trip and sleeping in the car with your best friend, or whatever other slightly irresponsible but ultimately harmless thing you're tempted to do but most times don't have the guts to.
    (Do it.)

19. Waiting for something outside to fix your inside.
    For the next year, job, relationship, paycheck, piece of clothing, new apartment to fix whatever discomfort or dissatisfaction you feel. (The latter will follow you into the former until you fix it on its own terms.) Always.

20. Only wanting happiness.

There's so much more in a life than just feeling content all the time. The most important things you'll experience will have little to do with your happiness. They'll be about suffering, and heartbreak, and joy, and panic, and fear, and love, and what you come out as having been through those things.

You will not remember the days when you were just "okay" and "happy." You will remember the moments of joy, and the pangs of ache, and the things that were defining and changing and miraculous and incredible and made you feel alive.

Stop numbing your life because you're afraid of yourself. The only beast there is to tame is the one who doesn't want to really live.

68

THE HAPPIER
you are with
A DECISION,
the less you
NEED OTHER
PEOPLE TO BE,
and 11 other things
TRULY FULFILLED
PEOPLE KNOW

Fulfillment may seem like the elusive desire that's driving an entire consumerist market, but that's only because some smart people are capitalizing on something inherent of us all (or at least, inherent of us by the millions): We all have an aching desire to live a meaningful life, and yet none of us seems to know how.

Somewhere along the line, we confused happiness for what we have as opposed to what we do. We thought that the solution to an incomprehensible emptiness was to fill everything else around us. Needless to say, this has mostly, if not entirely, failed.

To be truly fulfilled is to be happy because of your own self-realization. It is to come to such a genuine understanding of what you want that not doing it isn't an option anymore. It's seeing beyond the mindsets you adopted, or the ideals that are not inherently your own. It is the humble simplicity of what you want to offer the world each day, and it is the love you awaken as you do it.

01. Success is falling in love with the process, not the outcome. It's making your dreams about the journey, about the "doing," about the day-in-day-out routine and minutiae. The life you want is within the simplicity of your everyday tasks. You can't only focus on writing the synopsis and then wonder why you don't have a book yet.

02. Only some happiness is valued in society.

Not everybody will applaud that you left your job to work at a coffee shop because it's what you love. There is really only one kind of happiness that society values, and that's the kind that society is comfortable with: the kind that is far enough removed from genuine contentment that nobody feels pressured to consider how unfulfilling their own lives are. Do not let other people's demons decide what your happiness is. Do not let other people's fear of them make you afraid, too.

03. Love and success are not expendable. They're not non-renewable resources. Someone else's doesn't take away from your own.

This belief registers for most people in elementary school: We see that some people are popular, and some people aren't. Some people can be happy, some can't. This is often what begins the lifelong competition that only ever exists in our heads. Someone else's success doesn't make you less successful. Someone else receiving love or praise doesn't mean you aren't love or praiseworthy. You are not only as good as you are better than someone else.

04. The happier you are with a decision, the less you need other people to be.

The happier you are with what you do, the less you need other people to support you. Ironically, it's also in being happier with what you do that you'll find the support you were looking for before you knew how to give it to yourself.

05. The end goal is to see how the simplest things are the most extraordinary.

When the end goal is to have something tangible, the "end goal" has not actually been identified yet. Tangible goals— money, books, job titles, and so on—are mile markers. They are the products of your life, not the goals of your life. The goals are to be truly fulfilled. The book you write to do that is not your fulfillment, it's one expression of it. Don't confuse the radio for the sound wave.

06. You don't "have" to, you "get" to.

This is one of the simplest changes in perception, and yet also something truly fulfilled people master: the knowing that everything is an opportunity to experience. You don't have to go to work; you get to go to work. You don't have to wake up early; you get to wake up early. When you start considering things not as obligations but as opportunities, you start taking advantage of them rather than trying to avoid them.

07. Easy does it, and does it well.

It's a phrase used so frequently and yet rarely ever with understanding: Anything that is genuine and wonderful and most probably successful is effortless. The state you're in when you're creating will be what the outcome is. The more ease and love you put into it, the more other people will get out of it.

08. Anything that exists in your life exists because you created it. Anything that persists does so because you are feeding it.

Consider this: Every one of your actions feeds something within you. It feeds your desire for control, your love for your job, your spitefulness toward your sister, your complacency with your marriage. Every action creates and compounds upon something that already exists. With this in mind, ask yourself what it is you feed each day...your life will make more sense if you do.

09. It's not about whether or not you listen to yourself; it's about what part of yourself you listen to.

Most people find it almost impossible to listen to their instincts because they don't know what they're saying. Or, worse, they've listened to them before and they've been destructively incorrect or shortsighted. That's because at any given time, there will be many different "voices" that drive you to different outcomes. Your immediate instincts may be geared more toward protecting you rather than expanding you. They could be speaking out of a place of lack or fear. You have to ask yourself: What is the root of this reaction, where does it come from, and what is its outcome in the long-term?

10. Even when you justify your judgment of people by how right you are, you're still wrong.

It doesn't matter how awful someone is being or how correct you are in your takedown of their mental-emotional state, you're still wrong for doing it. It's not your job to police for the universe; it's your job to take care of why you feel more comfortable attacking assumptions you make about others rather than the assumptions you fear they're making about you.

11. Your soul knows what to do to heal itself; the challenge is just to let it.

Most mental and emotional healing comes from first completely addressing the problem. You'll find that, throughout your life, you'll create situations again and again that all but force you to address some long-standing issue. That's because you necessarily want to torture yourself, but that you want to address it and bring it to your conscious awareness so you can deal with it and let it go. Trust in your nature. It knows more than your physical mind.

12. You probably can't be whatever you want, but if you're really lucky and you work really hard, you can be exactly who you are.

…Which is all most people ever want, anyway. Grandiose visions of being something spectacular—and spectacularly removed from someone's skill set and personality, etc.—can be measured in proportion to how much they feel they are lacking. The funny reality is that people who accomplish incredible things never think of them as incredible; they think of them as normal. It's that integration into "normalcy" that makes it a pattern, which makes it a routine, which makes it a habit, which ultimately makes it a product. That drive and consistency is born of one thing and one thing only: doing something in alignment with who you truly are. It is a privilege, albeit an extraordinary challenge, to awaken to yourself. Even more so is to have someone who loves that person, a job that utilizes that person, and a life that fully realizes that person, even if you denied them along the way.

69

WHAT PEOPLE
who have
LOST LOVE
KNOW

The people who have lost love know that someone else's love isn't yours to lose.

Someone else's love is yours to experience, but anything beyond that is just becoming attached to an idea, a hope, a big ol' "supposed to be." The people who have lost love know that right there is the point at which you lose yourself—when you start believing someone else will carry some part of you with them when they walk away. When you start seeking salvation in the very person you have to be saved from, believing that someone else—someone other than yourself—can save you.

The people who have lost love know that you can lose things you never really had, end relationships that never really started, that never ran the course of all the dreams and plans you had together. They know that you can mourn people who were never really there at all.

The people who have lost love know what it means to fill the empty spaces in your bed with pillows and in your life with work or dates that don't matter much or just the acknowledgement of sadness. They know the therapeutic quality of embracing it.

They know what it means to be absolutely certain there is no feasible way you could ever love somebody as much as you love that one person. They know what it's like to have your concept of logic and sense and justice and fairness and "supposed to be" turned all the way on its ass.

They know that you don't always spend forever with the person you love the most, but you can spend forever trying to reconcile that fact in your mind.

And more importantly than those things, they know that moving on isn't a conscious choice, but rather what happens when you stop trying to. When you stop forcing yourself to forget. You forget about them when you start thinking about you.

They know what it's like to look back on the things they thought they'd never get over, and to realize that even the hardest things somehow dissipate with time, ease with understanding, release with awareness.

They know there is incomparable strength in having seen yourself through the worst.

They consider their actions before they're reckless with other people. They know what it's like to be on the receiving end of carelessness. They become the gentle lovers and cautious suitors whose hesitation and timidity might be confused for indifference—but it's not, and this is significant. They gain a reverence, and an understanding, of just how deep a human heart can love and how fragile an ego can break.

The people who have lost love know that tight, stinging, burning feeling in your chest and throat and legs. They know what depths panic can drive you to when you've exhausted every option.

They know that soul mates aren't what people think they are—they aren't happily ever after most of the time. They are a love that lights every part of you up and exposes the unhealed layers; your true soul mate is the one who shows you to yourself.

And they know that's the point.

They know that you can love a person, but never as much as you can miss them. They know what it's like to have no choice but to live in the moment, to have to mentally walk yourself through every hour of the day, because otherwise your awareness will be pulled from sifting through what happened and worrying about what will and wondering about where they are and if they even cared at all.

They know to appreciate what they have while they have it.

They know that there may be no deeper pain than seeing someone you love be in love with someone else. Or, more accurately, someone you thought belonged to you suddenly belonging to someone else. That simply. For all the great oceans of depth that you could feel running between you, that it can be over in a simple drop.

They know what it's like to carefully daydream running into that lost love again. They know what it's like to be picking out clothes with them in mind, rehearsing conversations alone in your bedroom, cutting their hair and running a mile longer as though a simple shift of appearance could make someone fall in love again.

They know what it's like to actually run into them when they're with someone else. Someone else who is in so many ways not what they are, for better, for worse.

From that extraordinary pain, they learn that someone's love for you isn't lessened or greatened by how much they love someone else. It's not a singular, expendable thing.

And that knowing this may be the greatest lesson of all.

They know what it's like to live with the ghost of what would have and should have and maybe-still-could-be. To be walking down the street with the constantly running narrative of what they'd be saying, what they'd be thinking, if only they were there. To be out at the bar when the conversation seems to drift from your awareness and all of a sudden all you can focus on is the faint thought of what it would be if they were sitting next to you. To be holding your basket in line at the grocery store and hear your song come on and all of a sudden, to be imagining all the ways you once thought they imagined you, and how they must think those very same thoughts, send those very same texts, act that very same way, just with someone else.

They know what it's like for there to be strangers in the world who once knew everything about you.

They know that you somehow always call into your life exactly what you need—the most painful, the most changing amongst it.

They know you never lose love. They know that what you experience, how you grow, what you take and learn and see and do because of it, is the point. Not to have it forever, but to become what it was meant to make you.

They know that—at first—you'll spend your time trying to figure out what to do with all the love that is left lingering.

And they know that you're supposed to give it to yourself.

70

SIMPLICITY.

Learn to like what doesn't cost much. Those are the things worth your time. You can buy your way into things and places, but you can't actually buy the experience of them. It's not what you do; it's what you perceive. A meaningful life isn't how often you can saturate your senses, but how you grow to think of even the simplest, most unassuming daily things.

Learn to like reading, whatever it is you like to read. Learn to like talking and people, even when they're not the same as you. Learn that truths can coexist. That's the one thing that will set you free in this world.

Learn to like simple foods and cooking them. Learn to like fields, trees, camping, walking, fires, watching the day break and end. Learn to like writing and burning candles on rainy summer early evenings. Learn to like clean linens and washing dishes and hot baths and drinking water and long, meandering drives.

Learn to keep your needs simple and your wants small.

Learn to breathe deeply. To taste food when you eat it, to sleep deeply when you sleep. When you laugh, let it carry on until you're sweating and out of breath. When you get angry, get really angry, just let things burn through you. The less you push these things away, the less they come out in inappropriate and debilitating ways. It's not anger or the sadness that controls you; it's the resistance of it that keeps them tucked in their place in your soul.

Learn to let negative thoughts drift back to where they came from—nowhere.

Do the things that are effortless. Let them be effortless. Find love that's effortless. You'll be instructed to believe that success comes from grueling, soul-bending hard work, but that's more something we impose on ourselves because letting effortless things also be successful ones makes them feel unmerited. That's how we create problems where there are none.

Decide to keep nothing but what is meaningful and purposeful. When you cycle and circle around your space, touching, seeing, and using only things that evoke a feeling of security, purpose, meaning, joy...your everyday life becomes grounded in happiness. When there's not enough to make a mess, no more than you can clean and wash and handle, everything feels settled.

Complexity is often the easiest choice. It's easy to let ourselves get wound up and bound down to the ways we let our thoughts and fears run narratives into storylines into realities we live out.

Simplicity is difficult because it requires clean thinking. It's the long, hard way to a cleansed perception (that is: not shadowed by conditioning or negative thoughts). But it's yours, and yours always. You can keep all of one hundred belongings for the rest of your life, and every one of them will be used, broken, replaced, taken, thrown out, rendered obsolete. But your perception of how meaningful and useful those temporary things were, how much you appreciated and enjoyed them—that's yours. And that is what choosing a life rooted in simplicity does: makes the ordinary miraculous.

People like to make big claims of what will bring you happiness. And happiness, in some form, is what we're all seeking, even if we don't place that word on it. Stability, love, money. Happy psychology, the phenomenon of the last 25+ years, has come about really for the fact that we pioneered a country for the sake of unbridled, radical happiness: religious liberation, freedom, democracy.

Yet these things, these houses that hold us and companies we run, these relationships we fail at because we're constantly expecting them to be more—the desire to max out pleasure—has not made us happier.

Because we have not changed how we think—and that's the only real change that ever happens, because it's the basis of how we feel. The magnitude of one's life is directly parallel to how deep their perception of it is. Your life grows as you do. What you experience is a reflection of what you are.

Do not forget that you do not have forever to do this, to change this.

It's easy to let another day, week, month, year slip by, letting yourself keep seeking the light in people and money and more and more and more. It's easier to spend that time seeking the light in yourself because you think that's the right thing to do. You don't find the light—the ability to perceive—because you already are it. The work is getting rid of everything that stands in the way.

71

18 LITTLE
REMINDERS
FOR ANYONE
who feels like
THEY DON'T KNOW
what they're
DOING WITH
THEIR LIFE

01. Nobody knows what they are "doing with their lives." Some people have a better idea of what they're working toward, but ultimately, none of us can accurately anticipate or summarize what our existence is about. Not yet.

02. You decide what your life is defined by. The feeling of being "lost" isn't what happens when you go off-path, it's when you forfeit control. It's what happens when you don't want to accept the course of events that have unfolded. Being found again is a matter of owning what happened to you and continuing to write the story.

03. J.K. Rowling didn't know she was going to be one of the most famous writers in the world; she was just writing a story for her kids. Steve Jobs didn't know he'd be a pioneer of how humanity interacts with technology; he was just a guy in his garage making a computer. Oprah didn't know she'd become the poster woman for self-improvement and success; she was just trying to do a job. You don't need to know what you're doing to still do something extraordinary.

04. There is no way you will be able to predict or plan what will be happening in 5 years from now.

05. If you can predict and plan for that, dream bigger. Try harder.

248

06. Planning your life (or having a cohesive idea of "what you're doing") isn't necessarily ambition; it's more just a soothing notion. Focus instead on what you want to do with each and every day of your existence. That's noble. That's worthwhile. That will get you somewhere.

07. You owe nothing to your younger self. You are not responsible for being the person you once thought you'd be.

08. You owe everything to the adult you are today. You owe it to yourself to ask yourself what you like, what you want, what calls you, what you need, and what you deserve.

09. Do you know why you don't have the things you once thought you wanted? Because you don't want them anymore. Not badly enough.

10. It's likely that you're between realizing you don't want what you once did and giving yourself permission to want what you want now.

11. Give yourself permission to want what you want now.

12. If you want to change your life, stop thinking about how you feel lost and start coming up with actions you can take that move you in a direction—any direction—that's positive. It's a lot harder to think your way into a new way of acting than it is to act your way into a new way of thinking.

13. Nobody's life is as good as it looks online.

14. Nobody cares about your social media presence as much as you do.

15. Social media has uniquely and distinctly made us evermore concerned with the next big "goal." If you feel like you don't know where your life is going, it's likely because you don't know what you want your next big impressive "goal" to be.

16. You don't need to accomplish anything to be a worthwhile human being. Very few people are actually meant to be extraordinary. That does not mean you cannot know contentment, love, joy, and all the real wonders of life.

17. Your life is only ever as good as your perception of it is. Feeling lost or like you "don't know what you're doing" is only solved by learning to think about things differently. That's all.

18. Stop asking: "What am I doing with my life?" and start asking: "What am I doing with today?

72

THE ART OF
AWARENESS,
or how to
NOT COMPLETELY HATE YOURSELF

All hatred is self-hatred.

And everything is feedback.

I really hope you remember those two tiny sentences every time your chest is pretzeled up and you feel hopeless and helpless and as though you're spiraling into a bottomless bucket of shit.

Everything is a reflection of you because all anything can ever be is what you take from it and all you can ever take from it, and all you will ever take from it, is what you are aware enough to perceive. The expanse of your experience is directly in line with your consciousness. Nothing is as it is; it is as you are. (That's a play on an Anaïs Nin quote.)

Unless you are there to touch and smell and see a flower, it is nothing but random matter vibrating in a void. Your recognition gives it its beauty and its presence. You are not in the world; the world is in you. And though that sounds like another abstract platitude, it is not. It is reflective of a greater, deeper, truer truth, and in these tiny moments of recognition, of awareness, we find that what we immediately perceive is not all there is, and that anything that feels dense and heavy and "wrong" and "negative" is not a matter of what's going on outside but what we're not healing and changing inside.

Awareness is the antidote to solving so many seemingly unsolvable problems. Just the simple knowing that your egocentric mind is deriving other people's actions and assuming other people's thoughts to torture you is enough to silence it.

The art of learning to be is unassigning "good" and "bad" and "right" and "wrong" to what you feel and what you see and what other people show you. After all, even the heaviest, darkest things ultimately serve you and open you to a truth you wouldn't have considered before had you not been put in the context to see it.

Here, all the things to consider and reflect on and read over again when you're feeling particularly terrible. (It was requested numerous times that I write a follow-up to this, so here you go.)

01. Your actions are more powerful than what anybody can ever say of you.

The thing about spiraling downward into a fit of helplessness is that it's usually accompanied by the feeling that we are completely out of control of how other people see us. Of course, this is nothing more than a mechanism of how we see ourselves, but bear with me, because the point here is that not one word anybody says is more powerful or true than how you behave and who you really are. You hold the power here. You call the shots. How other people want to perceive you is their problem, which they will have to come to terms with eventually. How much you want to allow their perceptions to affect you is yours.

02. What you think others think is more important than what they actually think. (It shows you to yourself.)

Once you gain the awareness that the whole concept of "what other people think" is one grand illusion that you're always at the short end of, you start to realize that "how other people see you" shifts as your mindset does. Funny how that works, huh?

03. Your reactions matter more than other people's actions do, and you can choose how you react.

Your opinions/thoughts/feelings/emotions/mental states do not have to rest on what you find out or simply imagine people do or don't say/think or believe about you. The reality of it is you will never know the entirety of what people are saying or thinking or believing, and those things are none of your business. They are carrying on, and always have been, whether or not you're made aware of it. The only thing that changes here is how much you want to change yourself based on that hypothetical. They can say what they want. You can react how you want.

04. In terms of romantic relationships and sex and love and body types and attraction and all that, the people worth loving and dating and sleeping with are far more accepting than you're giving them credit for.

There was never a true love story in the history of ever that blossomed because somebody thought somebody else's abs were flawless. As long as you're seeking validation from somebody who is inherently never going to give it is as long as you're withholding yourself from someone who will love you regardless.

05. You're supposed to be embarrassed of your younger self—really.

It's a mark of progress. (It doesn't mean you have to stay embarrassed, though.) It's good because it means you're able to look back and wonder, "How was I ever at that place?" indicating that you're no longer there. I hope you never reach a point in which you look back on your younger self and think, "Wow, I had it all figured out!" That means you stopped growing. (And that means you stopped living.)

06. There are overarching problems and then there are the symptoms of those problems that crop up again and again.

Most people spend their whole lives only addressing the latter. For example: Losing weight isn't going to fix your body-image problem, no matter how much you convince yourself you're doing the right thing. You're doing what will make you fit into your perception of "correct" as opposed to realizing that genuine body love doesn't have your mental stability hinging on whether or not you miss a class or eat a piece of pizza. It is a matter of evaluating not how the actions look on the surface, but where they are rooted. I'm not saying addressing those roots is easy or finding them fun—I'm saying you'll have to do it eventually. You can choose to now, or you will be forced to later.

07. There is no fear or worry or concern or paranoia or insecurity that you could possibly muster up that a million and five other humans haven't already felt.

The thing about self-loathing is that it's isolating in nature. It makes you the "other" and everybody else the "judgy normal people." I know this may be a little disheartening for your ego, but take it in stride: Generally speaking (and acknowledging logical exceptions), there is nothing you've ever done that hasn't been done before—somewhere, somehow, at some time. The story of the human condition is universal in nature. It's the separation and thought that we're the only ones experiencing it that intensifies the suffering element of that. (Interesting how that works, right?)

08. At any given time, you're mostly just concerned with how one or (maybe two) people perceive you.

Those people also tend to be the ones who we feel unaccepted by in one way or another. We're trying to prove something. We're worried about who will see us in an unflattering way and report it back to them. They're usually the almost-relationships, slightly disapproving parents, certain someones who we've dreamt of impressing for years on end. We're incapable of having our lives revolve around more than a few people at a time, even if it seems like we're worried about "people" as a whole. Try to put a face to that worry every time one crops up and you'll find that the faceless crowd of people is really just one or two who are very, very familiar to you.

09. Nobody is thinking about you as much as you are thinking about you.

So much of our internal conversations with ourselves revolve around quelling fear and panic about how we're being perceived at any given time. What we seldom realize is that the X factor here is that we're thinking through other people's mindsets. We're just making predictions and assumptions which are heavily if not entirely influenced by our own assumptions of ourselves. To put it shortly: Everybody else is

254

running around worrying about themselves as much as you are worrying about yourself.

10. There's too much at stake...
    ...to waste your time on worrying about things that are impermanent, unimportant, and ultimately just distractions from the things that bring you joy.

11. Your feelings of panic are directly related to wanting to change yourself to fit someone else's idea of who you are.
    If you didn't care to please someone else, if you didn't feel you needed to be okay with them to be okay, you wouldn't be worried about it. That sense of panic and concern with how they see you at all is directly, albeit not entirely, related to how much you feel you need to change or prove yourself otherwise. On a deeper level, it means you've externalized your sense of worth and purpose and therefore stability, and so long as it remains that way, it can never be genuine.

12. So if you want to get over these external, surface-level, shallow things, you have to turn your attention to things that matter more.

This is the truest solution and most effective antidote and secret of all secrets to renouncing your sense of whether or not you're going to be okay with yourself: Make something matter more than how other people see you. If all you have to care about, if all you think you can offer the world is a nice body or a fancy lifestyle or a lot of money or approval that makes you feel good, you're not doing everything you can and should be. Of course you're going to run into anxiety; it's all meaningless. The moment you know you're worth more than how you're seen, the moment you genuinely take stock in the notion that your life is more important than you, is the moment that everybody else's petty concerns fall to the wayside into the oblivion of unimportance. You become blind to them because you're only focused on what really does matter: you and whatever the hell you have to genuinely offer to the world.

10 QUESTIONS
TO ASK YOURSELF
when you don't know
WHERE YOUR LIFE
SHOULD GO NEXT

01. If you had the life you think you want, what would tomorrow be like? When you imagine the life you want, rather than focus on the elevator speech ("I am this, I do this..."), focus on the daily routine. If you had the life you think you want, what would you do tomorrow? How different would it be from what you're doing now? What from that vision can you actually start doing tomorrow?

02. If social media didn't exist, what would you do differently? Would you dress differently, feel bad about where you live, care about what your apartment looks like? What choices would you make if you didn't feel they were being silently policed by the faceless mob of people that lie behind the screens of social media? What would matter? What would you do? Who would you be?

03. If nobody would know what you did with the rest of your life, what would you do? If your life wasn't the slightest bit performative—if there was nothing you could get from doing something other than just the act of doing it, how would you spend your time? What would you be interested in doing? What would energize you?

04. If you died yesterday, what would you most regret? Forget imagining if you died tomorrow...what if you were already dead? What would you regret the most? What would you wish you had done differently, saw differently, responded to differently?

05. If you could choose five things that matter most to you, what would they be? Whether you realize it or not, your life will fundamentally be built off of the few things you care about the most. When it's not, it will feel out of alignment at best, or off-the-rails at worst. Fulfillment is living in accordance with what we genuinely value.

06. To what in your life do you feel a subtle, unexplainable "nudge?" What gives you a feeling of subtle, unexplainable enjoyment? What do you like, even though you don't understand why you like it? These are the things to pay attention to. These are the things that are real. Your mind is responding to what you think you like, your emotions are responding to what actually resonates.

07. If you knew nobody would judge you, what would you do with your days? If you would only be praised for your work, for your life, and for your choices—which would you make? What would you do?

08. What are you struggling with the most right now? Interestingly enough, the things that plague you the most deeply are signals toward where you must move next. If your deepest issue is not having a romantic relationship, the next phase of your life will likely need to involve at least trying to develop that. The things that you're struggling with the most right now can tell you what you really want and toward which direction you should step.

09. What do you already have going for you at this present moment? The mantra of any major life change should always be: "Start where you are, use what you have, do what you can." There is no other way to get anywhere.

10. If you had to live tomorrow on repeat for the rest of your life, what would you do? Or, put another way: If you lived today on repeat forever, where would you be? What would you have accomplished? Would you be thriving at work? Would you have made time for the people you love? Would you have written a book, or played music, or be spending your money

in a healthy way? Would you be dressing like yourself, and enjoying the sunrise, and eating in a way that will sustain you over the long-term? Your life exists in its days. Not in your ideas about those days. Your habits accumulate and begin to default. Imagining that you'll never grow out of them is the fastest way to a reality check.

74

THERE'S NO
SUCH THING
AS LETTING GO;
there's just
ACCEPTING
what's already
GONE

All things are good.

All things are ultimately designed to serve us. All things are good.

I know what you're thinking. What the hell? That sounds like just another nonsensical platitude that you're trying to pass off as a truth that cannot possibly be true.

But what is it that makes something "bad?" It's what we've decided (or have been conditioned) to believe "isn't right." What makes a feeling "bad?" We have lots of feelings—why are some good and some bad? Some show us that we're on the right path, and some show us how and when and where we need to redirect. How is the former better than the latter? Isn't the latter actually more important?

Bad feelings become bad when we fight them.

When instead of listening to ourselves, instead of permitting whatever feelings are going to transpire, even if they aren't necessarily comfortable, we fight them—the things that are meant to serve us and show us the parts of ourselves that need to be healed or the places in our paths where we need to take a turn, become "bad."

In the grand scheme of it all, good and bad are value assignments, and they're subjective. To a person, to a family, to a culture, to a country, to a nation, to a race, etc. What's right to one is wrong to another; what's good for someone is tragic for someone else. History isn't taught the same way in classrooms around the world. The second you realize you can define what "good" is in your life is the second you can start to free yourself. Because everything—even the hardest things to get over—can be good, if we choose to see why they're present, what they need to show us.

It's a rare thing to love somebody unconditionally. The very basis of love is finding someone who fills a set of preconceived conditions. When the object of our affection doesn't abide by them as we once thought they would, our feelings begin to falter. That's why the deepest relationships become the hardest—someone fills an idea of what you wanted and needed, and then as soon as they don't, you're absolutely taken aback. You aren't doing what I think you are supposed to be doing; therefore, how could you do this to me?!

This isn't actually loving someone. And the key to getting over that kind of half-assed love is realizing that much of what we fight and fall apart over isn't a matter of whether or not we love someone as a being, as a person, as a presence in our lives—but how much we do or don't approve of what they do for us.

We're finicky that way. We say we want unconditional love and happiness, but we don't behave as though we do. We want love and happiness when we get someone or something. Why? Because it puts the responsibility of choosing happiness, working on it, and toward it on something else.

The first step in regaining your locus of control, your embodiment of self, is to permit all things. Allow the love, allow the loss, allow the ebb and flow. Don't harbor intention; just be. How quickly do even our deepest troubles fade away when we center ourselves on this?

In the Tao, it says that softness is the equivalent of life. Bodies stiffen in death. Trees that harden are cut down. Therefore, hardness is death and softness is life.

When our hearts harden, when parts of us are blocked and filled with unfiltered emotions, we're forced to break them. The trees are chopped, the bodies decay. Hardness can only exist for a time.

The brain has a mechanism where it focuses on the most severe pain and blocks out all the others. It focuses on the hardest part and forces us to face it. Even though it feels like we're dulling all the other pains by focusing and concentrating on one, we're not. We're just furthering ourselves on the path of openness.

There is no such thing as letting go; there's just accepting what's already gone. There's losing ourselves in the labyrinth of the illusion

260

of control and finding joy in the chaos, even when it's uncomfortable. It's not forever. It only remains as long as we hold on. As long as we fight. As long as we control. As long as we don't accept what's already gone.

75

YOU ARE A
BOOK *of* STORIES,
NOT A NOVEL

Who you were doesn't have to bleed into who you will be.

We often stunt ourselves by tying who we were into who we think we need to become. We can't map a trajectory for our futures without considering what would make sense for the people we used to be.

Realizing this was tying together three habits I've picked up about myself, and about people in general:

First, we make problems where there are none. As though for our lives to have meaning, we need to overcome something. Happiness is something that we have to consciously choose; otherwise we'd create the reality that we subconsciously think we deserve. Not because we assume that who we are deserves it, but because somewhere along the line, we were conditioned by other people (and our own assumptions) to believe that we are only as good as the things they said about us.

Second, we avoid things that are too perfect. We destroy them, mentally or otherwise, if they are.

Third, we summarize in our heads. Whenever we're about to make a choice (about anything, really) we say in our heads what that will sound like. "She graduated and started this job at 20..." or however it goes. It's as though our decisions can only be acceptable if they sound right, and how they will continue sounding years down the line, whether or not they are right for who we are in that moment.

But the synopses we spend so much time writing are for characters we no longer are. You cannot always draw lines between what was and what is and what should thenceforth be. You cannot always make sense of your coexisting truths; you can only know that they are both valid. And you cannot avoid good things because somewhere along the line, the character schematic you outlined for yourself doesn't believe it deserves what you have.

When we avoid—when we evade—we cap off our happiness.

You weren't meant to be a story that plays out in a nostalgically pleasing way. Life isn't a sepia-toned flashback. Life is vivid and changing and real and unpredictable. Unchartable. With no plot other than the one we're living in the moment, here and now. We don't even realize how often we choose our current experiences based on old beliefs we are still subconsciously holding of ourselves. Because what we think of ourselves translates into what we allow of ourselves, and what we allow is what we experience, and what we experience is what amounts to our lives as a whole. A whole of which is a book of stories that don't need to seamlessly transition into one another. Which don't have to be narrated the same way. Which can be as short or long or staggered or confusing or exciting as you want.

The point is that you are in control of how it plays out—but the recurring inner narrative, the little voice that's telling you the story of your life, has to let go of the old chapters to genuinely write the new ones.

263

76

EVERYDAY SIGNS
the world is
EXPERIENCING
a shift in
CONSCIOUSNESS

There's a social theory that mankind's development is not a linear progression, but rather, it occurs in cycles. Civilizations rise and then fall; collective intelligence peaks higher each time it does. A brief mental sweep of history and a general understanding of nature would make this seem logical enough—we evolve spectacularly, and then catastrophe strikes.

It didn't come from nowhere. It's an ancient belief that Earth is subject to its position on its procession of the equinox. Each time it reaches the closest point to the center of the universe—where the concentration of energy is highest—we inch closer to awakening. We are currently on the upswing.

Regardless of the mythology, there's something interesting happening in the world today. Our collective consciousness is expanding. We're more aware of what's going on (for better and for worse), we're striving to understand ourselves, we're learning to work with our emotions and build lives that represent what we value, not what we're obligated to. Whatever the cause, here are some of the everyday effects:

01. People are beginning to recognize their power. Self-empowerment, individuality, and autonomy are seen as fundamental to living a whole and fulfilling life.

02. Positive psychology, emotional intelligence, personality typing, and other concepts for self-understanding are becoming increasingly popular. Positive psychology has been having a media heyday over the past 15 years, and between The Big Five, Myers-Briggs, astrology, Enneagrams, and the

like, we are starving for self-awareness, and this is how it's presenting itself.

03. Social justice issues are making headlines like never before, and "ignorance" is being defined as anyone who doesn't consider all beings to be equal. Certainly this is not the first time in history we've wanted to liberate ourselves from oppressive constructs, but with the help of technology, it is the first time that we think of healthy social "norms" as being those that are equal and accepting.

04. Yoga and meditation have become common practices in the West. Whereas just a few decades ago they would have been seen these things as strange, yoga classes are available almost everywhere, and research is showing that meditation actually changes the brain.

05. "Common knowledge" is expanding at a rate untouched before the Internet. Whereas we once only knew as much as we could remember, now we can research virtually anything. Mainstream media has us consuming articles and ideas at record speeds. We're learning in ways we never could before, and faster than we ever could, either.

06. There's a newfound interest in organic foods and homeopathic remedies. People are suddenly concerned about GMOs, antibiotics, and the other plethora of chemicals our foods are being drenched in.

07. Everyone can have a voice. Whereas the only messages that were communicated through media were once curated by a select few gatekeepers, now everybody can speak and share their perspective. For better and for worse, everybody can share what they think, and while it may seem frustrating at times, it is crucial in recognizing where we are collectively.

08. People are questioning the system and learning to think for themselves. While some conversations are more constructive than others, we're theorizing more than we're accepting things as "truth." We are becoming evermore skeptical of major social structures, and with good reason.

09. We're basing relationships on compatibility, not obligation. Gone are the days of marrying and parenting because you're "supposed to." Now, we want compatible life-partners, deliberate childbearing, and happy (non-nuclear) family structures.

10. We're talking about issues that have otherwise gone ignored —depression, sexual abuse, etc.—publicly and honestly. We're slowly removing the shame and stigma around mental illness and abuse and becoming more understanding of those who need help by sharing, relating, teaching, and healing with them.

11. We've just about had it with the employment model as it stands. We recognize that working ourselves to death does not make for a good life, yet we also realize that we are essentially enslaved to capitalism for our survival. While part-time work and freelancing and work-life balance are becoming more popular topics of conversation, the overarching structure still stands.

12. People are becoming more intuitive. As well as empathetic, and curious, and informed, and tolerant of those who are different from them.

13. We're recognizing the imbalance of feminine energy. We're seeing how deliberately femininity has been oppressed in society, and the crucial importance the lost balance serves us in every aspect of life (and society).

14. We're breaking out of the gender binary. We're no longer defining ourselves simply by what we appear to be—it's becoming increasingly more acceptable to discover who you identify as being rather than just accepting who you seem to be on the outside.

15. We're becoming more concerned with the effect we're having on natural climates. We treat the Earth as a thing, not an actual, living entity.

16. We're dealing with the effects of long-suppressed emotions. Over the past five or so years, you've likely been a friend or family member of someone who has gone through radical, intense changes in their life and in their person—if you didn't do so yourself! It wasn't that we came upon hard times and got through it—we came upon hard times and awakened to something deeper.

WHY
do we value
OUR SUFFERING
SO MUCH?

Suffering is a necessary evil.

But its inevitability is not the result of it being something that we naturally have to process out of due course. It's not something we take a passive role in. It is the result of a lack of our own growth; it is a catalyst to signal to us there's more to be done. This is to say, we're in control of it. We cultivate and experience it because we allow it. Rather, we allow the unhealed parts of us to control everything else. If we remain unconscious of this—and that its origin and, therefore, solution is external—we start to believe that we deserve it.

Any one of us can recall instances in which we've unnecessarily ruined a day that was otherwise going well with a flurry of worry and ungrounded paranoia. We start forcing ourselves to panic almost out of necessity. If there's nothing, fill it with something—something we deserve.

Where does that assumption come from, though? It usually has a lot to do with repressed emotions. We accumulate these feelings that we don't accept or deal with and they become the foundation on which we accumulate our beliefs about ourselves. As long as we attach ourselves to an idea of what's "wrong" and then allow ourselves to be conditioned by it (a friend lashing out is an outer projection of what they're dealing with; a failed opportunity usually makes way for a better-suited one), we become conditioned by the idea that we're not good enough. The key is realizing that we do this to ourselves.

We live trapped in the mental structures that we allowed external circumstances to construct, because we never realized we could dismantle them. As soon as we're in a situation that activates one of those memories, taps into an unhealed, unresolved issue, we don't stop to see it objectively; we lash out at what aggravated the problem.

Our pain can't dictate our internal dialogue, and we can't let ourselves run with compulsive, involuntary thoughts. Every time we do this, we allow that emotion to infiltrate our awareness and transmute itself into our current experience. We project what was onto what is.

There's an element of disidentification that has to happen. The realization that what's being experienced isn't a matter of what's at hand, but just a subjective, temporary projection of whatever it is you currently believe—in this case, that you should suffer.

Ironically though, the opposite of pain isn't joy—it's acceptance. Resisting only adds more fuel to the fire. It sets you back to where you were when you initially repressed it. It's not dismantling the structure; it's strengthening it. You permit it by fighting it.

It's hard for us to believe we deserve happiness, and so we continually go out of our way to attract and inflict pain. That dichotomy is natural, and it's human, but there's something to be said for transcending it. If you want to think it's impossible, you'll only continue to suffer because of it. If you want to keep valuing that suffering as something that makes you more human, then so be it—but the reality is that what makes us human is not what destroys us, but what we build ourselves with again.

As Marcus Aurelius has said: Choose not to be harmed, and you won't feel harmed. Don't feel harmed, and you haven't been.

78

WHAT YOU FIND
in SOLITUDE

Loneliness is just an idea.

It is the implication that you are ever disconnected from those around you. It's what happens when you depend on interaction to understand—and be okay with—yourself.

Because interaction has less to do with how other people treat you and more to do with how you perceive yourself based on that treatment. It's not about how many people are actually around us, or giving us love; it's what that love means to us and how it alters our mindset toward whatever it is we're doing or focusing on. Companionship seems like the reinforcement of oneness and connectivity, but it is also the idea that you not only need someone else's presence, but their approval, their acceptance.

You can be more alone in a crowded room and feel more connected in complete solitude.

To the extent that we are separate beings, or to the extent that we are aware that we are separate beings, is how "lonely" we can ever be. Essentially: You are only as alone as you think you are.

Getting past that idea that aloneness is lonely is chiefly important because there is something phenomenally foreign and elusive that you find in that kind of sacred idleness. When you stop working and start being. When you stop defining yourself by the roles you play for other people—and for yourself. You stop seeing yourself within the context of a society. You stop judging yourself by comparison. You start diffusing your mindset of thinking through what would be acceptable to others. You don't just start to hear yourself talk, but you realize that you are a person, hearing a mind.

And you begin to communicate with yourself in ways that are so much deeper, more fathomable, more understandable, than language can ever permit. As Huxley again once said: "In spite of language, in spite of intelligence and intuition and sympathy, one can never really communicate anything to anybody. The essential

271

substance of every thought and feeling remains incommunicable, locked up in the impenetrable strong-room of the individual soul and body. Our life is a sentence of perpetual solitary confinement."

This is not a bad thing, though.

It shows you who you are because you're no longer being someone else to someone else. You are only to yourself. You stop behaving to fit a standard and start acting for the sake of survival, of being alive, of humanness. You don't realize how much of your daily life, how many of your rote actions, are contrived solely by the means of being "acceptable" to the world around you, and how much these actions that are not founded in genuineness can disconnect you from yourself.

Solitude is the most important practice of all. It grounds you in what is and helps you escape from what you think should be. It is both infuriating and freeing for just that reason: It leaves you alone to see who you are and what you do; more importantly, it leaves you alone to see the real essence of what it is to be a person, the good, the bad, the downright odd and ugly. It leaves you no choice but to contemplate the bigger picture, the underlying reasoning, the way things are.

The only time we see the whole structure clearly is when we step away from it.

79

HOW TO RAISE
A GENERATION
OF KIDS
who don't have
A PROBLEM
WITH ANXIETY

Most people don't think they're obsessed with controlling their emotions because they aren't consciously thinking about their feelings. Instead, they are thinking about everything else that needs to be "right" so that they don't have to feel at all.

They imagine their worst nightmares to life. They worry incessantly about how much money they have to make to be "successful," how much food they must constrict to maintain their size, the minutiae of how other people respond to them so that they may behave in a way that makes them likable. They think about their social media presence, whether or not something is "right" for them, how nice their home appears to be.

They use fear to police themselves into being "good."

We don't think of these things as emotional control because they are the physical or mental parts of our lives. Yet we don't control the physical things in our lives when we can't control our emotions; we control the physical things in our lives to control our emotions. We think that if we find a "soul mate," we can't get heartbroken, if we're attractive, we'll be respected, if other people think of us fondly, we'll always think of ourselves that way, too.

As anyone who struggles with heightened or irrational emotions can tell you, the root of most anxiety and panic is a fear of experiencing anxiety and panic.

We deny our feelings not by refusing to feel them, but by using other things to try to avoid them. When we are obsessed with trying to control outcomes and reduce risks and ensure that we do not experience anything "bad," we are not living whole lives. We are fragmented selves, expressing only the parts we are momentarily comfortable with.

We don't control the physical things in our lives when we can't control our emotions; we control the physical things in our lives to control our emotions. We think that if we find a "soul mate," we can't get heartbroken, if we're attractive, we'll be respected, if other people think of us fondly, we'll always think of ourselves that way, too.

This emotional disassociation begins in childhood, as the product of being punished for "bad" feelings. Children do not know how to self-regulate their emotions. They don't understand them, and like the way they don't understand how their bodies work, or what it means to have manners at the dinner table, or treat others with respect, they must be taught, yet very often, they are not.

Instead, kids are taught that acting out will get them punished, and so begins the cycle of suppression. They learn that their parents will love them more when they are "good," they shut down the parts of themselves they fear are unacceptable.

What they are responding to is a lack of feeling loved. What they are wired to chase is their parents' love. If it is not being given naturally, they will try to manipulate how the parent sees them so it is created. Unfortunately, in this process, they disassociate from a crucial part of themselves.

And this is how they evolve into panicked, judgmental, anxious adults who cannot function in relationships. This is how they learn that it's crucial to control everything around them—if they don't trigger a feeling, they don't have to deal with it.

The way we raise adults who don't struggle with anxiety is by being adults who accept anxiety. We must be the voice of reason that they do not have yet. The voices they hear from us—especially in their most fearful and vulnerable moments—will become the voices in their heads someday. The way we raise adults who don't struggle with anxiety is by being adults who are loving and kind and nonjudgmental. Kids do not do what we tell them; they do what we do. If we want the world to change, we have to change ourselves. If we want to inspire them to cope with their feelings, we must learn to cope with our own.

274

And right now, we have the very unique privilege of learning how. Without the emotional intelligence to cope with anxiety, we have the opportunity to consciously grow to understand it. We have the potential to give our kids and their kids and the kids after that the gift of self-knowledge, but it can only come from giving it to ourselves first. (Ain't that how it always goes?)

the idiot's guide
TO EMOTIONAL
INTELLIGENCE:
WHY WE NEED PAIN

Pleasure cannot cure pain. This is one of the largest psychological misconceptions out there. Pleasure cannot cure pain because they exist on opposite ends of the same spectrum. Biologically, both our pleasure and pain responses are headquartered in the same part of the brain. The "pleasure chemical" that brings us joy is involved in the pain response as well. Alan Watts says that is the price we pay for increasing our consciousness. Simply: We cannot be more sensitive to one emotion and not also then experience the others to the same degree.

You know how people say that if you didn't have rainy days, you wouldn't be able to appreciate the sunny ones? The truth is that if you didn't have rainy days, the sunny ones wouldn't exist. This is called duality. We live in duality. We exist because of duality. That sounds like a buzzword, but this a very important thing to understand. Our bodies exist in duality: our lungs, hearts, gonads, they all function because they have an opposite and equal half. The same is true of nature: It sustains itself through a cycle of creation and destruction, as does human life. It's important to understand that we are not separate from the anatomy of the universe. There is no good without bad, high without low, or life without pain. The problem is not the presence of pain. It's the inability to see the purpose of it.

We believe that "happiness" is the sustained state of feeling "good." It is because of this belief that we are not happy. Happy people are not people who "feel good" all the time; they are the people who are able to be guided by their negative emotions rather than paralyzed by them.

Happiness is not about "how good you feel," but why you feel it. A life built on meaning and purpose feels good, though so does a life built on greed and selfishness. Yet one is better than the other. Why? Greed and selfishness are quintessential traits of someone seeking a high to eliminate pain. Meaning and purpose-driven work or ideologies are traits of people who have accepted their pain and have chosen to work with—not against—it. The former is destructive and unfulfilling. The latter is more difficult, but worthwhile.

Our pain serves us. It is a crucial, guiding force. Suffering begins to thrive when we don't listen to it. Imagine what happens when you place your hand on a burning stove. You feel pain because your body is signaling for you to move your hand before it disintegrates. Our emotional lives are no different, except for the fact that we understand the consequence of keeping our hand on the stove. We do not yet understand the consequence of what our emotional pain is guiding us from.

We see pain as being in opposition to our well-being rather than a key component in creating it.

The first thing that's required to fix this is understanding that we don't inherently want to avoid pain. In fact, a lot of what we think we want is not what we want at all. (Some of the most emotionally empty and unfulfilled people are those we idolize for being rich, or "successful.")

Next, it's shifting our goals from wanting to transcend the pain to aiming for a more neutral emotional pH. Some call this "shifting the baseline." We usually avoid the actual work of adjusting our mental/emotional receptivity because doing so eliminates the possibility of attaining the external "high." We think we're giving up on the dreams and hopes we assumed would make us feel incredible. In reality, what we are giving up is simply the illusion that those things will bring sustained happiness, in favor of a shift in perception, which actually will.

In the absolute simplest terms possible, we call this peace: when neither the desire for a high or the suppression of the low is present. When you've shifted your baseline from "survive" to "thrive" and have detached from outcomes, you can enjoy what each day brings.

Once you step out from the endless race of chasing elusive happiness, you realize that you were never running toward something better, you were just trying to outrun yourself. You will also realize that it was only because of pain that you were able to understand this. Your pain lined the pathway; it was guiding you to that understanding all along.

81

EVERY
RELATIONSHIP
you have is
WITH YOURSELF

It's interesting enough that human beings are the only (known) species that have relationships with themselves, but it's even more to consider the fact that human beings are the only species that have relationships with themselves through other people.

That is: Our perceptions of other people's mindsets largely dictate how we see ourselves.

What binds us in love, in companionship, in friendship? Familiarity. The sense that you understand each other at a visceral level. It's just being able to see yourself in someone else, and more importantly, being able to change your inner narrative when you know, see, and feel that someone else loves and accepts and approves of you no matter what. Ergo: You can do the same. (It's a survival mechanism, I'm pretty sure.)

The most meaningful relationships tend to be the ones in which we're completely reflected back to ourselves, because this is what relationships serve to do: open us. We only recognize this in the big, overwhelming, usually heart-wrenching ones, but it's true of every relationship. And it's the crux of our issues beyond basic survival: how we are in relation to other people. How we are in relation to ourselves.

The relationships we tend to be most happy in are the ones in which we adopt that other person's supposed narrative—what we think they think of us.

We feel most loved when we feel understood, when we are thinking that someone else is thinking in alignment with what we need to hear and believe. We feel most loved when we think someone thinks highly of us—their efforts and displays of affection serving to prove this.

This is why not just anybody can affirm for us that we're okay, only people to whom we've placed meaning. Someone to whom we already feel a physical or psychological connection. Someone we are looking at as a partner for ourselves, someone who is like us, someone who understands us.

It's why "loving yourself first" is the most common, the most confusing, and yet the most profoundly solid advice anyone can give. Because it's not really about feeling love for yourself; it's being able to feel stable enough that your mindset doesn't rest in the narrative of a supposed other's.

This is why things hurt so badly when we identify with them. All hatred is self-hatred. This is why we become so goddamned heartbroken. We cannot lose people; we can only lose ourselves in an idea of them. We decided how we felt about ourselves through them—for better and for worse—so when we perceive that their mindset changes from loving us to loving someone else, our own stability goes out the window, too.

The most freeing, liberating thing you can do is to realize that we are all a collective one and that each fragment of a bigger light refracts on one another in just a way that reveals what you need to see and understand, but that the light is always your own. Every relationship you have is with yourself. Every person in whom you feel you return "home" to is just coming back to yourself.

It's always yourself you find at the end of the journey. The sooner you face you, the less you need other people to fill voids. (You cannot squeeze someone into your brokenness and expect that to make you whole.) The sooner you face you, the sooner other people's actions don't affect you negatively—your mindset doesn't depend on them. You don't depend on them. Relationships do not serve to give you eternal, perpetual happiness. They serve to make you more aware. The sooner you realize that said awareness is your own, the easier everything else is.

82

15 LITTLE WAYS
to deepen your
RELATIONSHIP
WITH ANYONE

01. Spend a Sunday with them. Not a Saturday night, when everything is bustling and loud and socially seamless. Spend a Sunday morning with them, tired and hung over and without plans for the day. Eat breakfast together and don't fix your hair. Experience each other without needing to entertain.

02. Be comfortably silent. Go for a long drive and allow for bouts of quietness as they naturally happen. Existing in someone's silence is existing in the most intimate part of their life.

03. Call them when you're not okay. Take them up on the promise to be there for you no matter what. Tell them the truth. Let them comfort and console you. Tell them that you're there for them if they ever need it. Hold true to that promise.

04. Hold space for them. Listen to what they have to say wholly. Without anticipating your response, without checking your phone, without wandering eyes. Give them the entirety of your energy. There is nothing more precious and sacred and rare.

05. Talk about ideas. What you believe in. What you theorize about existence or what fate could have in store for you in the next five years. Just move beyond discussing people and events and petty, daily grievances.

06. Read each other's favorite books. Trade your personal copies —the ones that are highlighted and marked up, where the binding is almost completely breaking loose from having been flipped through so many times. Share with them something that opened your heart and fed your mind.

07. Create something together. Start a little business or work on a story or paint pictures for fun. Go on a service trip or build a coffee table or redecorate your respective kitchens. Do something where you team up for a greater cause.

08. Pay attention to the little things. Notice what they're often most bothered by, what their favorite flavor of ice cream is. Know their Taco Bell order so you can surprise them with it. Not everybody is naturally detail-oriented, so make it an intention to be. People appreciate it more than you realize.

09. Attend your respective religious/spiritual services/practices together. For the sake of understanding, go to their church service one Sunday, or show them how you meditate, or ask them what they believe and why. Let them be your guide through something you otherwise wouldn't know. There is something absolutely extraordinary in learning about someone else's culture or dogma or lifestyle, in practicing what it means to lovingly coexist.

10. Plan a short trip. It doesn't have to be elaborate or expensive. Explore a neighboring city for a day or go for a hike. Plan in advance so you have something to look forward to.

11. Integrate them in your other social circles. Merge your friends together for a wine night, no matter how deeply you're convinced they'll have nothing in common. There's something so intimate and special about gathering all the separate parts of your life in one place.

12. Always show up. To their baby showers and art exposés and graduations and moving days. Not because that's what "good friends/boyfriends/girlfriends do," but because that's what you do when you care about someone else's happiness as much as you do your own.

13. Plan your heart-to-hearts. The older you get, the more inconvenient it becomes to talk until 3 a.m. (There's work to do and groceries to buy and parents to call and you get the picture.) So plan ahead if you must. Decide to have a

sleepover and keep the next day open so you can stay up and sleep in and relive your middle school glory days.

14. Talk about your families and what it was like growing up. It's one thing to meet your friend/boyfriend/girlfriend's relatives, but it's quite another to hear the whole story, the reality, the not-ready-for-company-imperfect-picture of what they experienced. This isn't a call to needlessly air the dirty laundry, but rather understand that you won't really know somebody unless you understand the truth of their foundation.

15. Be filterless. Don't mince your words or tailor your opinions or only present the side of you that you feel is "acceptable." If they don't want the whole of you, the truth of who you are, they're not right for you anyway. And more importantly, people can sense genuineness and will subconsciously take it as a cue that they're free to be who they really are as well.

83

LET YOURSELF
BE HAPPIER
than you think
YOU DESERVE

If all great things are done by a series of small things put together, then great lives are created by a series of small moments put together, most of which we miss out on because we're writing the synopsis rather than the paragraphs of the chapters.

It's as though we live to write our eulogies. We get degrees and spouses and desire storylines and unfolding fates that make sense and flow well and ultimately write beautiful and admirable stories, but only ones that we will ever tell ourselves. We're never actually remembered for more than who we were and who we loved and how we lived in a moment-to-moment sense. The rest—the big, overarching, milestone kind of things don't matter, and maybe they never did.

We miss the moments because we're distracted. Distracted by the one person we search for in a crowd, fearing they're there, even when they're hours and states and other impossibilities away. By the someone who is always on our minds when we're writing or creating or choosing or riding the train or falling asleep—and we behave as though they are with us, and narrate our lives by what they'd say and feel and think if they were with us, though we know we'd never know that.

There's always one daunting task, always one to-do list that fails to include anything surrounding what we actually want to do. Not for work, not for the credit, not out of responsibility, but just because we want to be happy. Always one more promotion, one more move, one more great love to find before we can be happy.

But we aren't. We don't choose. We don't think we deserve it. We keep searching, and we keep narrating, and we keep living as though we have a tomorrow to live out all these grand fantasies and promises to ourselves, when the reality is that unless we stop today we'll live forever on the promise of tomorrow. These are daydreams. They're visions and hopes and issues that don't exist. The minute you start thinking of the past or future, realize that it's only a thought of a thing, a thought that's happening in a now. A now that we're missing.

Tomorrow never changes us. Our jobs never change us. Our relationships don't, either. Our problems change as the things in our lives do. The issues we take are reflections of what's wrong with us, the people we hate reflections of our insecurities. No matter how many things come and go, we take the same issues and hate the same people for the same reasons, and never stop to realize that it's not them that we hate; it's the parts of us they force us to recognize.

You have to stop living for how other people will remember you. Stop living by telling yourself the story that you think other people will be happy reading. Because it's an empty and lifeless one, and it robs you of the thing you're most seeking when you do it. The most important thing is that you do what makes you happy—and that you understand that your happiness is your choice and your responsibility alone. It is not a day or a job or a relationship or a change away, it's right now. The only work to do is to remove the blocks that prevent you from living it out. The only change that has to happen is to you.

The untold millions of little moments are what matter. It's not about having a job; it's about having a life that you want to live. It's not about having a degree; it's about the nights you finally felt the opposite of loneliness. It's not about having a relationship; it's about being in one. And it's not about living a life that other people can sum up comfortably; it's about having a life wherein those millions of moments build and corroborate with one another—and you follow them—and have more. You won't be there to hear the stories and eulogies they tell of you—you're only here to know them now.

84

HOW TO THINK
for yourself:
AN 8-STEP GUIDE

Most of the thoughts you experience in a day are not unique or self-generated. Our minds are like computer programs: They seek out, repeat, and believe what they are told to.

 Few people recognize how deeply their thinking is conditioned, and they assume their thoughts and subsequent feelings are a part of who they are (and so they defend them, passionately). Learning to think for yourself is something you must consciously choose, and very few people do. Here are a few steps to guide you through it, assuming you dissect one idea (or opinion) at a time:

01. Decipher the origin of the opinion. Recall the first time you experienced it.

    For example, if you remember being in second grade and hearing a parent say that anybody who isn't pro-life is a murderer, you probably had a very strong reaction to it, being all of seven years old. Figuring out the origin of your thoughts, ideas, and beliefs shows you how often they are not your own realization or discovery, but someone else's imposition.

02. Determine whether or not your evidence is based in emotion or reason.

    What are the supporting arguments for your opinion or idea? If they are emotion-based, are the feelings yours or someone else's? If neither, what are the facts that inform your belief?

03. Ask yourself who the opinion benefits.

    Is it anybody (or anything) but either you or the general good of humankind?

04. Consider why opposing ideas could be valid.

This is probably the most crucial part, and yet very few people have the wherewithal to consider and discuss opposing ideas without feeling absolutely enraged. (It's what happens when we identify with our thoughts too deeply.) Regardless, seriously sit down and try to understand the logic, reason, or fear of opposing opinions without passing judgment.

05. Recognize why you feel the way you do about it.
Unless you are a trained expert on the topic, any strong emotions that accompany your opinion on it are usually strictly personal (and therefore keep you away from being objective and realistic). It would take years and an extraordinary amount of research (at the level of Ph.D. candidacy) to be in a position to truly understand a nuanced issue enough to have an extremely strong feeling about it.

06. Research.
If you are as passionate as you claim to be about a particular idea, research it and make sure your ideas aren't unfounded. Then follow a few reputable newspapers, unbiased news sources, and research centers to keep yourself up to date with what's being discovered and discussed in the world.

07. Ask yourself what the outcome would be if everybody in the world thought the way you do.
It's the best way to determine whether or not an idea only benefits your ego.

08. Envision your most actualized self: What would they think, if not this?

Imagining what your best self would say about an issue is a pretty good way to determine what you should shift your mindset toward.

287

85

THE VERY
IMPORTANT
REASON WHY
we choose to
LOVE PEOPLE
who cannot
LOVE US BACK

The purpose of a relationship is not to be loved perfectly, or forever. It is not to have our every whim and wish met and fulfilled. It is not to be completed, or to have our minds and hearts fueled by the hormonal stimulation we think is the feeling of love. The purpose of a relationship is not the universe's way of saying, "You're worthy, and here's someone to prove it."

The purpose of a relationship is to see ourselves completely. It is to see the parts of ourselves that we are otherwise unconscious of. The purpose of a relationship is to infuriate and overjoy and destroy us so we can see what angers us, what thrills us, and where we need to give ourselves love. The purpose of a relationship is not to fix us, or heal us, or to make us whole and happy; it is to show us where we need fixing and what parts of us are still broken, and perhaps the most brutal of all: that nobody can do this work, or make us happy, but ourselves.

We choose to love people who cannot love us back to teach ourselves that we are, in fact, worthy of being loved back. We choose these people because they represent the parts of us that we don't love—why else would we waste our time on people who don't return our affection? We choose to love these people because they are the only ones with whom we share an intimate connection deep enough that it can awaken and illuminate the darkest corners of ourselves, and they are the only ones who can leave and let us do what we are here to do: resolve and actualize and heal them on our own.

It is not the nature of love that people struggle with, but what it is designed to do. Most of our turmoil simply comes from never having been told that love will keep breaking our hearts until they open, and that we will be the ones throwing ourselves in again and again.

Our life partners are the people who come after the love that opens us. Our big loves are the loves that emerge after we think we've lost them already. They come after we're ready, after we've already cleared out the damage and debris, only after we've learned what it means to love ourselves. It is in this we realize that love is sharing what we already have, not relying on someone else to give us something to supplement. It is in this we realize how crucial it was to love the people who could not love us back. They were never meant to, and the rest only depends on how long it takes us to realize this.

86

NOT EVERYBODY
WILL LOVE YOU
in a way you
UNDERSTAND

So much of the tension that turns to friction and so much of the friction that creates the fault lines that erupt in our relationships has to do with the ways we perceive love, the ways we expect it, and how the love we think we deserve does or doesn't match up to what we get and, oftentimes, give.

For a lot of people, it's not about whether or not they're in love with someone; it's the nuances that come along with being in love. It's how they're in love with them. It's the ounce of uncertainty we're told we shouldn't have. The notion that they're so young. That someone without such-and-such an issue could come along and be better than what they have now. That there is better out there. The ex who's more convenient, the distance, the fear of commitment. The timing, the distractions, the impulse to try something else.

And every last one of us can admit to knowing what it's like to be circling through these notions, trapped between loving someone and wanting to choose otherwise.

The problem is that we seldom realize that the heart is not a one-time-expended thing. You can't put someone in it and expect that to heal the scarred contours. You have to realize that often, the struggle is that we leave, even though we love them, and we fight, even though we love them, and we do wrong by them, even though we love them, and it's not because we don't love them enough, but that all of these things can coexist within us, and the presence of one love doesn't make another go away. But it doesn't heal the hurt at its root, either. It can just mask it for a little bit.

We can expect that our hearts are able to hold more than one thing, more than one person, more than one feeling—but we cannot expect that they'll all coexist perfectly. Love grows, and it grows you from the inside out. It expands you, but the expansion doesn't eliminate whatever else was there beforehand.

So it doesn't always look the way we think it should. There are hidden spaces and depths within us, and love sometimes comes out differently when it creates the echo of going through those parts of us as well.

Some people love silently. Some love without ever realizing they're in love—love doesn't look loving at all. It's masked by fear, forced into remission, and acted on in bouts of anger and disappointment. Sometimes it's not being able to look at someone after they're gone, sometimes it's not being able to stop, and most times it's not being able to tell them either way. It sometimes comes out punishing like the parents who try to force us into compliance, not realizing that you cannot shame people into changing. That their expression of anger is a mechanism of their ego, not of their love. We are not inherently whole once we've found another person to fit into us. Nobody can do that for us. We have to fill those spaces ourselves.

So sometimes it goes misunderstood. But the comfort is in knowing that it's not what we misunderstand about love as much as it is about how we let the misunderstanding open and expand us. You let the love, and all the twisted ways it's morphed and sullied, push you into transforming yourself and your life out of necessity. You eventually realize it was love that created you, not the pain that is the byproduct of lost love. And it wasn't the love someone didn't give; it was the love you had to find in yourself.

The only matter is that we let love do what it's supposed to: give us more of it, even—and probably especially—when it means we have to take it for ourselves. Sometimes we choose people to show us the hidden parts of ourselves. Sometimes we choose people who we know will hurt us. Sometimes it's the only way we can be acquainted with our inner beings, and even though we don't understand it, it's often the most honest, beautiful way we love ourselves, too.

87

HOW TO TAME
your inner
DEMONS

I used to think that taming your inner demons was a matter of transcending them. I used to believe that the gnawing notion of "not good enough" would be silenced when I was able to move past my mind's eye, because of course, our inner demons do not base their case in reality.

Our inner demons strike us at our sore spots. They recite to us all the things that we fear people will interpret us to be. They keep us stuck in the place where what other people perceive is reality, though of course, those perceptions are extensions of those people, and these ones are ours.

I thought they would dissolve as soon as I stopped looking at my life analytically and started going through the motions as the person experiencing my thoughts and feelings, not the person who is my thoughts and feelings. But what I came to realize is that every part of you must work in tandem. And as soon as I needed to do something requiring thought and process, I was back to square one.

It's nothing to get over and it's nothing to disregard. It's only something to acknowledge and understand and then cultivate differently. Because mindset is a cultivation, and to that end, it is ultimately a choice. We can change it. If we don't, we will remain at the whim of other people's actions and our own irrational gremlins that do nothing but prevent us from living out what we know to be true. And when these two forces collide and disrupt one another, we'll find ourselves in the pits of anxiety and depression, because something is trying to make its way out of us, and something else is preventing it from doing so.

The antidote here is awareness. As soon as you realize your thought is coming from a place of irrationality and fear, you've taken a step toward silencing it. As soon as you discover that you don't have to listen to that voice and that you are not that voice, you no longer have to be controlled by it.

You'll start to understand that having self-doubt is human. Irrational fears are, too. There's no part of this that's weird or strange or wrong. It's simply nature. But if we want to step beyond it, we have to reach beyond it and start choosing. Choosing what we consume, how we structure our days, and what we give our time to. What we assign value and meaning to, and how much.

Our natural, default setting isn't the one we have to operate on for the rest of our lives. The longer we stay in allowing ourselves to be completely overtaken by every deprecating thought that runs through our minds, we'll continue to cement ourselves beneath those beliefs, and they'll become real.

Because this isn't about believing that one day, we'll never have passing thoughts of judgment toward ourselves. This isn't about thinking we'll ever not care what other people think, even just a little. These aspects of humanness are universal and unchanging and programmed for a reason. But those reasons have little to do with us finding happiness. And we have to make the choice for ourselves. We'll never not care and we'll never not hear them. It's only a matter of whether or not we'll act based on them.

293

WHY WE REJECT
positive THINKING

A large reason why people write off self-help or positive psychology as "fluff" is because of how impossible it seems to accomplish. Positive thinking seems simple enough, so why is it that we have such a difficult time with it?

Well, the answer is simple, and it's not: There's a lot of subconscious bias against positive thinking, and that accumulates after long periods of time reinforcing your negative beliefs. To shift to a more positive mindset requires getting past that first period of angry disbelief. Here, a few other reasons why we reject positivity:

01. We see it as naïve.

    We falsely associate "negativity" with "depth," and so to be aware of the negative (or to be unenthused, under-emotional or passive) is to also be "cool." (This is why we think of the "cool kids" in school as not caring much.)

02. We're constantly reinforcing our subconscious belief in the negative.

    The very nature of personal belief is "that which experience has proven true to us." This is impossible, however, when we are subconsciously seeking out evidence to support the negative ideas we are constantly entertaining.

03. We are more inherently fascinated by the negative in the world because we do not understand it.

Because we do not understand the purpose or reason for pain and negativity, we find it unknown and mysterious, therefore, more crucial to attend to. We're fascinated by the intensity of something we don't understand, so we end up fueling it more and more simply by paying attention to it.

THE PHILOSOPHY
OF NON-RESISTANCE:
THE DIFFERENCE
between
"GOING WITH
THE FLOW"
and becoming
A DOORMAT

When the Western Zen renaissance began in the 50s (a movement to which many have credited Alan Watts's work for inspiring) it was a manifestation aligned precisely what ancient teachings hoped and intended for humanity: to adopt it into our lifestyle. Yet an essence got lost in translation. We began to interpret spirituality from the perspective of the ego when it was not designed for that, and we do not realize we are doing it because it is the only thing we know.

Take, for example, the concept of non-resistance. From our understanding, it is the process of consciously releasing expectations and attachments to outcomes (which the Taoists argue is the root of all suffering).

Yet we don't really know what it means to be non-resistant, so we regard it as a sort of "ego surrender," where our idea of "letting go" spirals into "surrounding control of life and simply allowing whatever, no matter how terrible!" This is how the misperception that spirituality is passive and lazy is born.

The way that non-resistance was intended to be practiced was by striking a fine balance between what you can and cannot control in your life. To put it metaphorically, it is to steer the ship along with the current, not against it. It does not mean to surrender all control or effort, it simply means to wield it more wisely.

This is such an exemplary way to characterize the nature of the ego, but as tradition would teach, the ego is not "bad" (that is another

Western stereotype). The ego serves an absolutely crucial purpose; it is simply a matter of recognizing that and surrendering to it, rather than our fear and lack of awareness. In this case, it is realizing that the path of non-resistance does not call for us to completely surrender to "whatever" happens in life. Rather, it is to be discerning about how we exert control and realize the fact that the "current" is more powerful than we are. We can either stage a fight we'll always lose or let ourselves be carried.

90

YOU HAVE TO
BE KINDEST TO
YOURSELF
when it seems
LEAST DESERVED

We believe that being cruel to ourselves is a self-preservation tactic. We pick out our flaws because we are survivalists by nature. We have an itch to be aware of what other people could deem unworthy and insufficient. So we dwell on every possible flaw someone could rip apart and use against us. But it never makes us stronger. It doesn't make us immune to someone doing so simply because we got there first. Believing what other people could say before they say it doesn't give us a defense against it.

You have to stop believing that you need other people's permission to be okay with yourself. That however you do or don't align with what other people value determines your worth. That however the world does or doesn't show you kindness is a direct reflection of how much you deserve it. You have to be kind to yourself. Even, and probably most especially, when it seems least deserved.

Telling ourselves everything other people could possibly use against us doesn't numb us to it. It only makes us believe we are worth those words and that those accusations would be valid. Besides, there are so many variables to whether or not someone will grace you with their approval and praise that it's nearly impossible to blanket over everyone and everything completely and universally. And that's what's required if validation is to be sought: certainty. The exact kind we can't find in ourselves.

But people's opinions, especially negative ones, largely stem from what they know they don't have and can't do. You eventually have to stop basing your self-worth on the insecurities of others and start basing it on your own genuine convictions, no matter how long it takes for you to find them. I always knew that my belief that I wasn't worth it wasn't the reason I played my own antagonist. My fear of being hurt by other people was.

The only way you can ever really heal or find some sense of genuine contentment is in narrating your life as someone who loves you would. Because you should love you. So today, while I was getting down on myself for something writing-related (because that's how life works sometimes), I was about to text my one friend who always encourages me and tells me to keep going, but I realized: Why can't I tell myself what she's going to say? Why do I have to wait for someone else to give me those words? It's not that I shouldn't appreciate her encouragement, but why do I value the thoughts and opinions of other people more than I do my own?

It's a shift of mindset. In that respect, it's a choice. It's choosing to get help, to move away, to end a relationship, to rekindle one again. It's feeding yourself and making sure you get enough sleep. It's tenderly, constantly reminding yourself that you are going to be okay; not because you're delusional, not because that's what everyone says, but because "okay" is where we all end up. Not because anybody else tells us that we will. But because we find it on our own and learn to believe it for ourselves.

91

THE 15 MOST
COMMON
types of
DISTORTED
THINKING

To think well is to think objectively and factually. The human brain is wired to affirm itself; we are programmed to find evidence that supports what we most want to believe. Unless our subconscious is clear, it's how we create our most compelling convictions. If we were raised believing we are social outcasts, we're always seeking out evidence that we are, in fact, disliked by peers.

Like most things, distorted thinking tends to happen in patterns. We aren't alone in the things that most deeply plague or fascinate or panic us, and in fact, you'll probably find comfort in the fact that there are terms for them. In 1981, Dr. Matthew McKay, Dr. Martha Davis, and Patrick Fanning outlined exactly what these are[17] and how they tend to manifest.

Here, 17 of the most prominent types of distorted thinking:

01. Filtering. Filtering is choosing to have a selectively informed perspective. It is to take the negative details of a situation and magnify them while filtering the positive aspects out. Picking out a single detail and coloring entire events by it isolates "good" and "bad" experiences from one another, and therefore, they become larger and more awful (or better) than they are in reality.

02. Polarization. The hallmark of distortion is a hyper-reliance on dichotomies. Things are either good or bad, right or wrong, and no in-between. It is to perceive everything within extremes and be closed to a middle ground. This tends to manifest most strongly in self-perceptions: You're either perfect or you're a failure.

299

03. Overgeneralization. You come to conclusions based on a single piece of evidence or a single experience. If something bad happens once, out of fear that it will happen again, you expect it so you can "prepare" for it. The language this kind of thinking usually entails is the use of "always" or "never" to illustrate a problem. This kind of distortion can lead to a restricted life, as you avoid experiences because you gauge failure on a single event or instance.

04. Mind-reading. You assume to know what people are feeling and why they act the way they do, especially when it comes to how they feel about you. This is usually due to your own projections and biases. You can only comprehend that people feel the way you would and respond the way you do to certain situations, simply because you aren't familiar with anything else.

05. Catastrophizing. You always assume that the absolute worst will happen. It is to take random circumstances and to imagine they are indicative of the most disastrous outcome. It is a symptom of not trusting oneself and not believing you have the capacity to adapt to change. If you imagine the worst is always happening, nothing can shock or surprise you.

06. Personalization. You interpret everything that happens within the context of how it affects and applies to you. You think that everything people say or do or infer is for or against you. It is the inability to realize that a world exists outside of how you engage with it. Other symptoms are trying to compare yourself to others, as though someone else's intelligence or attractiveness means something about your own. The basic thinking error is that you interpret each experience, each conversation, each look as a clue to your worth and value.

07. Control fallacies. There are two ways control fallacies work: Either you feel externally controlled (you see yourself as helpless or a victim of fate) or you feel internally controlled, which means you think of yourself as responsible for the pain and happiness of everyone around you. Both are usually

symptomatic of not taking control of your life in a healthy, productive way.

08. Fallacy of fairness. You believe that you know what's fair, right, and just, and that the only problem is other people don't agree with you. You do not understand that truths can coexist, and by virtue of seeing your own opinions as valid (experience has proved them to be), you assume they are valid for everyone else as well, and if they would only adopt them, their problems would be solved.

09. Blaming. The sister issue of projection. When you blame, you hold everyone and everything responsible for your pain. On the flip side, you blame yourself for every problem that comes up. Regardless, it's a distorted way of holding someone or something accountable for an issue.

10. Shoulds. You have a list of rules about what people should and shouldn't do that you grew up believing were unquestionably true. These were imposed on you through culture, family, religion, schooling, etc. People who break these rules anger you, and you do everything to avoid doing so yourself. Because you believe the rules are indisputable, you put yourself in the position of being able to judge and find fault in everyone else around you.

11. Emotional reasoning. You believe that what you feel must be true, without evaluating it at all. If you feel bored, unloved, unintelligent, unsuccessful—even momentarily—you assume it's true just because you have felt it. A lot of internal conflict arises out of the inability to reconcile our emotions with our thinking processes.

12. Fallacy of change. You expect that other people can change and that they must, because your hopes for happiness depend on it. This leads to you putting a lot of pressure on people, when in reality, you are simply corroding your relationship with them. The underlying assumption of this thinking style is that your happiness depends on the actions

of others. Your happiness actually depends on the thousands of large and small choices you make in your life.

13. Global labeling. You generalize one or two qualities that you see in your immediate social circle as being a judgment about all of humanity. Global labeling creates a world that's stereotypical and one-dimensional. Labeling yourself in such a way is an impediment to self-esteem; labeling others in such a way results in relationship problems and prejudice.

14. Being right. You feel as though you are always on trial to prove that your opinions, actions, and choices are correct, or at least, more correct than an alternative. Being wrong is associated with being "bad" or unworthy. Your need to be right often results in closed-mindedness, as defensiveness does not leave room to consider another idea, perhaps one that is more informed than your own.

15. Heaven's reward fallacy. You imagine that someone is keeping score of all the wrong and right doings in your life. You expect that your sacrifice, good-doing, or self-denial will pay off, even if there is no clear, logical way that it will. You are constantly doing the "right thing," even if you don't feel like it. This leads to feeling physically and emotionally depleted, because there is no actual reward in the sacrifice and denial.

---

17 Davis, Martha; Fanning, Patrick; McKay, Matthew. "Thoughts and Feelings: Taking Control of Your Moods and Your Life." 2011. *New Harbinger Publications*.

92

101 THINGS
that are more
IMPORTANT THAN
WHAT YOUR BODY
LOOKS LIKE

01. How kind you are to the people who can't do anything for you.

02. That you are aware of the fact that the last thing someone will remember after you are dead is what pant size you wore.

03. The understanding that what we are beneath our skin is more real than what's on it or how many layers of cells lie between.

04. The knowing that someone else's judgment of what your body is or isn't does not make it any more or less of that thing.

05. How gracefully you can accept the things that aren't meant for you.

06. How hard you are willing to fight for the things that are.

07. That you accept other people's bodies for what they are.

08. That you accept other people for who they are.

09. That the greatest thing we can do with our bodies is let them facilitate us lending ourselves to the people who need what we can give.

10. That you can taste your favorite food and treat yourself to it as often as you want to.

11. The knowing that nothing is permanent here, especially our physicality. This is a ride. The car needs to work to get you through it. People will judge you as much as they want, but their judgment will be theirs to reconcile, not yours.

12. The knowing that what we really need, on a core level, is the love and acceptance of other people, unconditionally. Maybe

not everybody. Maybe not many people. But in principle, by someone. Our ability to give that far outweighs how we look while giving it.

13. THAT YOU CAN TASTE PIZZA.

14. That you cannot only be okay with your body when it looks and feels the way you want it to. That you find comfort in sometimes being very uncomfortable, and that you know it is not your responsibility to defer to anyone else's level of comfort (or lack thereof).

15. That you have a mind to comprehend whom a person is and a body to show them that you understand them.

16. That you can cuddle with your pets.

17. That you pay your own bills.

18. The fact that we do indeed have these internal atlases, and that when we feel an unexplainable pull, we follow them, for they know much more than our minds can conceive.

19. That (some) people can create another human life if so they choose. (That in itself is a freaking miracle.)

20. That you can swim and run and cry and scream and dance and float on water and feel weightless and free.

21. That your mouth can tell the people you love that you love them...

22. ...and kiss some of 'em, too.

23. That you are able to evolve and change.

24. That you can make conscious decisions for yourself.

25. That you are conscious as a principle.

26. That you know how to let go and have a goddamn great time.

27. That you have the ability to let go of your attachment to how you believe things should look and embrace them as they are.

28. That beauty is not quantifiable.

29. That you realize food is not the enemy.

30. That you understand how contrived our idea of beauty is, how it has been engraved in our minds silently, in photos and side comments and expectations we learned from peers and mentors, unintentionally or not.

31. That you never have to accept a narrow definition of what's beautiful.

32. That you understand that people will love you more for loving yourself.

33. That you know to love yourself means to be okay with not being totally okay with some parts of you all the time.

34. That you can cultivate your beliefs through your own experiences, learnings, and to whatever rings true.

35. That you can, and do, make decisions for yourself.

36. That you can stand up for yourself when passivity is no longer a choice.

37. That you can stand up for others when passivity is no longer a choice.

38. That it is only very small people who feel the need to make comments about other people's appearance. That such an act comes from a very deep, very insecure place, and is not someone you should get angry at, but show love to, because they need it.

39. The fact that you can use your body to read your favorite books and read this right now.

40. That your body facilitates the things you love most in your life. Your legs let you travel and your arms hug the people you love.

41. That you will never really know what great things lie ahead, and though the unknown may seem scary, that you aren't supposed to. It's elusiveness that makes things feel incredible when they arrive.

42. How honest you can be with yourself about yourself.

43. How honest you can be about yourself to other people.

44. That you can use your body to play with the little kids in your life and to tell them (and show them) that you love them.

45. That through your body, you can feel happiness and joy.

46. That through your body, you can feel sadness and pain and can grow and learn from that.

47. Being able to experience the unprecedented high that comes from realizing the million things that seemingly didn't work out in the past was some universal conspiracy to bring you to exactly the right place, somewhere far beyond where you could have imagined for yourself. (It will happen if it hasn't yet. Just wait.)

48. The ability to process the kind of unprecedented compassion that is displayed in the world daily but is sometimes overshadowed by the alternative.

49. Having eyes to see the love of your life, hands to hold them, and a mouth to speak to them, a gut instinct to know they are your soul mate, and a mind to understand that they agree.

50. How well you perform at your job.

51. How adamantly you stick to what you believe.

52. How fiercely you pursue that which you feel most called to.

53. How earnestly you can laugh at yourself.

54. How honest you are willing to be in regards to your shortcomings, and what you do in light of them, not in spite of them.

55. The tiny acts of kindness and courage that we perform daily, because at the end, that may be our only purpose here.

56. How often you make time to do the things you want, not the things that are expected of you.

57. That you stop judging and berating people for their own imperfections.

58. That you have the ability to hear the music you love.

59. That alternatively, you have the ability to feel the vibrations of music if you can't hear it.

60. The knowing that the lack of one sense, one talent, one ability, does not lessen you; it defines you as someone cut out for a challenge above others.

61. The understanding that the pursuit of physical beauty will eventually be futile—we all sag, wrinkle, and age the same in the end.

62. The genuine understanding that most of the time, you cannot equate your health to your appearance.

63. The genuine understanding that you have no right to judge someone else's health by their appearance.

64. That you can use your body to perform the things you most truly love to do (write, dance, sing, what the hell ever).

65. That you use your body for sex: for good, consensual, wild sex when you want, where you want, and never for any other reason but that.

66. That your body is not for the consumption of others, and that there is never a reason to do something to it that doesn't make you happy but will appease others.

67. That you are not at fault for how society views physical appearances, but you do have a responsibility to yourself to defy it consciously.

68. That you know what to say when the people you love are most hurting and need those words of comfort.

69. That you know when to shut the hell up and just be present for them.

70. That you know how to grieve and mourn the things that will inevitably pass.

71. That you know how to embrace and enjoy the things that will invariably pass.

72. That you donate the things you don't need to the people who do need them.

73. That you don't adopt other people's confining, cruel words as your own.

74. That you make your own money to spend as you see fit.

75. How often you tell the people who you love that you love them while you have them, every day, in every way you can. Because you never know.

76. That you sacrifice when a sacrifice needs to be given.

77. That you have the ability to feel warmth and smell your childhood home and have your senses act as transmitters back to the things and people you would have otherwise forgotten about.

78. That you embrace love, no matter how scary it is.

79. That you are an honest person: in word, promise, work, and heart.

80. How able you are to put your ego aside and apologize when an apology is due.

81. How genuinely you apologize—it says a lot about a person.

82. How well you take care of yourself when you most need to be taken care of.

83. That you make gifts and mix CDs and write notes and send letters to people just for the sake of making them smile.

84. How genuinely you see all people as equals.

85. That you stop apologizing for doing what you want with your body.

86. That you realize your mind's capacity is limitless if you so choose to pursue it.

87. That you embrace releasing your mind from having an input on the things that inherently require your instinctual feelings.

88. That you have little things in your life that genuinely make you happy.

89. That you have the courage to go back and reconcile when you are at a standstill and someone needs to cave.

90. That you can rejoice in other people's successes.

91. And not rejoice in other people's failures.

92. That your body is capable of understanding when someone is giving you that very specific "I love you" look, and that you are so lucky to ever have had it in the first place.

93. That you spend your life doing something greater than just making yourself happy in the moment.

94. That you realize that to help others, you must first help yourself.

95. That you understand how the last two points both contradict and necessitate one another.

96. That you give yourself enough sleep.

97. And enough vegetables (sorry to nag you, but that shit is important).

98. How you feel about your body.

99. That you forgive the people who are cruel to you over your body and realize that they are hurting somewhere too, and that people only ever lash out at what strikes a chord within them.

100. That you forgive yourself for being cruel to yourself over your body.

101. That you use it to write things like this and send the message on.

93

7 ZEN
PRINCIPLES
(and how to
apply them
to modern life)

Our biggest aversion to psychological guidance systems—religious or not—tends to be skepticism bred out of (assumed) inapplicability.

We'll trust lifestyle magazines and blog posts and cultural norms. This is simply because they make sense to us. They become self-evident "truth" when we can easily apply them to our issues.

But we don't often consider the source, or the intention, or the long-term significance of what it is we begin to believe in. When the extent of our personal philosophy is, essentially, to just do what we're told without questioning, we end up serving consumerism, or ego, or misguided religious figures or someone else's desire for control.

Despite being a derivative of Buddhist teaching, Zen is simply the art of self-awareness. It does not dictate what you should feel or believe in; how you should be or what you should do…only that you should be conscious of your experience, fully immersed in it.

It's for this reason that Zen principles are universal—they can apply to any dogma or lifestyle, essentially. So here are eight ancient teachings of Zen and how to navigate them in the modern world.

01. Your experience is constructed by your mind.
    The Yogācāra discourse essentially explains how our mind's perceptions create our experiences. Therefore, we must realize that, even despite our disposition, we can create a different experience simply by shifting and choosing what to focus on. We are raised to believe that we cannot choose what we think about, when, in fact, we can. Not every fear feeling or negative thought is an invitation to explore it to a resolutive end.

02. Your concept of self is an illusion (and construct) as well.

"Who you are" is an essence. An energy. That's it. That's why it's never "one thing" for too long or in any given context. That's why it's so difficult to understand yourself—you're more than the limiting definitions and titles repetitive habits and jobs and roles provide.

However, most of us only understand ourselves as we imagine other people see us. (Writer, teacher, mom, student, basketball player, "good person," etc.)

Most of our issues surround trying to manipulate the ego; trying to inflate or immortalize the self. Trying to shift and change how we think other people see us (therefore, how we believe we exist in reality, and so how we should see ourselves).

Mastering the idea of self is knowing that you can play out the illusion of who you are and what you do while not being so lost in it that it controls you.

03. You need not believe in anything; you only need to follow what feels true in the moment.

The trouble with adhering to a certain, set belief system without question is that when you value (or consider) the voices that were implanted into you by someone else's dogma or teaching, you start trusting that more than you trust yourself, and you'll end up either very lost or very confused, battling between what you think is right and what you feel is true.

If you aren't living your life by what you know to be true, you aren't following your highest good. Allow yourself the ability to expand and grow by thinking (and feeling) beyond what your current dogma "allows."

04. The ultimate path to happiness is non-attachment.

And before you get all caught up in the impossibility of not caring about the outcome of your life, understand that non-attachment is much more (and yet much simpler) than "not caring" how things turn out.

It's about the simple understanding that all things serve you. The "bad" things teach you and show you how to heal to open even further to the "good" things. It cannot be put much simpler than that.

05. "Doing" is not as important as simply "being."

Meditative states can be achieved though a variety of practices, but perhaps the most underutilized among them is just "sitting." The art of doing "nothing" is profound. It quiets the waters of your mind, brings forth what needs to be immediately acknowledged and healed, and keeps you connected to yourself, not the attachments and responsibilities you have in your life.

The point is: You are not what you do; you simply are. Aside from a meditation practice, giving yourself the time to relax, recuperate, and reflect is of the upmost importance.

06. You can be an objective observer of your mind and your life.

It's one thing to know that you can choose your thoughts, but it's really more to realize that you can also decide which ones you value, if only you are able to see them all objectively.

Guided meditation practices will often have you observe thoughts as they pass, as a third-party viewer. The point being to teach you that you are not those thoughts. You are not your feelings. You are the being that experiences those thoughts and feelings, who decides which to value and act on.

07. Your natural state is oneness.

The reality we will all return to eventually is that everything is one. (This is the basis of enlightenment.) It is in the illusion of separateness that we suffer. It is playing out the ideas of individualism that we learn. It is to our natural state, unification, that we eventually return.

94

6 SIGNS YOU
have a healthy
SOCIAL
SENSITIVITY

In a world that seems to assume that extroversion is the norm and introverts exist within a counter-culture that needs to be justified and explained at every step and turn, it seems we've begun to overthink what a normal, healthy amount of social sensitivity is.

Not liking everybody or desiring solitude or preferring one close friend to a group of many is not social dysfunction. We're overgeneralizing what it means to be "antisocial" or "socially anxious," when those are extreme, if not clinical terms that we may want to think twice before throwing around. Here, a few ways to determine whether or not your social sensitivity is normal:

01. You experience a degree of social anxiety in unfamiliar situations.
    Social anxiety is usually having enough foresight to recognize what people may be judging or assuming about you. If not kept in check, it can paralyze rather than keep you self-aware. It is normal, if not indicative of a high intelligence.

02. You desire solitude because being alone is emotionally enriching.
    You do not isolate yourself when you'd prefer to be with others, simply because you're afraid or feel unworthy of keeping company.

03. You only enjoy the company of a few, select people.
    You're not supposed to like everybody. To say that you "like everybody" would be to deny and reject the parts of you that may not genuinely feel that way, and as we all know, disassociation isn't good. We're only meant to really love and enjoy a few people and tolerate a few more.

04. You say "no" to plans when you want to say "no" to plans.
    You do not go because you feel obligated or pressured. You
    are able to say "no" to people who you don't want to see, and
    to doing things you don't really want to do, when the cost
    would be your mental or emotional well-being.

05. You analyze situations because your snap judgments may not
    be well-informed, not because you'd like to reinforce your
    anxiety or make yourself feel better through delusion.
    You self-evaluate as a means of becoming aware of what
    (may perhaps) be unconscious choices and habits. You do
    not over-evaluate with the intention of arriving at a different,
    made-up conclusion, or to create an alternative perspective
    that supports an irrational idea: "He looked at me funny; I
    knew he hated me."

06. You worry that your social anxiety is abnormal.

Worrying about whether or not you have too much anxiety about
being in social situations is probably the most normal thing there is.
That's not a product of "having a severe problem"; it's a product of
wanting to be self-aware enough to handle it if there is.

95

NOW
is ALL
you HAVE

From all the time I spend overanalyzing (an arbitrary act I can't be the only one guilty of), I realize that I'm able to routinely trace all of my issues back to the same core problem: I don't know how to be uncomfortable. I don't know how to be able to feel the good things without being completely deterred from the experience by the inevitably bad. It's something I have to outgrow, because it's certainly not something that is resolvable. It's just...life. And I think we live in a world that's all but curated that mindset for us.

I have the issue of seeing parts of my life as just precursors of time to facilitate getting to where I want to be next. And the sickening reality of that is, given enough of those days, your entire life becomes a waiting game. Now, I've been able to resolve a lot of that nagging, lingering need to escape, but of course, it creeps up on me now and again. So I can't help but be interested in it.

Because it comes from the idea that there will be a happily ever after. You get through the pain and then you bask in having been healed and reconciled and changed and made once again whole and new. But there is no swift motion of starting in darkness and moving toward the light indefinitely. There's a lot of in and out. There's a lot of grey area. There are days you're so far back you can't believe you let yourself get there, and then there are days you forget you were ever miserable to begin with. Getting stunted by this —being fearful of moving forward and more fearful of going back—is the only guaranteed way that it will ruin you.

Because it's a succession of "nows" that will add up, lifting us from awareness of one experience to another, that will be all we have in the end. So what we see in the experience is what we have to appreciate before we're lifted away from the monotonous routine, because the alternative is that we cease to exist. We're done. And we let things pass because the discomfort made us feel like we were backtracking away from that "light" state we're perpetually moving toward. We made a bad life out of a few bad experiences because we weren't able to check off the list of things we had in our minds as prerequisites for feeling content, dare I even say...happy? But happiness isn't a contrived mental process that you allow yourself in when things are thought to be right. It's an experience, it is an emotion, and all you have is right now to experience it.

And I see such patterns of thinking facilitated largely by our society. Not only that there will be a happily ever after that we are all entitled to after we've suffered enough, but that joy is in planning for tomorrow. To be very, well, millennial about it (God, I can't believe I'm using this as an example), it's like the Tumblr posts and Pinterest boards that are all images of what we want, hope for, and are inspired by. And it's lovely to look at those beautiful things and decide you want them. But how many of us actually get up and get them—even something as simple as a pretty coffee and book to read by a windowsill? Not many. We get up to complain about not having the lives we dream of and carry on, day after day, rinse and repeat.

Now is all we have, my friends. You have to choose now. You have to live in the heartbreaking reality that is what you see and perceive in this moment...the mess, the beautiful schisms that make for wars and love and peacemaking and harmony and change. The rawness of being so low some days that all you can muster up as your purpose is just to keep breathing—and then realize that's all there is either way. Maybe it is about diving into the deep end and letting now be more than just enough. Realizing that things are only ever as boring and mundane as we let them be. That there are mysteries and experiences and fascinatingly foreign parts of life that we won't see until we take a step out on the wild side, the side of us that isn't concerned about tomorrow.

316

96

THE ART *of* MINDLESSNESS

Many people have written beautiful pieces about the importance, and their experience, with mindfulness: the ancient practice and supposed modern anecdote to our perpetual dissatisfaction. Live in the moment; be conscious of every sensation of your daily experience. This kind of awareness, in my opinion, is more than just a proposed solution to our human condition, it's the final frontier, it's the place we will all find ourselves, at one point or another: either embracing each moment as it comes, or letting them all wash by us —mindlessly. So when I say that what we really have to work on is mindlessness, I by no means am actually talking about not being mindful; it's just a play on the phrase. (I wanted to clarify in case there was any confusion.)

We talk about the importance of mindfulness in the context of being conscious and present, completely immersed in our experience. That is crucial. But what is also crucial is realizing that much of that has to do with how we can transcend the mind. We live in a culture, and a period of human existence, that is far too concerned with what we think about things. Though reason is crucial to our development, it sometimes denies our instincts, desires, and pleasures in place of expectation and "normalcy." We can't be surprised that when we try to confine the fluid, natural, untamable reality of a human soul that we end up suffering as we do.

We are a species disconnected. For all the technological advancements we've made, our ability to connect on a human level is miles away from its natural, primitive state. Our daily discussions are so deeply imbued with value placed on manmade means, we are focused so much on what man can do and not nearly enough on what man is. We are steadily moving away from concepts of religion, associating faith and trust with ignorance as opposed to spiritual intelligence. We simply don't value the reality of our human existence, the part of us that is up for interpretation, partially because it's unknown, and mostly because we can't agree on anything or know for certain, so we deny it rather than embrace its unknownness.

What we think, we become. And if what we are becoming is any indication, we are thinking far too much about the things that don't matter and not making room for uncertainty, for discomfort, for the things that are indeed unknown but which yield the best outcomes. The ones that are indeed larger than our mind's comprehension.

In our incessant mindfulness (not in the meditative way, but just in the fact that we process everything psychologically), we start labeling, categorizing, and defining things. We become used to what's known and disregard what isn't. This doesn't leave room for the acceptance of people and things that aren't like us. We relinquish responsibility by putting other people beneath us. We declare their sentiments wrong and unjust, and therefore we are superior. We live in a culture that makes means and commodity out of ripping each other apart, and it functions healthfully because we buy into it. We love to see how other people aren't as good as we are, how we can place them beneath us and find comfort in the knowing that we are okay because we are better than them. But we end up caging ourselves. We inevitably fall within what we once said was "wrong," because we're human beings, and dangerous territory is the mind that doesn't leave room for the soul to falter.

We need to teach our children not to have screaming fits because it makes us look bad as caretakers but because learning to process negative emotions without being scolded and shamed for them is important. We need to become actively, consciously aware of what we are buying, clicking, associating with and inevitably supporting, especially when it serves to do nothing but harm another person (even if we don't realize it at the time). We have to stop defining people. We have to take our discomfort with the unknown and settle into it firmly, because the fact that we will be uncertain is a certainty. We have to realize that major change can only happen on a minor scale. One individual at a time. We have to move on from our minds and move into our hearts. What makes us the same is something our minds may never be able to understand. We have to let go of trying to understand everything else that's collateral to suffice for it.

318

97

THE DIFFERENCE
between
HOW YOU FEEL
and how you think
YOU FEEL

Imagine the last time you had a strong emotional response to something. Was it the product of having sat with the experience for a moment, processing and internalizing it, and then scanning your body to determine how you felt? Probably not. When we ask one another: "How do you feel about that?" it's essentially interchangeable with, "What do you think about that?"

Emotions are simple and subtle. When we scan our bodies, we find that they are sensations, and ultimately they boil down to one of two things: tightness or openness. It's how we interpret that tension or ease that we create thoughts that then exacerbate intense, joyous, debilitating—any extreme—emotions.

This is to say: we create the way we think we feel simply by assigning meaning to sensations. There is a difference between how we feel and how we think we should feel. This is the reason for everything from mob mentality to social conditioning. It's also largely why people feel "stuck" in inescapable, emotional turmoil. No emotion lasts for any significant period of time—that's not how they're designed. It's only the cognitive patterning that keeps us re-inciting a feeling over and over again, or that keeps us from choosing the course of action that the emotion is guiding us toward.

We are taught how we should feel about roughly everything in life. Our cultural, religious, familial upbringings dictate a set of things that are "good" and "bad." Our egos, our desires for survival, superiority, love, acceptance, etc., fill in the rest. We end up with a mental ecosystem of actions and reactions.

These "mental emotions," as I call them, are by and large the reason we suffer, despite being more evolved than ever before. It is no longer our fleeting sense of hunger, or desire to mate, that controls us: It's our thoughts about what it means when someone doesn't love us, and how our subconscious minds seek confirmation that this is true, and how this repetitiveness creates a belief, and how that belief creates our lives.

We're taught that either which way you go, a life worth living is one that is highly emotional. It's full of love, or full of passion, or one in which you persevered through incredible suffering. We believe we should have an opinion on things to know who we are, and worse, we believe we should have an emotional response to feel as though our voices are counted. This is what makes us feel worthwhile—this is what makes life feel worthwhile.

The next time you feel like you're in an inescapable circumstance, honestly scan your body and see what's present. Even a tightness or uneasy feeling in your gut is just that—a little bit of stress. That's it. That is all. That is all that feeling can do to you. Check back in after an hour, after a day...it will probably be gone.

What you'll realize is that even your "gut feelings," your instincts, are not overpowering, huge emotional waves. That's why it's called the "little voice within."

Sometimes we aren't comfortable with the inherent quietness within us and so we create layers of chaos to distract ourselves from it. But once that chaos becomes exhausting, all you have to do is sit back with yourself and just let yourself feel what you feel, not what you think you feel.

What you'll realize is that even when your emotions are telling you the worst: "this is not right," "you need to change," the manner in which you inherently communicate with yourself is always soft, it's always gentle, it's always loving, and it's always trying to help you.

What you'll also realize is that you don't have a natural aversion to your emotions. They aren't "bad." They don't feel "bad," even though your brain wasn't taught to label them as "good." We enjoy sadness, and pain, and everything else, at the appropriate time, to the appropriate extent. We enjoy it because it is an aspect of simply allowing our emotions to be.

It's not our thoughts that create our lives, it's how we use our thoughts to dissect the meaning of our emotions, and how based on

320

our assertions, we decide what's "good," "bad," "right" and "wrong." None of these things inherently exist. The symphony that results from our orchestration of them is what creates our perception of whether or not we're living a good life.

98

THE POWER
of negative
THINKING

If you want to be emotionally free, there is only one thing you need to understand: Whatever problem you think you have right now is not the actual problem. The problem is that you do not know how to think about your problem correctly.

You're sick of platitudes. But this isn't really something you can afford to ignore. This isn't just advice that may perhaps be applicable to some people, sometimes, in certain situations. It is not just a kind notion that can soothe you on a hard day. It's not just something you can lean on when you've exhausted all other options.

The point of experiencing anything is learning how to think about it differently. When you do not do the work of learning to think differently, you become stuck.

The more we experience, the more capable we are of seeing the world with varied lenses, thinking with more dimension, considering possibilities that were previously inconceivable. Real education is not learning what to think about, but how to think in general.

Learning how to better ignore negative thoughts is not learning how to think; it's learning how to disassociate. Our negative thoughts inform us as much as positive ones do. Rather than becoming afraid, we can learn to see them as directives, or at the very least, if we can be discerning about what we ascribe meaning to, we can decide what matters to us, and to what degree.

Therein is the power of negative thinking.

As the Stoics practiced negative visualization (imagining the worst possible outcomes and then preparing for them), learning how to think is the simple art of recognizing that you choose how you apply meaning and emotion to your life.

And if you don't consciously decide what matters and what doesn't, you'll spend the rest of your life in feeling patterns, responding to what you were conditioned by when you were young.

The solution is not a hyper-focus on positivity (as mainstream pop psych would have you believe), but learning how to turn the shadow aspects of your mind into forces that ignite change and inspire growth.

Emotional freedom and inner peace come from knowing what to do when those negative thoughts and feelings arise, because they will.

As Jonah Lehrer explains, we regulate our emotions by thinking about them. Our prefrontal cortexes allow us to think about our own minds. Our brains think about themselves. Psychologists call it metacognition.

We know when we are angry, because each feeling state must come with a degree of self-awareness, so we can figure out why we're feeling what we're feeling. Without that awareness, we wouldn't know we are afraid of the lion that's charging at us in the wild, so we wouldn't run to escape it. If we didn't run away, what would be the point of the feeling in the first place?

But more importantly, if a feeling doesn't make sense—if the amygdala is responding to a "loss frame," then it can be ignored. "The prefrontal cortex can deliberately choose to ignore the emotional brain"—that is, if it determines there is no merit in ascribing meaning.

What this means is that whatever problem you think you have in your life is not the problem, it's the fact that you see it as a problem, rather than a signal you refuse to respond to, or a product of over-ascribing meaning, extrapolation, irrational thoughts that created irrational emotions that continue to go unchecked, and so on.

It is the fact that you see the problem as a problem rather than a fallacy in your understanding, your focus, your perception.

The problem is not the problem, it is how you think about the problem.

If you want to function, you have to learn how to think about your feelings. The difference between the kind of anxiety that paralyzes you and the kind of fear that accompanies anything brave and worthwhile is discernment, which takes practice. The difference between the kind of people who turn their obstacles into opportunities and the kind of people who are crushed beneath the weight of their own uncertainty is knowledge and awareness.

Being uncomfortable forces us to think of options that we wouldn't have had to imagine before.

It is why heartbreak is crucial to human growth. The obstacle that becomes the way. Any idiot can enjoy the positive things in their lives, but it is only a few that can take the negative and find something even more profound.

WHAT YOU
need to do
TO HEAL YOUR LIFE
FROM ANXIETY

01. The opposite of addiction isn't sobriety, it's connection. The same is true for anxiety. Anxiety is being disconnected from the present moment, other people, or yourself. Usually all three. You must reconnect with your life.

02. You must give yourself permission to want what you really want. There is no way around this. Whether it's a romantic partner, a better job, some more money, recognition for your work, see it and accept it, even if you think society says it means you're shallow or broken or don't "love yourself" enough.

03. If you can't figure out what you really want, look straight at your deepest fears. What's on the other side of them? That's what you want.

04. Be grateful for your discomfort. The sad and weird thing is that happy people are complacent. Feeling uncomfortable is the signal that you're on the precipice of something new and better, but you must take action.

05. Your new best friends will be structure and productivity. It's not about checking off a 100-point task list; it's about knowing that you accomplished something (anything!) that contributes to your well-being each day.

06. "Irrational anxiety" is usually cured by doing very practical things. The nonsensical things you worry about are usually aggrandized projections of real concerns that you're not dealing with.

07. You must start where you are, you must use what you have, and you must do what you can. Anything else is running away from your problems and abandoning your life and yourself. Real change is a product of evolution; thinking otherwise is an illusion that will keep you separated from the very stuff you need to heal.

08. Make a conscious effort to connect and reconnect with the people you already have in your life—even if it's just one person you trust and connect with. This will begin to re-form healthy emotional attachments. It's not weak to need love.

09. Buy a notebook that is exclusively for junk journaling, which is what you're going to do whenever you feel pretzeled up inside. Write down whatever comes out—whatever gruesome, awful, self-hating, embarrassing thoughts come up, let them out. Once you do this a few times, you'll believe me when I say this will release them.

10. The only thing you should ever try to do when you're very anxious or panicked is to comfort yourself. You cannot think clearly and shouldn't make assumptions or decisions about your life in that state. Figure out what soothes you (a snack, a bath, talking to someone, doing something you really enjoy) and get yourself out that energy before you do anything else.

11. You will need to figure out how to live in the moment, even if that seems boring, impossible, terrifying, or all three. Anxiety is the warning sign that we're too much in the past or the future—and being there is affecting how we make choices in the present.

12. You will need to take action on the things that are holding you back from pursuing the things you actually want. As Cheryl Strayed says, "Real change happens on the level of the gesture. It's one person doing one thing differently than they did before."

13. Read. If you don't read, it's not because you don't like reading; it's because you haven't picked up anything that interests you. What you read now will affect the person you're

going to be for decades to come. Read articles and essays online about how people cope with their fears—in it you will find camaraderie, how many strangers feel just as you do. Read about things you don't understand, that scare you and fascinate you. Just read, damnit.

14. You can change how you feel. This is something you must remember. It's as simple as: "I want to feel differently about this, so I am going to focus on a different aspect of it."

15. If you want to buy into the idea that you cannot "choose" happiness or how you feel or what you think, you are condemning yourself to an extremely hard life and should stop reading now, because doing those things is the only way to save yourself.

16. You will always have anxiety. You will always feel fear. If you give a damn about your life, or if you're even playing the slightest bit of attention to what's going on here, you'll know there's a lot to be anxious and afraid of. The end goal is not to eliminate those feelings, but to strengthen the mental muscle that will allow you to choose to be happy in spite of them, not become paralyzed when they're present. That's all.

17. For some people, strengthening that muscle will require a simple shift of perspective. For others, it will be years of medication and therapy and more work and effort than they've ever put into anything before. It is the fight of all our lives and the thing we most owe to ourselves. If you're going to pick a battle, pick this one.

18. The problem is not the problem. The problem is how you think about the problem. Your internal guidance system is sounding off right now because something isn't right. This doesn't mean you're barreling toward a life of perpetual, inescapable suffering. It means somewhere deep down, you know there's another way—a better way—to live. It means you know what you want, even if you're scared of it.

19. You need to choose love. This sounds like annoying advice, but you cannot give up on the people who light you up inside,

on the things you love to do (even if they aren't work) on what you want for yourself. You must choose love even if it scares you. (In fact, your fear about doing something is proportionate to your love for it.)

20. You must learn how to express pain when you feel it. This does not mean you can justify reckless, unchecked behavior; it means you need to learn how to acknowledge your pain, communicate it clearly to others, and deal with it as it comes up.

21. You must learn how to unravel whatever emotional toxicity is built up inside you. For example: If you don't let yourself feel and accept that you were hurt badly by your ex, you will constantly be projecting ideas about how your new fling will hurt you and how you shouldn't even try, thus recreating the situation you're most afraid of. The unraveling is seeing, feeling, and accepting. Life is sometimes brutal and unfair and unspeakably horrendous. ("We are all in the gutter, but some of us are looking at the stars." —Oscar Wilde)

22. Separate sensations in your body from what you think they mean. When you're seriously upset, ask yourself, what do I actually feel in my body right now? Like, what do I actually feel? Chances are it's nothing more than just a little tension or discomfort. The rest of your panic is everything you've chalked that sensation up to mean.

23. Don't trust all of your feelings. Conventional wisdom says to, but that's insane considering how many of those feelings stem from irrational thoughts and past experiences and so on. If you blindly trust all of your feelings, you will be thrown around by them constantly. Decide which ones mean something and which don't.

24. Utilize the most powerful growing tool of all: "future-self work." If you're on the fence about kids, imagine your life at 75. Do you want your own family around you, or are you okay on your own? Imagine your life in three years from now. Will you be happy you didn't try harder in that relationship, or that you

didn't save any money, or that you wasted your time watching Netflix when you could have been writing the book or starting the business or playing music like you really want to? Imagine your life from the perspective of the person you hope to be. It will place many things back into alignment.

100

STOP CHASING HAPPINESS

Alan Watts taught that the desire for security and the feeling of insecurity are one in the same—that "to hold your breath is to lose your breath." Traditional Zen Buddhism would agree: To desire fulfillment is to not have fulfillment, happiness is not something you seek, but that which you become.

These ideas are nice (albeit likely just platitudes for most people), but they illustrate the madness behind the common wisdom of "chasing happiness." As Andrew Weil has said: The idea that human beings should be constantly happy is "a uniquely modern, uniquely American, uniquely destructive idea."

It is our desire for perpetual happiness that drives consumerism, eases the fact that we're all barreling toward uncertain death, and keeps us hungering for more. In many ways, it—alongside our existential fear of death and suffering—accounts for why we've innovated and developed the society we live in. Our lack of fulfillment has driven us because the quest for happiness does not and will not cease.

This is largely due to hedonic adaptation, which is really just the fact that human beings get used to what happens to them. We change, we adjust, we adapt, we crave more. Psychologists also call it the "baseline," the way in which we regulate ourselves to come back to "neutral" after different life events occur.

Chasing happiness is trying to keep ourselves sustained by "positive" life events, rather than adjusting the baseline as a whole. Motivating ourselves with the hope of achieving a sustained feeling of "good" is not only unhealthy, it's impossible.

If you want to be happy, you need to stop chasing happiness. Happiness is a byproduct of doing things that are challenging, meaningful, beautiful, and worthwhile.

It is wiser to spend a life chasing knowledge, or the ability to think clearly and with more dimension, than it is to just chase what "feels good." It is wiser to chase the kind of discomfort that only comes with doing something so profound and life-altering that you are knocked off your orbit. It is wiser to tip the scales over rather than balance things you don't like only because you believe balance will make you "happy." It is wiser to do things that are hard and make you feel vulnerable and raw than it is to avoid them because comfort makes you feel temporarily, fleetingly good.

At the end of the day, to avoid pain is to avoid happiness. (They are opposite forces within the same function.) To numb ourselves to one side of our feeling capacity is to shut down everything. It leaves us chasing the kind of empty happiness that never really fills us and leaves us shells of the people we are really destined to be.

101

WHAT YOU
should know if you're
EXPERIENCING METANOIA:
a change of
MIND, HEART, SELF
OR WAY OF LIFE

Whether it's a simple shift of committing to treating people with more kindness, the brutal (and liberating) realization that you're responsible for your own happiness, trying to better make sense of the world is a heavy-duty task, and we're called to do it numerous times in a life. There's a beautiful word for this: It's called "metanoia," and it originates from the Greek word for "changing one's mind or purpose." It really doesn't matter what you're changing from, or to, only that any kind of massive psychological or emotional shift tends to heed similar circumstances and common struggles. Here are a few things you need to know if you're going through one of your own:

01. If it's a relationship that prompted a revolution in your worldview, know that this relationship has likely served its purpose. A lot of people hold on to the catalyst of their personal "awakenings" because they confuse "big love" for being "forever love." They're not the same thing.

02. You don't need to be mad about your limiting, old beliefs: Change is in building what's next, not in dismantling what was. You don't need to ruminate in disappointment for how long you spent not realizing there was more to life than you assumed. The point is that you figured it out eventually.

03. The base of any personal catastrophe or desire for deeper understanding is usually the same: It's the realization that you, and only you, are responsible for your life. You cannot depend on anything—anything!—to do the real, grueling work

of what it means to find comfort in a world that's entirely impermanent. No job, no amount of money, no relationship, no accomplishment can supplement that for you. It's a peace you must come to first; then you can enjoy the rest.

04. "Loving yourself" is an action, not a feeling. When we think of romantic love, we think of the flush of hormones that gives us an ooey-gooey emotion. We rarely think of the daily tasks and commitments necessary to make someone else's well-being as important as our own. The same goes for loving yourself: We think it's the emotion that comes with holding yourself in high regard, when most of the time it's more like standing up for yourself, having the courage to keep going, having the courage to quit, finding happiness despite the impermanence and unreliability of things, and so on.

05. You don't need to have every answer, nor will you ever have every answer. It's never about how certain you are, it's about how willing you are to try anyway. Nobody knows the mysterious abyss from which we come and eventually go back to, and yet so many people's lives—and our society/culture in general—are crafted and dictated from teachings about this unknown. Everything is speculation for now—but some speculations lead to a happier, kinder, more peaceful world (and some don't). The point isn't who knows what for sure; the point is who is willing to do what it takes to make the best version of the reality we have now.

06. You don't need to believe in anything, but you do need to be able to listen to what feels true in the moment and hold enough objectivity to speak and act with respect and kindness toward yourself and those around you. And if you're instructed or pressured to believe in anything that doesn't resonate with you at basically every cell of your being, know that it is your internal guidance system saying: "not quite."

07. Your struggles will be what make you what you are. Discomfort is the pressure usually required to make us act in a way that we wouldn't otherwise. This, on the surface, feels scary, because it is unknown. But the most difficult moments

of your life will be the catalysts of your becoming. The challenges will grow you into someone you never imagined you could be. The "bad" things in your life will be the necessary leeways into things better than you can imagine. You will be grateful things didn't turn out the way you wanted. You will be grateful for what you struggle with once you get to the other side.

ABOUT
the
PUBLISHER

Thought Catalog Books is a publishing house owned by The Thought & Expression Company, an independent media group based in Brooklyn, NY. Founded in 2010, we are committed to facilitating thought and expression. We exist to help people become better communicators and listeners in order to engender a more exciting, attentive, and imaginative world.
Visit us on the web at:
www.thought.is or www.thoughtcatalog.com.

ABOUT
the
AUTHOR

Brianna Wiest is a writer and author. You can find her work on *The Huffington Post, Teen Vogue, Thought Catalog, Glamour, Medium, Soul Anatomy, Bustle,* and others.
Facebook: facebook.com/briaeliza
Twitter: @briannawiest